TEACHING ACADEMIC WRITING IN
EUROPEAN HIGHER EDUCATION

STUDIES IN WRITING

VOLUME 12

Series Editor:

Gert Rijlaarsdam, *University of Amsterdam, The Netherlands*

Editorial Board:

Kluwer Academic Publishers continues to publish the international book series Studies in Writing, founded by Amsterdam University Press. The intended readers are all those interested in the foundations of writing and learning and teaching processes in written composition. The series aims at multiple perspectives of writing, education and texts. Therefore authors and readers come from various fields of research, from curriculum development and from teacher training. Fields of research covered are cognitive, socio-cognitive and developmental psychology, psycholinguistics, text linguistics, curriculum development, instructional science. The series aim to cover theoretical issues, supported by empirical research, quantitative as well as qualitative, representing a wide range of nationalities. The series provides a forum for research from established researchers and welcomes contributions from young researchers.

Teaching Academic Writing in European Higher Education

Edited by

Lennart Björk
University of Göteborg, Sweden

Gerd Bräuer
Emory University, Atlanta, U.S.A. and
University of Education, Freiburg, Germany

Lotte Rienecker
University of Copenhagen, Denmark

and

Peter Stray Jörgensen
University of Copenhagen, Denmark

KLUWER ACADEMIC PUBLISHERS
DORDRECHT / BOSTON / LONDON

A C.I.P. Catalogue record for this book is available from the Library of Congress.

Dr. Effie Maclellan
Department of Educational Studies
University of Strathclyde
Southbrae Drive
GLASGOW   G13 1PP
Tel:- 0141 950 3355
e-mail:- e.maclellan@strath.ac.uk

ISBN 1-4020-1208-X (HB)
ISBN 1-4020-1209-8 (PB)

Published by Kluwer Academic Publishers,
P.O. Box 17, 3300 AA Dordrecht, The Netherlands.

Sold and distributed in North, Central and South America
by Kluwer Academic Publishers,
101 Philip Drive, Norwell, MA 02061, U.S.A.

In all other countries, sold and distributed
by Kluwer Academic Publishers,
P.O. Box 322, 3300 AH Dordrecht, The Netherlands.

Printed on acid-free paper

Printed in the Netherlands

TABLE OF CONTENTS

PREFACE

DAVID R. RUSSELL

English Department of Iowa State University, U.S.A.

I was fortunate to attend, as a visitor from the U.S., the first European Association for the Teaching of Academic Writing (EATAW) conference in 2001 at Groningen. I was struck by the similarities in the challenges higher education faces on both sides of the Atlantic in terms of developing students' academic writing, and students' learning through writing. It is indeed an international 'problem.' But I was equally struck by the profound differences in responding to these challenges – among nations, institutions, disciplines, and even within disciplines. The essays in this extraordinary volume address a growing demand for help with academic writing, on the part of students and academic staff alike. And they do so in ways that bring fresh approaches, not only to Europeans, who have only recently begun to study academic writing, but also to researchers and academic staff in the U.S., where we have a century-old tradition of attention to the problem – but are much in need of these fresh approaches.

Academic writing has become a 'problem' in higher education – all around the world – because higher education sits smack between two contradictory pressures. On one end, far more students (and far more diverse students) come streaming into higher education – bringing in a far greater diversity of linguistic resources (often interpreted as 'standards are falling,' as Frank, Haacke & Tente point out). On the other end, students are leaving higher education to enter far more specialised workplaces. As the kinds of organisations and the jobs in them that students will enter have become far more specialised, the writing has become more specialised as well. Students need a greater diversity of linguistic resources to successfully enter professions and institutions. And they will have to have a greater linguistic and rhetorical flexibility to transform those professions and institutions as the pace of change increases – and with it the specialisation of writing. In the centre, often unacknowledged, sits writing – an immensely greater diversity of writing, the myriad genres of communication that disciplines and professions and institutions create to organise their work. So in the reports of various ministries and commissions, higher education is increasingly charged with developing students' writing.

Yet our understanding of writing has not caught up with these changes, in large part because academic writing has rarely been treated as an intellectually interesting object of study, much less teaching. In the institutional environments where we academic staff live and work, and in the wider political environments where ministers and commissions and the public at large live, writing is too-often assumed to be a single, easily-generalisable set of skills learned once and for all, usually at an early age – like riding a bicycle.

This is one aspect of what Brian Street has called the autonomous view of literacy. That one set of writing skills fits all, regardless of the discipline, the profession, and the genre. There do seem to be some commonalities in academic writing across the curriculum, and in the challenges students face in developing their writing (as this volume shows). Yet a growing body of research suggests that writing is not a single generalisable set of skills, but a very complex, developing accomplishment, central to the specialised work of the myriad disciplines of higher education, and to the professions and institutions students will enter and eventually transform. Each new specialised genre a student or new employee encounters means learning new strategies – strategies that have become second nature to academic staff, and are therefore merely expected, uninteresting.

Our ways of talking about writing development in academic culture at large have for so long centred on surface features (poor spelling and so on) or on broad generalisations (students should write more clearly and coherently) that we do not have a widely shared vocabulary in higher education for talking about writing development in higher education. We tend to be like the blind men and the elephant in John Jeffry Saxe's poem. One blind man had hold of the tail and thought the elephant like a spear, another the leg and thought the elephant like a tree, and so on. Each of us thinks he or she is describing the same thing when we talk about writing, or the essay, or an argument, or clarity. We do not realise how different our expectations are. As Lea and Street from the U.K. have found (as well as researchers in North America) when one asks academic staff to point to features in students' writing that make it 'poor', there is very little agreement in what they point to. Thus an important theme in this volume is creating an intellectually interesting discussion of writing and learning – and serious research on it.

For this reason, it is refreshing to see many of these essays take very seriously the question of what academic writing is, its varied forms and functions within particular disciplines, institutions, and education systems (unlike many popular U.S. approaches). Analyses of genres, text types, and discipline-specific argument help us understand the difficulties students have in writing, difficulties that are too often invisible to academic staff – and of course students.

Academic writing, in this view, is not invisible, something that students should have learned elsewhere, but rather intellectually interesting – something partnerships across the curriculum can form around. The 'bad' writing of many students becomes not merely a deficit to be remedied, but a necessary stage in students' understanding and entering powerful institutions and professions. Focusing on writing becomes a way of focusing on the methods, practices, and social-psychological processes of intellectual inquiry, of innovation, and of learning. The study of academic writing is thus part of deep higher education reform.

Many of the essays in this volume offer new ways of addressing this central problem: How to simultaneously raise the awareness of students, specialised academic staff, and policy makers to writing's powerful and varied role in learning, teaching, work, and citizenship, while at the same time integrating efforts to develop writing into the specialised studies and activities writing serves – instead of holding academic writing development on the invisible margins of academic work.

Raising consciousness of writing through co-operation among academic staff is crucial, whether through student support units working with academic staff in the disciplines, or through courses in academic writing that are designed with a close eye to the demands of writing in the disciplines. In this way it is possible to reveal tacit knowledge, develop a shared vocabulary for discussing writing, and contribute widespread reform of higher education at a much more profound level than the ministries and commissions can ever achieve with top-down structural reforms.

Many of the essays here speak to the difficulties of this slow, bottom-up educational renewal. Each department or faculty, each institution, each national system will have to evolve its own ways of approaching academic writing development. And in this volume are many ideas for constructing useful cross-curricular dialogue and collaborative pedagogical projects.

In that regard, this volume also shows the value of cross-national comparisons and dialogue for building collaborations. All of these studies have been influenced (more or less, positively or negatively) by North American research traditions. But each also grows out of its own institutional, regional, and national roots. It is crucial for researchers and program developers in academic writing to sometimes see with others' eyes the problems they confront. As I found in co-editing, with David Foster, *Writing and Learning in Cross-National Perspective: Transitions from Secondary to Higher Education* (NCTE Press, 2002), cross-national dialogue is most valuable not in providing solutions but in 'making the familiar strange' (as Clifford Geertz says), helping researchers and program developers to adapt not adopt practices.

For example, for over a century now we in the U.S. have mainly tried to deal with the problem of student writing by requiring students to take a general writing course during their first year – with very mixed success. This volume shows that the debate over general versus discipline-based writing development is very much alive in Europe, which has no tradition of 'first-year composition.' But even where writing is taught special, separate courses in Europe, in large classes, it is done so with a much greater attention to the demands of writing in the disciplines than is usually the case in the U.S. We in the U.S. have much to learn from European research and pedagogical innovations, borne out of very different educational systems. Similarly, the U.S. efforts over the last 20 years to research and teach writing in the disciplines through co-operating with academic staff (called in the U.S. Writing Across the Curriculum) have influenced much European research and program development. And I look forward very much to a fruitful transatlantic dialogue as we in the U.S. learn from European research and pedagogical innovations.

This volume will bring to light – for Europeans as well as North Americans and others world wide – the interest and importance of academic writing. And it introduces the young but strong national research traditions that make writing visible, and offer new prospects for higher education reform world-wide. I look forward very much to the next EATAW conference and to continuing the cross-national dialogue this book admirably furthers.

TEACHING ACADEMIC WRITING IN EUROPEAN HIGHER EDUCATION: AN INTRODUCTION

All roads lead to Rome – The Texts, the Writers or the Discourse Communities in Focus – Same Goals, Different Pedagogies and Organisational Forms for the Teaching of Academic Writing in European Higher Education.

LENNART BJÖRK*, GERD BRÄUER**, LOTTE RIENECKER***
& PETER STRAY JÖRGENSEN***

*Gothenburg University, Sweden, **Emory University, USA & Freiburg University of Education, Germany,
***Academic Writing Center, University of Copenhagen, Denmark

Abstract. The introductory chapter gives an overview of and provides background for the implementation of the array of European writing programs and pedagogies represented in this volume. The development of teaching academic writing in Europe is compared to the development seen in the US where the teaching of writing is further integrated into the educational institutions. The chapter discusses the striking diversity in the European program designs as well as the approaches to teaching and tutoring academic writing in the light of the shared background and also shared inspirational sources from the US in Europe. The integration with the disciplines is depicted as a prominent issue for the still quite small European writing programs and writing centres – a theme which is discussed in many chapters. The introduction lastly concludes that while the expertise in teaching academic writing is now established in Europe, deeper integration between the disciplines and the writing programs/writing centres (in the US known as WID and WAC-programs) has yet to be developed.

Keywords: Development of writing program design in Europe, Models for teaching writing in Europe, Teaching academic writing in Europe, Writing in the disciplines in Europe, and Writing pedagogy in Europe.

Björk, L., Bräuer, G., Rienecker, L. & Stray Jörgensen, P. (2003). Teaching Academic Writing in European Higher Education: An Introduction. In: G. Rijlaarsdam (Series Ed.) & L. Björk, G. Bräuer, L. Rienecker & P. Stray Jörgensen (Volume Eds.), Studies in Writing, Volume 12, Teaching Academic Writing in European Higher Education, pp. 1-15.
© 2003 Kluwer Academic Publishers. Printed in the Netherlands.

1   AUDIENCE: STUDENTS, TEACHERS AND ADMINISTRATORS OF TEACHING ACADEMIC WRITING

If you are a student of (the teaching of) academic writing, what are the current pedagogical and content discussions of what should be taught students about writing in higher education (HE), and how?

If you teach writing in higher education or if you plan to set up a writing program or just a course on academic writing, *how* should you do it? What models have higher education teachers of academic writing in Europe adopted, transformed, or invented to suit the needs of their particular circumstances? What theories and methods underlie the existing facilities and programs and the teaching of academic writing offered here?

If you are a study administrator in higher education, *why* should your institution have a writing program or a writing centre and how could it be designed and implemented, based on the existing European experiences?

The questions mentioned above are at the core of this first European anthology in English on teaching academic writing in higher education. In this volume, we feature concrete pedagogies, samples of actual teaching, of papers and student writer case stories – *the texts and the writers* – and the writing projects where these pedagogies are housed – *the contexts*. Teaching methodology and the organisational frameworks of academic writing are intertwined: the pedagogy depends on the wider social context, the characteristics of the students being taught, the staffing and the resources available, as well as on the theoretical and methodological underpinnings fore grounded by those who teach.

2   PURPOSE AND USABILITY

We hope the present volume will be useful as a source of inspiration to present and future teachers of teaching academic writing in and outside of Europe[1], and to students writing about and entering the practice of teaching academic writing – an emerging and expanding field. You will find that the chapters offer a wide spectrum of concrete suggestions for teaching and curriculum design, for working directly with texts, for cooperating with subject teachers and for project implementation, as well as a list of references with a wealth of European as well as American resources. Students new to the field may start here. The first part of the book *Text and Writer* is equally useful for teachers of academic writing and for any other discipline. Many teaching and feedback strategies and reflections are just as applicable to classroom teaching in the disciplines, it is not solely activities for special designated teachers of writing.

---

[1] *A European forum for the exchange of teaching and organizational models for higher education writing programs was formed in Bochum, 1999: EATAW (European Association for the Teaching of Academic Writing, http://www.hum.ku.dk/eataw) a contact-organization for teachers of academic writing. The editors of the present anthology are past and present members of the board of EATAW.*

We hope to inspire writing project planners and a wider audience of those working with pedagogy in higher education, of which writing pedagogy is or should be a central part.

And we hope to further our communication and exchange especially with American academic writing teachers and writing program administrators, who have influenced the European writing projects greatly with their expertise.

3   CONTRIBUTORS OF THIS VOLUME

The contributors are pioneers in setting up some of the first writing courses, writing centres and writing projects in Higher Education in their native countries: Scandinavia, Germany, the Netherlands and the UK. They share their experience and present their instructional and organisational models. No facility described in this book is older than 10 years; all are small in terms of positions available (1 – 10 full/part-time employees) – but not necessarily small in outreach. Not all have a permanent status. They come from a range of academic disciplines: Mother-tongue language studies, literature, pedagogy, psychology, rhetoric, and medicine. All have a long history of teaching and tutoring academic writing in universities and other higher education institutions. The contributions foreground very different aspects of what the writers perceive as main student difficulties and main pedagogic targets in the teaching of academic writing: Epistemological, motivational, social, cognitive, linguistic, aesthetic, emotional.

Most European writing projects are not accompanied by research positions, but as this volume testifies, the teaching of academic writing in the represented facilities is certainly research-based teaching, in the sense of research of the practice and theory of teaching academic writing.

4   INTRODUCTION TO THE CHAPTERS

4.1 Part One: Text and Writer

Part one *Text and Writer* centres on the texts and genres – the essays, papers and theses – written in higher education, and on the challenges the writers face. The chapters focus on the teaching and tutoring pedagogies in use to help create better texts and writers. In this part of the book, the reader may find concrete advice as well as theoretical and methodological underpinnings for some of the current European work in the teaching of academic writing. The sequence of the articles follows the course of studying in higher education in order to place an emphasis on beginning and finishing studies.

It is no coincidence that writing programs often address first-year students and thesis-writers foremost. Many chapters reflect the work with these two rather different groups of writers. In the context of the demand for writing courses when entering and finishing university, two gaps appear as needed to be bridged: one between high-school level and higher education, and the gap between higher education and working life and continuing education. The first three chapters address the writing difficulties of beginning writers in a higher education context new to them, and on introductory courses to academic writing. The remaining chapters in Part One focus on general writing classes, individual tutoring and feedback strategies, and subject-teacher-oriented activities, across and within disciplines. This part features a number of concrete descriptions of how academic writing is being taught, and it may be of equal interest to teachers of the disciplines in higher education and to academic writing teachers.

Chapter 1
Otto Kruse outlines some typical problems that university students face when they start to work on their first writing assignments without being taught to understand the differences between writing at the high school level and the university level. The writing skills required will be discussed as something to be taught at the university, not in high school, as they are inherently connected to the traditions, forms of thinking, modes of communication, and research methods of the academic world itself.

Chapter 2
Lennart Björk discusses the rationale of an introductory writing course for first-term students at the Department of English, Gothenburg University. In this course, a distinction is made between text types and genres. The first part of the course focuses on three basic expository text types: causal analysis, problem solving, and argumentation. Students work with model texts and produce their own texts within a process-oriented model. The term is finished by a genre – *i.e.,* discipline-specific-paper in literary studies.

Chapter 3
Stella Büker introduces the concept of the 'PunktUm' project at University of Bielefeld, which assists international students in academic writing. Based on the major L2 writing research findings, she develops a scheme that categorises the students' individual problems. A practical example from a consultation sequence demonstrates how extra-curricular writing assistance can respond to the individual writing difficulties effectively. Büker argues for a combined programme of individual tutoring and workshops.

Chapter 4
Lotte Rienecker and Peter Stray Jörgensen describe how they use genre specific excerpts from student's texts as model examples in across the disciplines large class teaching. The pedagogical purpose of having students comment on model examples is to have students internalise an understanding of the features and qualities of the overarching academic genre, the research paper. The large class teaching meets the needs and constraints of the mass universities on the teaching of writing.

Chapter 5
Signe Hegelund and Christian Kock propose that students' problems with genre and task definition in academic writing may be helped with an adaptation of Toulmin's

argumentation model. They suggest that student should be encouraged to apply the model as an assessment criterion and, at the same time, as a heuristic tool during text work. This involves a 'macroscopic' or 'top-down' approach to the evolving draft, not a 'microscopic' analysis of individual passages. The paper suggests a number of appropriate class activities.

Chapter 6
Mary Scott and Kelly Coate's primary aim is to highlight an aspect of feedback, the relation between teacher and student, as realized in samples of written response from a postgraduate college within the Federal University of London. They regard this kind of feedback as especially important in view of the increasing number of students with a widening diversity of past learning experience and of assumptions regarding the roles of teachers and students. They suggest that examples of feedback such as examined in this paper should form the substance not only of seminars with students but also of staff development sessions.

Chapter 7
Lotte Rienecker and Peter Stray Jörgensen describe two traditions of writing which are evident in European HE writing: The continental (topic-oriented) and the Anglo-American (problem-oriented) tradition – and their corresponding writing pedagogies. The authors describe and discuss the problems that arise for students writing in a continental tradition, when writing in the mass university with its very high student-teacher ratio. Suggestions are made for tutoring and teaching academic writing to students writing in the continental discourse communities.

Chapter 8
Kirsti Lonka describes a process-writing course with PhD. candidates from a medical school in Finland. The approach of the course combines cognitive strategies with generative writing and shared revision. The aim of the intervention is to reveal and then revise practices and ideas of writing that usually remain tacit. Lonka points out how to put writing theories into action within the participants' own writing practices.

4.2 Part Two: Teaching Academic Writing in Context

Part two moves from the text-writer-teacher level to the larger contexts of the historical background behind the need for writing instruction:
• The organization of the writing centre/program
• The implementation within the mother institution
• Different models of integrating the teaching of writing
• Cooperation between academic writing teachers and subject teachers.
In this part, those who set up, finance, work in, maintain or cooperate with writing facilities will find inspiration. Here, we learn about different models of European writing programs and the institutional framework and perspectives.

Chapter 9
Gerd Bräuer outlines institutional structures that can enhance the emergence of successful academic writers. He suggests the development of writing (and reading) centres at both ends of the educational pyramid: in high school and at the university. For
each writing (and reading) centre type, he provides a description of possible content,
working methods, functions, and goals. He develops a set of recommendations for
how to initiate interplay between these places of producing and reproducing texts
that would prepare not only successful writers but also better learners.

Chapter 10
Olga Dysthe explains the historical and contextual background for why writing has
not had a prominent place in Norwegian higher education. She tells the story of what
strategies the professional development unit at the University of Bergen has chosen
in order to increase and improve the use of writing. The choice of the 'Integration
model' for strengthening writing is underpinned in socio-cultural theories of learning. Three strategies are represented: writing-to-learn and learning to write, the initiation discipline based action research, and workshops and writing groups. Finally,
Dysthe discusses the state of writing at Norwegian universities, particularly the effect of the evaluation system on writing.

Chapter 11
Andrea Frank, Stefanie Haacke and Christina Tente present the Writing Lab of the
University of Bielefeld and report in particular about their effort to make academic
writing an explicit subject of teaching in the faculties. The authors describe their
experience of cooperating with the academic staff and discuss the phenomenon that
the interest in the Writing Lab grew constantly, contrary to the initial fear that the
lab would eliminate itself over time by establishing writing instruction within the
individual departments.

Chapter 12
Susan Orr and Margo Blythman discuss current discourse about student writing
from a 'standards are falling' – and an 'academic literacies' approach, in which literacies in HE are understood as social practices. Taking the latter as their point of
departure, they problematise subject lecturer's discourse about study support. The
authors conclude that success in study support depends on how subject teachers con-
ceive the functions of study support. By engaging in dialogue with subject teachers
and their understanding of student needs and study support activities, the study support teachers can improve the cooperation with subject teachers.

Chapter 13
Femke Kramer, Jacqueline van Kruiningen and Henrike Padmos discuss the main
features of a writing project at the Faculty of Arts, University of Groningen. They
describe how the project gradually developed, the problems they encountered and
the ways in which they adapted initial goals. In conclusion, the authors outline rec-

ommendations for the development of a teacher-oriented writing programme within the setting of a European academic institution. The basic idea behind these recommendations is that educational renewals need a time-consuming, bottom-up approach to change attitudes and raise consciousness among faculty members and administrators.

Chapter 14
Margo Blythman, Joan Mullin, Jane Milton and Susan Orr outline the principles of study support in two of the five colleges of the London Institute. They identify the micro-politics of implementation, thereby focusing on the process of moving policy to practice. The key argument is that study support must be understood by staff and students, effectively situated organizationally and firmly linked within the wider institution.

The two parts of this volume give some examples of the current work done in Europe (Part One) with writing processes and products of student writers in HE, the teaching and tutoring, instructing and responding to student texts, and in Part Two the work with integrating this work in the contexts where the writing is designed, advised and finally evaluated.

5   WRITING COURSES, WRITING CENTRES, AND WRITING PROGRAMS: RESPONDING TO PROBLEMS IN EUROPEAN HIGHER EDUCATION

Writing centres and writing programs date back only to the early 1990's in continental Europe, but in the UK and the US writing programs already started in the late 19th century, and by the 1970s, hundreds of writing centres in the US had been more or less firmly established.

Although the teaching of academic writing as a separate entity of higher education is rather new in continental Europe, writing instruction as a means of individual feedback, term papers or degree theses has always occurred, even if the main method applied there has been more or less learning through trial and error. In such a scenario 'students reinvent academic writing' (Kruse, this volume). One may claim that much of European university pedagogy tradition is adversarial in principle toward any explicit teaching and instruction of writing – as well as other skills such as teaching any presentational skills and teaching HE teaching. 'Universities in Europe are very ambivalent and do not endorse the teaching of academic writing' (Kruse, this volume). The underlying rationale for this position is that content is married to form, teaching is married to research, discipline is married to formats for texts, good writing to good thinking, and that all of these are so closely tied together that instruction which separate these marriages may in advance be deemed as fruitless endeavours. The idea of the ability to write as a gift, an inborn intellectual and sometimes even artistic talent which is in its nature unteachable is not far away when the notion of teaching academic writing is discussed in many a HE setting outside the narrow circles of the academic writing teachers.

5.1 From Elite to Mass Institutions

The shift in higher education from elite to mass institutions, but staffed by people with similar training as decades ago, the widening of participation in higher education, has led to a need for substantial reforms in teaching. Higher education in many European countries currently sees significant cutbacks on the tolerated length of studies (for instance Holland, Norway, Denmark), and less patience on the part of politicians with high dropout rates and other signs of 'inefficiency' in higher education. Retention of students is mentioned as an overriding institutional concern in several articles (see for example Orr & Blythman, and Kramer, van Kruiningen & Padmos), as a major impetus for investing in teaching academic writing. At the same time, the amount of writing done in education, as well as the demands made on writing skills by employers has increased. Within higher education institutions, we likewise witness a movement where more weight seems to be placed on the writing of long academic papers already from the beginning of a student's career, and former professional educations become academic educations requiring university level writing. As a result, more students than ever before need substantial writing skills and, therefore, depend on regular and explicit instruction, advice and feedback. Learning through writing as well as developing writing ability is necessary today to complete a higher education. 'Skill' is a reductive term for what it is teachers of academic writing hope to enhance: The ambition shared by all the contributors to this volume is rather to strengthen the connection between writing, thinking and reading; teaching the disciplines through writing-to-learn and, as Bräuer puts it, the eventual goal is lifelong learning.

5.2 The Diverse Student Population

The original observation made by those who initiated the first generation of writing program/centres anywhere was that 'Johnny can't write'. European universities face a growing diversity of students from educational backgrounds, and the diversity as well as the widening access to HE represents a challenge to traditional higher education. Scott and Coate from the UK report that while the participation rate was 15% in the eighties, it was by the mid-nineties up to 30% and is expected to reach 50% in the near future (this volume). Several articles in this volume address the difficult process of integrating students into academic writing. It is as a result of the observation that many students are ill prepared for academic writing that all the contributing projects have been founded. Typical for the European writing projects, the scarce resources are being used for the students who have writing problems, and students in transition from one educational phase to another: new students (Björk, Bräuer, Kruse), international students (Büker), adult 'post-experience' students in teacher training (Scott & Kelly), 'standards are falling'-students in the rapidly expanding British educational system (Orr & Blythman), thesis-writers (Rienecker & Stray Jörgensen), starting doctoral students (Lonka). All of these are in a transition where writing has to be taught (again, anew) and social relations negotiated carefully. European writing facilities are mostly designed to meet pressing demands, and so the writing centre/project meets the academic writer-to-be in a phase of transition and under stress. In America, all college students will meet with writing courses in the introductory course Composition 101, and/or through writing across the curriculum or writing in the disciplines-activities. And as those of us who have American guest students will know, they will have a much lower threshold for dropping into a writing centre for some help with a paper, reflecting that they are accustomed to using such a facility. European higher education seems to be at a historical point where the pedagogy of trial-and-error is inadequate, but where a pedagogy of instruction is just beginning to evolve.

5.3 Implementing and Developing the US Inspiration

All facilities in Europe owe the 'idea of a writing centre,' citing a key article on writing centre development by Stephen North (1984), to the writing pedagogy in US higher education. Without the powerful inspiration from the American writing movement, there would not have been models to point to when asking administrators for funding the first European initiatives just a few years ago, and it is doubtful whether any writing project in Europe would exist today without the long history for such facilities in the US. In the words of Kramer, van Kruiningen and Padmos: 'Europe is going through a phase of initial initiative and implementation which America has been through years ago (…) Europe needs a gradual, procedural change in teaching methods and attitudes towards writing and education'. The development of the teaching of writing that has been under way in America for a century is now strongly needed in Europe, but this development has here only a history of a couple of decades.

5.4 Governmental Influence

Some of the writing facilities described in this volume have been initiated or spurred on by a government reform project in HE. This applies to the German, British, Norwegian and Dutch projects. Writing projects have come into existence as part of quality-reforms at the initiative of the state, and in line with international trends. One international trend in higher education is the professionalisation of pedagogy as witnessed in the advent of Centers for Teaching and Learning and Professional Development Centres of which writing projects/experts may become a more or less distinct part. Individual teachers and researchers who have recognised the needs of many students initiate others (examples in this volume come from Denmark (University of Copenhagen) and Sweden (Gothenburg and Stockholm universities).

6 DIFFERENT MODELS AND SHARED CONCERNS

6.1 The Diversity of Models for Teaching Academic Writing

The teaching of writing in higher education is geared toward the different functions of writing. Writing promotes thinking, learning and communication; writing expresses the self of the writer; writing socialises the students into the discourse communities of the disciplines. Writing requires and also develops a set of key skills, which may be transferred into many different contexts. The diversity of the models of teaching writing and of organising a writing course, writing program, or a writing centre mirrors these different functional aspects of writing. Different key concerns for the teacher or the curriculum result in different writing pedagogies, as shown in table 1.

Table 1: Pedagogies ensuing from a focus on text, writer or discourse community

The text in focus - academic discourse	The writer in focus - individual discourse	The discourse community in focus - discipline specific discourse
Key concerns		
- content - rhetoric of science - scientific genre and genre conventions - text types - linguistics - meta-cognition - "that" - form	- process - epistemology - identity, integrity, sponta- neity - writer types, styles, voices - blocks, procrastinations - cognition - emotion - "I, him, her" - self-expression	- social construction - academic literacy - discipline specific conven- tions - discourse "types" - discourse jargon - "us, them" - content and form within disciplines
Corresponding pedagogies		
- instructional guidelines - formats, templates - model examples - writing software - large groups/classes - feedback techniques - general academic writing courses	- teaching process-writing: learning logs, diaries, brainstorming, clustering, free-writing - teaching revision strate- gies - individual tutorials - feedback to individual writers - therapy - process-workshops	- advising - dialogue - discussion - socialisation - identification - small groups - peer response - team-teaching with sub- ject teachers - discipline-specific courses

Based on the different approaches mentioned above, you will find a diversity of teaching methods: individual tutoring of and feedback on writing, process-oriented courses, text-type or genre-teaching courses, dialogic peer-discussion, organised peer-feedback groups, discipline specific courses on academic writing, and net-based writing instruction for students and teachers. Any single writing program might be inspired by any of these understandings of what should be the central content and pedagogy of a university writing course, program or centre. In part, the different points of departure depict a historical development through the last thirty years of writing research and writing pedagogy, which itself bears witness to the diversity of theoretical understandings to which practitioners of this field adhere.

Over time, the main focus seems to have changed from normative instruction and developing the expressive powers and the writing processes of individual writers, towards the constructivist view of writing in HE seen as a development of academic literacies where 'the good academic paper' is a function of social constructions bound by sometimes very local discursive conventions, for instance around a single subject teacher.

One of the differences among teachers of academic writing is a classical pedagogical question of whether starting from parts of a text or from whole texts will promise a better potential for learning. It seems debatable whether to first present text types or genres, working from the conventions of a particular discipline or from overarching rules underpinning scientific writing at large. Some might also want to start right from the student writer's texts and experience.

6.2 Expert Model or Integration in the Disciplines Model?

Some teachers of academic writing – represented in this volume – work within an 'expert model' where a writing facility offers its own teaching and tuition. Some strive for an 'integration model' (using Olga Dysthe's terms), which brings tutoring and workshops right into the individual disciplines. Why choose one model over the other? There is the assumption that the 'expert model' rests on a text- or a writer-based centre of gravity in the work, whereas the 'integration model' follows the concept of academic socialisation into discourse communities, initiating a discipline-specific view of what needs to be taught and who may teach it. Quoting Kruse on this latter view: 'Writing is highly discourse-specific and should be integrated into the curriculum of the single subjects, as the writing-across-the-curriculum movement has proposed'. In this volume Kruse, Dysthe, Orr and Blythman, Kramer, van Kruiningen and Padmos, Scott and Coate emphasize the social context, where else Björk, Bräuer, Büker, Kock and Hegelund, Lonka, Rienecker and Stray Jörgensen focus more on the writer and text-based teaching of academic writing. This does not mean at all that there is no overlap: focusing on the writer does not mean to forget about writing in the disciplines and vice versa. In practice as we all know, there are no clear boundaries and dividing lines. And there are certainly also pragmatic concerns, such as resources and the possibilities of working within specific disciplines, behind the choice of either an expert model or an integration model for any writing facility. In addition, the differences in HE writing traditions appear not only as discipline-specific, but also within disciplines, as Rienecker & Stray Jörgensen show in their article on the continental and Anglo-American traditions of academic writing. Both traditions can thrive within a discipline.

How discipline-specific is academic writing? What are the differences and the similarities across disciplines? This question has a profound impact on who may teach what and to whom. If academic writing – or indeed any writing in the education system – has so many faces that it breaks down into teacher-specific discourses, then the teaching of writing can only be the domain of the subject teachers, requiring as Olga Dysthe has put as it 'dual competencies' (keynote speech, European Association for the Teaching of Academic Writing conference in Groningen, 2001) of all higher education teachers, rather than special expert units. Perhaps there is a truth to be found in the term 'comfort zone: We all have a comfort zone of teaching, beyond which we would feel out of bounds. (Susan Orr, keynote speech, Writing Development in Higher Education, conference in Leicester, 2002). Susan Orr expanded that for the academic writing teacher, the comfort zone may mean that he/she will teach writing within certain disciplines, but perhaps not across educational fields. And we might add: For the subject teachers the comfort zone may include more than the *knowing what* of the subject and the discipline, namely the *knowing how*, of which the academic writing is a part. What HE in Europe needs is for many more teachers to gradually expand their comfort zone towards an integration of academic writing and other literacies in the curricula of their disciplines.

The constructionist view entail different traditions within disciplines of a magnitude which might make common textbooks and other study materials in academic writing impossible, but this is obviously not the case: Protagonists of writing in the disciplines do write textbooks for cross-curricular academic writing. In writing instructional material, the author looks for what is thought to be the common features across disciplinary differences. Again, pragmatic concerns would necessitate this overlap of pedagogical approaches in Europe: It is unlikely that a textbook on academic writing for just one discipline in a small language would even be in print. The market would simply be too small. Thus, resources and markets are determining factors behind pedagogy.

Despite all these differences, let us take a brief look at what we noticed as the shared concerns across disciplines among the European countries contributing to this anthology.

6.3 Shared Concerns: The Writer and the Text

Despite the diversity of our national and educational backgrounds, the contributors to this volume have many shared practices and observations on both the individual writer/teacher level and on the organisational level.

First, what we all have in common is that we focus our teaching on writing processes. 'Process' can be taught without adherence to a discipline. Nevertheless, it is the teaching of product qualities ('What is a good paper in higher education?'), which is a controversial issue, an issue of the greatest importance for any teacher of academic writing to resolve. In the process of editing this book, the diversity of inspirational sources became very concrete in one point: We do not have the same theoretical framework in common, because over time different sources have influenced our scholarship and teaching. Throughout all the chapters of this book, there is only one reference shared by most contributors: Bereiter and Scardamalia (1987), *The Psychology of Written Composition*. The main idea expressed in Bereiter and Scardamalia's much-cited work is that writing development proceeds in phases, starting out with the ability to write narratively, where all material in a composition is related to its title, but not necessarily linked within the text through a task or problem. The so-called writing as knowledge telling is writer-centred, not reader-based, and it is the reader-based prose which is the teaching goal of any teacher of writing. The next stage is analytic writing, which allows for the needs of a reader and for a purpose-driven investigation of a problem or question, holding together every element of the text. Bereiter & Scardamalia call this level of writing development the knowledge transforming stage. There is a widespread agreement among writing researchers that knowledge transforming is a primary goal for writing instruction in secondary and tertiary education. Nevertheless, the ability to transform knowledge through writing must be consciously and continuously trained, it cannot be taken for granted, not even with adult learners in university education.

To this and to the finding that an argumentative purpose seems to be at the core of knowledge transforming, all the articles in this volume bear witness. Many university writing programs are designed to feature argumentation as the last and most challenging step within a series of writing tasks. Kock and Hegelund's article outlines a new way of utilising Stephen Toulmin's model of argumentation in the teaching of the writing of research papers.

6.4 Shared Concerns: Context

All writing practitioners in this volume aim to address academic writing as 'writing to learn' for all students, not just as a remedial service to 'weak students'. Nevertheless, the ways of how to put this goal into practice are different: Orr, Blythman, Milton and Mullins take writing across the curriculum as their models, they state that they would rather work with curriculum, with professional development and staff consultations than spend their time in endless tutoring sessions with individual students who share similar writing difficulties. Despite the obvious advantages of this approach, many authors in this volume report about the difficulty of engaging staff in the disciplines in academic writing pedagogy as seen in the article by Frank, Haacke and Tente from the Bielefeld Writing Lab, one of the oldest writing projects in Continental Europe (since 1993). Kruse, Dysthe, Orr and Blythman also report that staff in the disciplines still believes that writing should be learned in primary and secondary education and should not be the task of universities. Thus, it seems no coincidence that writing in the disciplines is repeatedly proposed using the modal verb 'should'. The fact is that there is no European example of a writing in the disciplines program in HE so far. All existing writing across the curriculum projects are small and not fully integrated into the institution.

There is hardly a writing centre/project that does not exert a great deal of effort towards integration. The expert model seems to be nobody's expressed ideal, but often what HE institutions are left with, unless there is a strong driving force supporting the integration in the disciplines of teaching writing. In the cases of Norway and the Netherlands, the driving force towards more integration of writing and writing instruction has been changes in higher education – in the Norwegian term – governmentally implemented quality reforms.

7   FUTURE PERSPECTIVES

A concern shared by many contributors to this volume is that writing programs and writing centres face isolation within the university. In contrast to the US, writing facilities in Europe have not yet developed structures for writing across the curriculum or writing in the disciplines. Both approaches take the teaching of academic writing back into the classrooms where many feel it is best taught. Therefore, a next step for European writing educators may be to work through and with higher education faculty to proliferate a more integrated approach to the teaching of academic writing. Existing programs and centers are so far – as some of them in Germany are called: Leuchtturm-Projekte, ('lighthouse-projects') – places where experts provide their expertise and service mainly to students. One exception to the rule of relative isolation is the Dutch writing program of the Groningen University, Faculty of Arts. This writing program addresses university staff only, in its first stage through an electronic handbook on the teaching-in-the-disciplines of academic writing and on the design of written assignments (see Kramer, van Kruiningen & Padmos). Representatives of the fields themselves contribute to the continuing writing of the handbook. The Groningen program is unique in its teacher-centred approach, where all other projects work from the writing problems of individual students, to addressing the faculty and a wider audience through handbooks, peer-tutor service; peer writing groups, and additional team-teaching and teach-the-teacher initiatives. The Groningen project also sets an example in having the design of written work at university as a major target, a key area in curriculum planning where resources and expertise on writing is all too often not used at all by the institutions, but are merely called upon to help individual students who 'cannot write'.

For writing programs with less far-reaching goals than the Groningen-project, the next step in development could be a gradual integration with members of faculty into the teaching of writing. Several of the contributors to this volume mention the already existing obligatory pedagogical courses for new university teachers as the best forum for establishing contacts and to teach research-based writing pedagogy to HE teachers.

Does the strategy of supplying the faculty with writing pedagogy know-how make the writing project obsolete? This hardly seems likely. Writing research and expertise in the practice of teaching has developed vastly and it can best be distributed through writing centers with their specific expertise and network within the professional field of teaching academic writing. Frank, Haacke and Tente observe that the learning needs seem to develop and to become ever more facetted as time passes and basic knowledge about writing becomes common ground for faculty and students. A future prospect is that research in academic writing and the teaching of writing should naturally have its home in writing centers or programs.

Based on the variety of models of writing programs, as introduced here in this book, we hope to inspire the foundation of new facilities, the further development of existing ones, and we hope for more communication across and beyond Europe concerning the teaching of academic writing. After roughly ten years of institutionalised European writing pedagogy, the consolidation as well as the implementation of new initiatives still very much depends on the visibility and success of the facilities already existing, as well as on the organisational support from home institutions (see Orr, Blythman, Milton & Mullin). From our own experience, we know that it is highly important to let colleagues, administrators and politicians know about 'what other universities already have.'

In the next few years, the teaching of academic writing may change dramatically, as much as instruction in higher education in general might change through the possibilities of computerized learning and teaching. Already today, 'learning to write from sources' is changing fast into 'learning to evaluate Internet sources'. Before we know it, the genres we teach today, the essay and the traditional academic research paper may be supplemented with new genres such as hypertext, calling for new ideas on how to teach and how to organize writing instruction.

ACKNOWLEDGEMENTS

We would like to thank all contributing authors for their creative ideas, scholarly excellence and collegial spirits during the long process of putting together this book. We are especially grateful to Gabriela Ruhmann, director of the Writing Center at the University of Bochum, whose advice and support encouraged us immensely during the early stage of our project. We also thank Gert Rijlaarsdam (series editor) and the team of Kluwer Academic Publishers for their continuing assistance especially in the final phase of this challenging project. We owe great thanks to Trine Lykke Gandil, student assistant at the Academic Writing Center, University of Copenhagen, for making the manuscript ready for print.

The team of editors

PART ONE:
TEXT AND WRITER

GETTING STARTED: ACADEMIC WRITING IN THE FIRST YEAR OF A UNIVERSITY EDUCATION

OTTO KRUSE

University of Applied Sciences, Erfurt, Germany

Abstract. This contribution outlines some typical problems that university students face when they start to work on their first writing assignments and the pedagogical implications for the learning and teaching of academic writing. The paper starts with a case study showing some of the experiences of a student trying to write her first scholarly term paper. Without being taught to understand the differences between writing at the high school level and the university level, she runs into a number of problems that can be considered typical for this situation. In the second step, a description of the most important demands of academic writing will be given. It will be argued that the writing skills which meet these demands are substantially different from the writing skills required in high school, and that they must be taught at the university, not in high school, as they are inherently connected to the traditions, forms of thinking, modes of communication, and research methods of the academic world itself. The third part of the paper will draw conclusions for the learning of writing and will emphasise the idea that writing should be an integral part of university teaching programs and deserves considerably more attention as a research subject itself.

Keywords: Academic learning, Communication, Discourse communities, Knowledge production, Language conventions, Learning difficulties, Writing skills, and Writing socialization.

1   THE START: AN ILLUSTRATION

Johanna[2] begins her degree in Education at a German university. In her first semester, she takes a course on the topic of 'fatherhood'. The course is a 'Pro-seminar', meant to introduce students to academic discourse and teach them about scholarly presentation and discussion of research materials. To get her credit points, Johanna must give a summarising presentation of one of the subtopics of the course and write a term paper about it. As she never had writing problems in school, Johanna is opti-

---

[2] *Please note that Johanna is not a real person, but a fictional character. All descriptions of her behaviours and problems, however, have been taken from observations of real students in writing counselling.*

19

Kruse, O. (2003). Getting Started: Academic Writing in the First Year of a University Education. In: G. Rijlaarsdam (Series ed.) & L. Björk, G. Bräuer, L. Rienecker & P. Stray Jörgensen (Volume Eds.), Studies in Writing, Volume 12, Teaching Academic Writing in European Higher Education, pp. 19-28. © 2003 Kluwer Academic Publishers. Printed in the Netherlands.

mistic that she will successfully manage this task. She receives a reading list about her subtopic 'The role of the father in infant education', finds most of the titles in the library, and starts reading. The paper has to meet the criteria of academic texts, she has been told, and she has been provided with a style guide showing the accepted forms of quotations and references.

In high school, Johanna has learned to write narrative texts about her own experiences, interpretations of pictures and novels, and argumentative texts about political or ethical dilemmas. Though she never knew exactly how she managed successfully to write a text, she enjoyed writing. The process of writing itself has not been discussed in any of her classes, but she knows that it is useful to start out with a draft, then write a rough text, and finally rewrite it. She has learned that an outline is important, and that exact spelling, grammar and punctuation are necessary conditions for good grades. She has a tentative understanding of the fact that texts are an important key to knowledge, and she is looking forward to delving into deeper levels of knowledge in her university studies. Altogether, she has been quite well prepared for the learning tasks that await her.

When Johanna starts reading, she first opens the book that looks most authoritative to her. It is a two-volume book called 'Fathers', which contains a 200-page section about the role of fathers in infant education. While she reads this chapter, she starts to get discouraged. Dozens of empirical studies are summarised here and she is unable to think of a way to add anything to them. Is she meant to summarise the summary? Or even reread the original sources? She looks into one of the shorter articles on her reading list, which is obviously written by a feminist. Here she finds the results of a few empirical studies, followed by a critique of fathers, who, according to the author, do not participate in infant education in the same way and with equal intensity as mothers do. That sounds interesting, but how can she combine this article with the first book? Still different is the third article she opens about the history of fatherhood, which claims that fathers today spend significantly more time in infant education and in interaction with their children than they ever did before. Obviously, fathers have improved considerably over time, but how does this go together with the aforementioned paper?

Johanna goes back to the two-volume book and slowly moves through the critical 200 pages, fighting against fatigue and discouragement. She underlines almost every second sentence. When she tries to summarise what she has read, she is dissatisfied with her own text. She keeps rereading, trying to copy the phrases used in the original source, as her own wording doesn't sound scholarly to her. She rewrites her paragraphs several times without finding the proper style that would make them sound 'right'. None of the criteria she has learned so far of what the terms 'academic' or 'scholarly' could mean seem to apply to the task of designing a text. Writing, for the first time in her life, becomes painful.

By mid-semester, as the date of the oral presentation approaches, Johanna starts to get nervous. She has no idea which aspects of the topic she should choose for her speech. She has read most of the articles on the reading list and summarised some of them, but she has not written any ideas of her own. She starts writing her speech, but runs into a dead end after one and a half pages, not knowing what has gone wrong. With the help of a friend, she sorts out her thoughts and decides to reduce the presentation mainly to a combination of the feminist and the historical article, which helps her to stay clear and concrete. To her surprise, she gets a positive feedback for her speech and her professor seems to be pleased about the vivid discussion that it gives rise to. Nobody seems to have noticed that she ignored a lot of the literature on the reading list.

After this experience, Johanna drops her work on the paper for a while. When she takes it up again she has to read most of the literature again. She decides that she would write short sections and collect useful quotations that she will then combine to make a coherent text. Summarising the texts continues to be a problem, as she never feels certain that her summaries are correct. Neither has she found a way to integrate her own opinion into the text. What she has written looks like a copy of the original, without anything of her own. Every time she uses the word 'I' she immediately feels that the sentence loses its power, so she adopts the impersonal 'one'. A large part of her struggle is connected with the selection of the right words, as she has found out that the terminologies of the texts differ significantly, and she never knows which term is the right one.

Despite these feelings, Johanna continues her work and writes many short pieces, which she then organises within a logical sounding outline. When brought into a coherent text and printed out, the result does, as Johanna notices to her surprise, have some of the 'academic' qualities that she was struggling for.

Some time after she has turned in her paper, she asks her professor about the result. She learns that the outline of her paper is not fully consistent, that her own opinion is missing, and that she has misunderstood some of the empirical research. Still, her professor likes the over-all approach of her paper, as she feels that a feminist position was a good addition to a pure academic treatment of the topic. Johanna receives credit for her work.

Though Johanna was relieved, she felt that she had not learned much about writing. She considered her work as a near-failure, for in view of the huge amount of time she had invested, the result seemed inadequate. She still did not know what a scholarly term paper is and what she could change next time in order to work more efficiently. Writing for her has started to become an arduous and stressful procedure without any personal significance, simply meant to fulfil her study assignments and to conform to the established academic standards.

2   THE TASK

Like Johanna, freshmen in German and probably most European universities start their careers as academic writers largely unprepared. Though they are usually fairly competent writers in sorts of text related to their recent school education and have enough general language ability to meet the challenges of academic writing, they run a great risk of failure if their learning is not supported by substantial writing instruction also at the university level. Let's have a look at what Johanna had to infer about academic writing instead of being taught:

- She had to produce a text but was not provided with any knowledge about what kind of text this should be. She did not know that she had to choose between

different text types and different genres of academic writing, as for instance
Björk & Räisänen (1996) have described. (See also Björk, this volume.)

- She was not prepared for the fact that she might run into problems with writing;
  she had to assume that she could solve the task with the same means and skills,
  which she had mastered in her writing assignments at school. Even if she had
  tried to look for help, she would not have known who to ask and what to ask
  (see Ruhmann 1996, 1997b for a further discussion). The only help she received
  came from her friend and, indeed, much of the writing know-how of students is
  passed on in this informal way.

- She was not aware that it was her own task to define the problem and to delineate the topic she would write about. Her approach was mainly knowledge-
  telling, as Bereiter & Scardamalia (1987) called this unsophisticated, simple
  form of knowledge reproduction. She certainly had the capacity for a more
  elaborate knowledge-transforming mode of writing, but did not know how this
  was done in the academic domain. Her paper did not contain a research question
  (or a problem formulation), which is the most natural academic tool to put the
  knowledge-transforming process into action, as shown for instance by Rienecker (1999).

- She did not know anything about the connections between writing and the research process. She simply assumed that writing is meant to spell out the results
  of research, not knowing what makes it a knowledge-producing act and how it
  is intertwined with the knowledge development of research (Kruse 1997a).

- She did have a rough understanding of the writing process, but was not prepared
  to understand in which way academic writing is a technology with its own rules,
  tools and strategies. She learned some of the techniques of academic work (like
  writing excerpts, using file cards, using bibliographies, researching in the library *etc.*), but was not informed about how they relate to the writing process.

- She was very conscious about the fact that academic texts do use a special language, but did not know anything about the construction of its style or rhetoric
  (Kruse 2001). So all she could do was to try to imitate the sound of it.

- She correctly assumed that academic text production requires a thorough
  appreciation of the existing publications, but she lacked a deeper understanding
  of the connections between reading and writing (see Jakobs 1994, 1995, 1997,
  Kruse & Ruhmann 1999). Transferring her experiences from school to
  university, she assumed that a correct reproduction is the main criteria in
  dealing with other's ideas, not knowing exactly what kinds of obligations and
  what degree of freedom she has in doing so.

- An academic text appeared to her as a kind of a container that has to be filled
  with knowledge, not as a means of purposeful communication. She only
  vaguely sensed what academic discourse could be and how writers in the academic world relate to each other by publishing their writings (Jakobs 1994,
  1995).

- She was confused by the existence of contradictory standards in the evaluation
  of texts and did not yet understand that different judgmental criteria might be
  equally valid.

Though Johanna was not prepared for academic writing, she did get her assignment done and she learned a lot about writing in doing so. What she was forced to do in a certain way, was to reinvent academic writing, partly as an intuitive process of language acquisition, partly as a rational reconstruction of how academic texts might be structured and partly as a process of trial and error as to how the writing process might be managed. We may assume that Johanna will eventually master her study program and that she may even proceed to write a doctoral thesis, as have many students before her without any formal writing training. But without a deeper understanding of the writing process, her learning capacity will be impaired by a set of obstacles that will slow down her progress in learning and may discourage her further. As reading, thinking and writing are closely interrelated in academic learning (Friedman & Steinberg 1989) she will not be able to live up to her capacities if her writing socialisation is not supported.

Many students are less prepared for the writing tasks at the university level and are less persistent in pursuing their goals than Johanna was. They are likely to face more severe learning difficulties and eventually fail to finish their studies at all, as is the case with about one third of all students in German universities. To gain a better understanding of their academic development, it is necessary to have a closer look at what 'academic writing skills' are. It is only by the co-operation of several distinct, but interrelated abilities that an academic text can be produced. These abilities have to be connected with a substantial knowledge of research procedures, as academic writing serves delineated purposes in this process. Unfortunately, however, academic writing is not only logically connected with scientific endeavour, but also traditionally, as it follows the language conventions established in the various discourse communities throughout the long history of scholarly activity (see Pörksen 1994, Ehlich 1995). These conventions do not apply to all academic communities in the same way, but vary from community to community.

For students, writing in the academic world is not only a learning task but also part of their larger academic socialisation. It teaches the students how to talk about subject-specific matters and how to produce the distinction between everyday and academic knowledge. It makes them members of discourse communities and allows them to communicate with their colleagues.

3   THE DEMANDS

Academic writers usually have to solve several different tasks simultaneously, and their writing process may be impaired if they fail in even one of them. Flower & Hayes (1980) proposed three general constraints that a writer has to deal with: the demand for integrated knowledge, the linguistic conventions, and the rhetorical problem. These constraints or demands of writing are useful for grouping the most important aspects of academic writing skills (Kruse & Jakobs 1999) that students like Johanna must acquire.

3.1 The Demands of Knowledge

Anyone who writes an academic text needs integrated and flexible knowledge, either cognitively represented or in external storage, in order to organise the writing process smoothly. This is what students like Johanna understand almost immediately: Academic writing refers to the body of existing knowledge and therefore asks for a thoughtful study of the existing sources. Before writing, one has to learn what one is writing about. Beginning writers in the academic field are first of all handicapped by their limited knowledge, which is usually accompanied by a feeling of being unable substantially to contribute to the existing knowledge.

But the relationship between knowledge and writing is more complex than it appears at first (Molitor-Lübbert 1995). Though knowledge is the most important factor for academic writing, its relationship to writing is obscured by the fact that it is hard to tell what knowledge really is. Following a constructivist viewpoint of knowledge, as is widely accepted in the contemporary theory of science; it is useless to look for any persisting 'true' knowledge. What is accepted as true in academic communities changes rapidly. Thus, writing cannot be considered a means of simply describing knowledge; rather it is a way to construct knowledge through the use of language. Language is not a passive matter, onto which knowledge is imprinted like a seal is imprinted on wax, but rather is an active device to produce knowledge (Kruse & Jakobs 1999, Kruse 2001). This fact is especially puzzling for beginning writers in the academic field, who in high school have grown accustomed to thinking in terms of true and false. This habit leads them to look for *true* knowledge and the *right* way to express it, instead of looking for what might possibly be said and what their own message might be.

Academic knowledge is discourse-specific. Academic texts can be understood only as part of a co-operative effort of a scientific community to gain knowledge. Each text refers to former knowledge and points towards the knowledge that will be produced in the future. Text composition should thus be viewed as a transitional phenomenon, as a kind of a bridge from existing to future knowledge. This means that a writer must accept his or her role of knowledge-transformer and refer to himself or herself as an agent of change rather than simply a knowledge-teller. Beginning students like Johanna quickly recognise that they are meant to do more than simply reproduce what they have read, but they do not easily find their role and the rhetorical means actually to transform knowledge and thus become authors of academic texts.

While writing a text demands a response to existing knowledge, in the academic learning process, writing also functions as a means of *acquiring* knowledge and at the same time of *demonstrating* the acquired knowledge (as well as the acquired writing skills). This is a difficult situation for writers, as it forces them to pretend that they have mastered the required knowledge and therefore does not allow them to communicate any problems with it or with the writing process itself. Still, the traditions of writing in German universities force the students right from the beginning to use the elaborate genre of the research paper (*'Hausarbeid'*) and does not allow them to use more personal and more communicative forms of writing, as proposed for instance by Fulwiler (1997) or Kruse (1999). It seems necessary to adopt ways that make writing a tool for learning and separate it from the demanding forms of elaborate academic writing.

3.2 The Demands of Language

One of Johanna's main concerns was to find the 'right' language for her paper. This raises two different questions: first, what is 'academic' language, and second, what happens to Johanna's 'own' language? Academic writing forces students to adopt a new kind of language, without helping them to master the transition from common to academic language. This limits their language capacity almost as if they were forced to think in a foreign language.

Language has always been a matter of utmost importance to scholars, as it is the basis of consciousness, thinking and communication. Writers who do not conform to the standards of academic language can hardly expect to be recognised in the academic world (Pörksen 1994). Using poetic language instead of academic terms, for instance, immediately discredits a text (and the writer) in the academic world. The 'right' language functions as a sign to the audience, signalling that the writer is a member of their community. As this is true for the language used in most social groups, Johanna sensed that finding the right style was an important part of her task of getting accepted in the academic world.

What Johanna did not know is the fact that even for most scholars the structure of academic language is not fully transparent. Though they usually know the prescriptions from style guides and publication manuals that exist in their fields, they are not aware of the more subtle linguistic dimensions that govern the language use in the academic field. The style of research is 'social' in nature, says Gross (1991: 954) and is not an individualistic, fashionable accessory of language use.

Johanna was confused by the fact that the language of the different texts she read varied significantly. The scholarly book on fathers, summarising the existing empirical research, was written in a different style from the argumentation of the feminist or the report of the historian. For Johanna it was a painful decision to conform to one of these three alternatives. She did not have meaningful criteria that could tell her which of them to prefer. This was one of the main causes for her long and painful struggle to find the style that sounded 'right'.

What, then, is academic language, and how much of it should be taught? Is it necessary to teach students discourse-specific language? Or is it more advisable to help them to rely on their 'own' language – which consists, in part, of ordinary language – and encourage them to express their personal inclinations. There is no simple answer to this question. Neither of the alternatives is completely satisfactory. What students must learn, and what probably constitutes one of the most important writing skills, is some kind of textual awareness that allows them to conform to academic discourse when necessary but also to stick to their own modes of thinking and writing. What helps students most is a positive definition of academic writing that defines the desirable properties of academic language (see for instance Elbow 1991).

3.3   The Demands of Communication

The rhetorical dimension deals with the purpose of writing and the effect a text is supposed to have upon the audience. This asks for a consideration of the communicative context of which academic writing is a part. For students like Johanna the first contact with this issue is usually connected with the question: 'For whom am I writing this paper?' They notice that many decisions in their writing process depend on the selection of a specific audience. How should I argue? What do I have to explain and what can I take for granted? How explicit or inclusive should I be? In order to give students a fair answer to these questions, it is not enough (though it may be useful at the beginning) to tell them to write for their fellow students. This would be no more than a short-term substitution for the larger truth, that an understanding of the audience in academic writing is connected with an understanding of academic discourse.

Academic discourse, on the surface, is based on the fact that academic writers read other's works and respond to them. This exchange of ideas leads to the result that the texts are connected with each other. Each text depends on the existence of many other texts, which themselves were written on the basis of former texts. Academic texts are, therefore, highly redundant, in that they repeat to a large extent what has already been published. Only a small portion of them is innovative. By the term 'discourse', usually both aspects are meant: the exchange itself and the textual forms of this exchange. In order to participate in this discourse, one must follow the accepted language conventions and use the traditional text forms in the respective academic field.

The dependency of academic texts on other texts is demonstrated most clearly by the use of references and quotations, and this explicit referentiality is probably the most outstanding of all characteristics of academic texts. Unfortunately, students are usually instructed only as to how to deal with the formal aspects of references and quotations and must simply infer the deeper meaning of these formalities as discourse-producing devices, which connect a text with other texts, like links in an electronic circuit.

Academic knowledge, it has been said, is produced in a collaborative effort by the scientific community. However, the kind of collaboration practised here differs from the collaboration in any other kind of human work, as it never comes to a halt or finds its final goal. Such collaboration is a never-ending process of adding new findings or ideas to the pool of knowledge, thus extending and transforming it. The people co-operating with each other rarely ever meet each other personally. The most important rule that governs the collaboration is the obligation comprehensibly to publish new research results, and the obligation to recognise others' publications on the same topic (Weinrich 1995). Learning to write in the academic world means to learn the rules of the game in order finally to be able to participate in it.

There is yet another characteristic of the academic text that causes students to misunderstand its communicative purpose. Academic writing is usually addressed to the scientific community and academic texts are a means of communication with this community. But as Kretzenbacher (1995: 34) has shown, the linguistic features of academic language disguise the communicative purpose, as the author or sender of the message ('I') is hardly ever mentioned, just as the receiver is rarely directly addressed. The message itself is kept in a transparent, windowpane-like style that makes it appear independent of the language by which it is formed. It is because of this transparency that academic texts tend to appear as mere containers filled with knowledge, not as purposefully designed messages addressed to someone.

4 CONCLUSIONS

What appeared to be Johanna's individual problem, must, in fact, be considered as a problem of the university level teaching in general. Unlike American colleges, European universities do not offer their students general composition courses and only in rare cases provide them with help in special, subject-specific training classes or writing centres. In Europe, the academic teachers traditionally teach academic writing *en passant*, while dealing with the content matter of the courses and by supervising the papers and theses of their students. The general assumption underlying this policy is that it is up to primary and secondary education to teach writing abilities, and that it should not be the task of universities.

When students try to write their first scholarly papers, they suddenly find themselves amidst a world of texts that is governed by rules and functions different from any type of discourse they have ever met before. It is within this context, that students like Johanna should organise their writing process and acquaint themselves with the scholarly procedures of reading, note-taking, recording, collecting data, argumentation, formulating ideas, finding structures, revising and so on. And it is in this context that they should learn to think and argue about the knowledge acquired.

If we want to understand how students learn to write and what kind of problems they face in doing so, we should remember that academic writing is a complex self-management process in which students must cope with nearly all aspects of research simultaneously. It is necessary to untangle the different aspects of writing in order to allow students to find an easier access to the learning contained in the single components.

Fully to appreciate the importance of academic writing for university education it is necessary to consider at least four aspects of writing education:

- To understand writing, it is necessary to look not only at the product, the text, but at the context and the process of writing as well. A process-oriented writing approach can help students to gain insight into the different uses of writing, while a context-oriented approach will help them to understanding their role as writers in the academic world.
- Writing is a technology of its own, and as such it is inseparably connected with the creation of knowledge. An analysis of the cognitive processes in writing discloses important heuristic and epistemological principles that underlie the production of knowledge (Molitor-Lübbert 2001). Writing thus deserves considerably more reflection as a methodological principle. Like other fundamental methodological procedures, as for instance empirical research procedures, writing should be institutionalised as an academic subject.

- Writing is a key qualification for all academic professions, not only for academic education. Writing is not simply a prerequisite for academic performance, but one of the core features that provides people with a set of powerful aids for the mastery of all intellectual tasks (Bean 1996). Writing thus should be part of all academic education programmes.
- The teaching of academic writing is not a task that should be limited to language specialists. Writing is highly discourse-specific and its teaching should be integrated into the curricula of the single subjects, as the writing-across-the-curriculum movement has proposed. In this context, the teaching of writing can be integrated with critical thinking and active learning to foster both intellectual development and subject-specific learning (Bean 1996).

European universities and research institutes must consider writing as part of the overall academic culture. The most urgent part of this task is to change the philosophy and the methods of teaching in order more effectively to apply the powers of writing as a tool for learning, inventing and communicating knowledge.

TEXT TYPES, TEXTUAL CONSCIOUSNESS AND ACADEMIC WRITING ABILITY

LENNART BJÖRK

Gothenburg University, Sweden

Abstract. The Department of English, Gothenburg University, has for over a decade offered an introductory writing course for about 150 first-term students. Due to budget restraints and availability of teachers, the department has found it possible to offer only four workshops (of three hours each) per term for all students at the same time in a lecture hall. In addition, the students have typically been divided into groups of about 25 for eight classroom hours spread over the whole term. A distinction has been made between text types and genres. The first part of the course has focused on three basic expository text types, causal analysis, problem solving and argumentation. Students have studied model texts in order to strengthen their meta-cognitive basis and produce their own texts within a process-oriented model. At the end of the term, students have also written a genre – *i.e.*, discipline-specific – paper in literary studies. The article describes the course and discusses the rationale for the focus on text types in an introductory academic writing course.

Keywords: Causal-analysis text type, Genre competence, Process-oriented writing instruction, Textual competence, Text-type competence, and Text types vs. genres.

1 BACKGROUND

The vast majority of Swedish first-term university students have not, or they claim they have not, received any help in secondary school to analyse or practise expository or discursive writing. For whatever reason, my experience over the past couple of decades tells me that the writing ability of most Swedish students entering university is inadequate. And, if I understand the signals from friends and colleagues abroad correctly, this is not an unknown phenomenon in the rest of Europe. In this context, an article in the German newspaper 'Die Welt' is worth mentioning. In the article entitled, freely translated, 'The Organisation of Thinking by Writing' the author maintains that 'according to assessment by experts, half the university drop-out rate in Germany is due to inadequate writing ability.'

29

Björk, L. (2003). Text Types, Textual Consciousness and Academic Writing Ability. In: G. Rijlaarsdam (Series ed.) & L. Björk, G. Bräuer, L. Rienecker & P. Stray Jörgensen (Volume Eds.), Studies in Writing, Volume 12, Teaching Academic Writing in European Higher Education, pp. 29-40. © 2003 Kluwer Academic Publishers. Printed in the Netherlands.

If university students in other European countries have had similar experiences, it is not surprising that there is an increasing understanding of the importance of writing support in higher education in Europe, an understanding testified to by a number of European conferences and publications in recent years. The present article draws on insights from these as well as US sources but primarily on my own experience of one particular writing course that I have been involved in teaching in the English department at Gothenburg University for well over a decade. It is part of the first-term syllabus, where it competes for teaching resources with other courses considered crucial to foreign language study, such as phonetics, grammar, language proficiency and culture studies.

Although modest in terms of teaching hours, the composition course has ambitious aims. The immediate and obvious ones are (a) to prepare students for writing in the field of English studies, and (b) to help students improve their English language proficiency. However, since English is a subject that many students (about 50%) study for one term only before going on to other disciplines, the composition course also tries to offer writing instruction that can serve as a useful basis for writing across disciplines. The first part of the course therefore focuses on non-discipline-specific writing, and it is this aspect of the course that is the focus of the present article.

2   THEORETICAL AND METHODOLOGICAL CONSIDERATIONS

In the context of our students' inadequate writing ability and the fact that most of them will pursue professional careers not related to the discipline-specific writing of English literature or language, the hypothesis behind the course was that a useful first step for the students to improve their general language awareness was to clarify the distinction between *text types* on the one hand and *genres* on the other. These terms are sometimes used as synonyms, but I am here making an important distinction between them, as can be seen in the following overview (table 1).

Briefly, *text type* is a general, inter-disciplinary typology whose main principle of categorization is located in the *overriding communicative purpose* of texts. For instance, if that purpose is to explain the causes of something, the text is an example of the causal-analysis text type; if the overriding purpose is to solve a problem, the text belongs to the problem-solving text type, and so forth. I emphasise *overriding* purpose since of course text types are usually mixed in any one concrete text. Thus, for instance, there are descriptive and narrative passages in a causal-analysis text, but they only serve the overriding causal-analysis purpose, and it is that overriding purpose that is the criterion for the text's text-type categorisation. Text-type criteria are text-internal criteria, derived from the text proper. It is important to note that text types are not discipline specific: they cut across disciplines, across university subjects and departments.

Table 1. Distinction between text types and genres.

Expository/Discursive Text Types	Expository/Discursive Genres
Causal Analysis (to analyse the causes of something)	Academic papers/articles/books in psychology, linguistics, literature, philosophy, physics, architecture, mathematics *etc.*
Problem Solving (to identify a problem and to propose solutions to the problem)	
Argumentation (argumentation for and against; to take a position on an issue)	

Genres on the other hand are defined by socio-cultural criteria, *i.e.,* by text-external criteria. That is, the criteria are determined from outside the text: '…the characteristics of a specific genre are defined by the conventions agreed upon by the writing communities within which each genre is used.' (Björk & Räisänen 1997:19). This is why, for instance, an academic paper in physics is very different from a paper in history, linguistics or literature. This means that genres are discipline and/or subject specific.[3]

Depending on our perspective, it is possible to see text types both as smaller and as larger entities than genres. In a strictly theoretical sense, text types coincide with basic language functions and are thus larger concepts than genres. As Seymour Chatman writes, 'By 'text-types' (…) I mean something other than genres (…) Text-types are underlying (or overriding) structures that can be actualised by different surface forms.' (Chatman 1990:10-11).

If we leave the strictly theoretical sense, however, it may in practical pedagogical contexts be helpful to see a genre as the superior concept. If, for instance, we look at a newspaper article as a genre it is easy to see how one part of it may be narrative, another descriptive, and a third section argumentative. Thus, the individual article makes use of various text types. In such a context, we might say that the text types are the *building blocks* of the article, of the genre.

In brief, the distinction between text types and genres is the basis for the two parts of the introductory writing course here described, with text types being the focus of the first and somewhat larger part, and genres of the second part. The underlying assumption, then, is that a key aim of a general, introductory writing course

---

[3] *Rienecker and Jörgensen (see this volume) present a compelling alternative: they posit the theoretical construct of 'the research paper' as a general super ordinate genre, which includes characteristics from different disciplines, and they argue that this genre should be the focus of introductory writing courses.*

is to promote *text-type consciousness* and *text-type competence* and that the purpose of a writing course in a discipline is to promote *genre consciousness* and *genre competence*. Practically, this has been implemented in the first part of the course by a focus on three text types, *causal analysis*, *problem solving* and *argumentation* (or position taking – *i.e.,* in as 'pure' a sense as possible, in just a *for* and *against* dichotomy).

The choice of these three expository text types calls for a few words of explanation. Linguists often distinguish between five text types (idealised norms): *description, narration, exposition, argumentation* and *instruction*.[4] Of these, I have chosen to focus on argumentation only, because argumentation is at the core of academic writing. But I have here subdivided argumentation into three sub-categories – causal analysis, problem solving and (pure) argumentation. The subdivision is intended to help clarify the textual implementations of three distinct and separate *overriding communicative purposes* of argumentation. In addition, these three text-type categories are, as far as I have been able to find out, the most common text types in expository/academic prose.

Table 2. Process-oriented writing instruction.

The Writing Process

---

1. *Prewriting* (the study of model texts, note-taking, discussions, inventio, memory search –anything in fact that precedes the writing of the first draft)
2. *First draft*
3. *Peer Response* (students are divided into small groups of three or four members; they share and comment on each other's drafts-after having received training in various kinds of constructive, *text-type specific*, response activities)
4. *Revising* (revision on the basis of peer response)
5. *Teacher Response* (teacher response on the second draft)
6. *Revising and Editing*
7. *Teacher Evaluation*
8. *'Publishing'* (copying for seminar discussions, student newspapers *etc.*)

---

[4] *See, for instance, Egon Werlich's classic study* 'A Text Grammar of English' *(1976). Seymour Chatman (1990) distinguishes between four basic text types: argument, description, exposition and narrative. Per Ledin (1996) asserts that there 'is an important distinction between genres and text types. This distinction can be described as a difference between sociocultural and linguistically-universal categories or as a difference between the classifications made by language users and those made by scientific classifications.' (Ledin 1996: 12; my translation). Tuija Virtanen (1992) constructs a two-level typology model with a 'superordinate level' which comprises 'discourse types' and a 'subordinate level' that includes 'text types' (Virtanen 1992a). Virtanen gives a useful discussion of text typologies from Aristotle onwards.*

Before turning to the article's more developed line of argumentation in favour of a focus on text types, let me consider some methodological aspects. First of all, the writing course has been given within the general methodological framework of what is known as *process-oriented writing instruction*. This is nowadays, of course, a widely accepted and practised pedagogy and there are many models of it. Our version is shown is table 2.

As research has shown, students need knowledge about writing – that is knowledge about written products as well as knowledge about the writing process (Schoonen & de Glopper 1996). In our course, therefore, we initially spend some time in explaining the views and pedagogical experiences that inform process-oriented methodology.

The analysis of model texts is central to the working process. Let us look at an excerpt from a concrete student text of the *causal-analysis text type*. The excerpt is taken from a text entitled 'The Increasing Number of Foreigners Living in Japan', which was the result of a writing task given as follows: 'Write as *pure* or *focused* a causal-analysis text as possible of a trend or phenomenon that you are personally familiar with and interested in.'

Student Text	*Analysis of the Structure*
'The Increasing Number of Foreigners Living in Japan'	Title: Announces the subject
(1) When I first came to Japan nine years ago I was, if not unique, certainly a curiosity. Japan had not yet been discovered by great numbers of travellers, and the few of us who were there then could fully enjoy the advantages of being strangers in a very hospitable country. When I left Japan this past spring the foreigners were everywhere. The number of foreign residents in Japan has been increasing every year this past decade. Why is this?	1. Establishes the trend on the basis of the author's personal experience and raises the question WHY which tells the reader that a causal analysis will follow.
(2) Nine years ago a number of foreign businessmen lived in Japan, and it would be easy to argue that the growing number of immigrants is just a natural development of the general internationalisation of the business world. But even though the number of businessmen has increased, another group of people has increased even more: young, relatively uneducated people from Europe and America are arriving in increasing numbers, and there are many more of them in Japan than in the neighbouring countries	2. One potential cause: the general internalisation of business. Counter-argument: other groups. Cause thus only partly accepted into the analysis
(3) An obvious cause is that, compared to other	3. Other possible or alternative causes:

Student Text	*Analysis of the Structure*
Asian countries, Japan is very rich, clean, safe and very well organised. In addition, you can buy food from every corner of the world in the well-stocked department stores. Thus you might say that Europeans and Americans must find life easier and more comfortable in Japan than in any neighbouring country. But people do not travel because they want to see the same things that they have at home or just to have the same comforts. There must be some other reason.	the civilised and international aspects of Japan. Support: life more comfortable than in other Asian countries. Counterargument or reservation: people do not travel to see what they have at home. Cause only partly integrated into the analysis.
(4) Could it be that Japan is particularly exotic? We have all heard of the Geisha, the Samurai, Japanese martial arts, Zen Buddhism and other manifestations of a culture very different from our own. To explore a new culture is undoubtedly the most common reason for travelling, and many people devoted to some aspect of Japanese culture have flocked to Japan in recent years. This is true for instance about some friends of mine who came to study everything from swordsmanship to doll making. Such study visits have been encouraged by the Japanese authorities who have been very generous in issuing special cultural visas.	4. Another possible cause is introduced: the exotic character of the country. Supporting arguments in the form of concrete examples are cited and the cause is partly integrated into the analysis: see counterargument in paragraph 5
(5) Still, most of the young foreigners arriving in Japan today do not fit into the image of a devoted student of culture. Instead, the typical foreigner is a young American with little or no interest in Japanese culture. It is when we analyse his motives for coming that we start getting closer to the main reason for the increasing number of foreigners in Japan.	5. Counterargument against the previous cause is raised: most foreigners are not interested in Japanese culture. This paragraph also serves as a transition to the analysis of the main cause in the following paragraphs
(6) Our typical American is very different from the travellers of ten years ago. Unlike them he knows all the practical details. His information is especially up-to-date as to the potential material advantages of the country: there is money to be made in Japan.	6. The main cause is introduced: money.
(7) The lure of the rising yen, then, is the single most important reason for more and more westerners settling in Japan. It is quite easy for a European or American to get work, teaching languages or working in the entertainment business. Often, no special qualifications are required, so for the young westerners unable to find a job in their own country Japan is	7. Main cause is developed. Supporting arguments offered and information added about the pleasurable life available to those with a good income.

Student Text	Analysis of the Structure
indeed a paradise. And, while making more money there than at home, they can also have a good time in Japan's enormous number of discos, pubs, restaurants and other places of entertainment.	

Example 1. Text of the causal-analysis text type. *Excerpt is adapted from Björk & Räisänen (1997). Copyright © Studentlitteratur. Adapted with permission*

This is not a perfect text: it is not very thought provoking and its structure is simple. But it has, I think, some useful *instructional* qualities, which help clarify a few basic features of the text type. First of all, its *overriding purpose* is clear: that purpose is to analyse the causes of the growing number of foreigners in Japan. There is no *competing* overriding purpose (for instance criticism or promotion of the trend). Still, some might think, is it not too elementary a criterion to emphasise *clarity of purpose* in a university student text? On reflection, however, I would expect that many readers share my experience of wavering, conflicting and digressive purposes in student texts. Even graduate students at times seem to have conspicuous difficulties in making clear in the text what the purpose of a thesis chapter – or a section of a chapter – is.

Naturally, the indication of a clear and focused purpose is only one important feature of expository texts and students need help to identify other basic features of each particular text type. With the help of concrete models like the one above, students improve their ability to generalise about text type characteristics – to improve their textual consciousness, which, it is assumed, will later help them to read and write various academic genres.

In the case of the causal-analysis text type, an overview of basic features might look like the listing in table 3.

Students need to become aware of the necessity of being able to recognise and define such features in the model texts, and in the texts by their friends that they respond to in the response groups. It is this text-type awareness – this textual consciousness – that they will themselves apply as they write and – above all – revise their own texts.

I should perhaps emphasise that the characteristic features of text types as exemplified above are not to be seen as merely *rhetorical* features when we consider the 'academic' quality of texts. That is, we should not make too absolute a distinction between *form* or *language use* (the textual manifestation of thinking processes) on the one hand and ('academic' or 'scientific') *content* on the other. In other words, the manner in which an academic text handles claims (for instance about causes as in the example above), arguments, counterarguments and support is inseparably part of what is 'academic' or 'scientific' about the text (cf. Hegelund & Kock in this volume).

Table 3. Basic features of causal-analysis texts.

Basic Features of Causal-Analysis Texts

A Clear Presentation of the Trend or Phenomenon
- making sure that the reader can easily understand what the trend or phenomenon is that you are offering a causal analysis of.

An Analysis of the Causes which
- offers convincing arguments in favour of the cause(s) you suggest.
- indicates awareness of possible objections to your suggested causes. Such objections can be just mentioned, or integrated or refuted.
- indicates an awareness of alternative causes (which can be just mentioned or integrated or refuted).

A Clear Disposition/Structure
- consider which of the two main patterns for structuring a causal analysis is the more effective one in your case (look at the model texts to see what strategy the authors employed):
  a) having the main cause(s) first.
  b) having the minor cause(s) first.

A Reasonable but Authoritative Tone
- avoid too strident or high-pitched a voice.
- do not be too cautious in your argumentation: too many 'perhaps' or 'in my opinion' undermines your authority on the subject.

In analysing, or writing and revising, their own expository texts students may also benefit from a reminder of a few elementary general aspects of argumentation that they may come across in any expository text type. One such reminder deals with the most common ways of handling counterarguments (table 4).

Table 4. Ways of Handling Counterarguments.

Ways of Handling Counterarguments or Alternative Views

- to mention or acknowledge (just showing awareness of alternatives)
- to integrate (incorporating into one's own line of argument)
- to refute (proving an alternative unacceptable)

This is very elementary stuff, but our experience tells us that such reminders are helpful for most of our students at this stage of their textual-analysis career. For later stages, a fuller use of the Toulmin model of argumentation is perhaps superior, as for instance developed at the Academic Writing Center in Copenhagen (Rienecker 1999: 101-102); see also Rienecker & Stray Jörgensen (2002) and Hegelund & Kock in this volume).

3   RATIONALE

There is widespread pedagogical belief these days that university writing instruction should start immediately with the specific genre of the students' discipline. This is how, the argument runs, students will be socialised into a certain discipline and acquire the communications skills required in their future professions. However, on the basis of my teaching experiences in the course briefly described above, I here wish to question the *dogma of genres* in university writing instruction and claim that a majority of first-term university students need to *start* their academic writing by practising *text types*. I emphasise *start*, for this is not a question of either text types or genres, but of both; my main claim is simply that the teaching of text types should precede the teaching of genre in a university writing program. Whether we dismiss this text-type focus and practice as a merely propaedeutic step or not is unimportant – as long as the need is recognised and acted upon.

Now, if I my assessment of the writing ability, and needs, of first-term university students is reasonably accurate so far, they are likely to benefit less from having to face genre writing immediately than from engaging with the more *limited* textual purpose set by one text type at a time. My bottom-line proposition is obvious: I am simply advocating the common-sense principle that it is easier to learn a less complicated textual operation than a more complicated one.

Let us return to the insight from Chatman that genres are the *surface forms* of text types. And, let me exemplify the relationship between the two concepts. An academic genre, an article in the natural sciences for instance, very often consists of different sections, each section having a separate communicative purpose: one section might be devoted to causal analysis, another to problem solving, and a third to argumentation for or against a position or point in previous research and so forth. Thus, in addition to keeping such different rhetorical purposes under control in the same (genre) text, the novice *genre* writer has to handle new and specific genre conventions of the discipline – not to mention the cognitive demands of a university level study of a new and complex subject. I suspect that the potential cognitive overloading of this combination of challenges may be one explanation why students often write so poorly in their first term when they start with genres right away.

Still, there is a potentially serious objection to the focus of such a course: since the writing instruction is *non-discipline-specific*, is there not a risk that a course of this kind will become yet another space for traditional, unrealistic, isolated writing assignments? It would be foolish not to acknowledge immediately that the risk is real, and that care has to be taken. The course outlined here, however, I believe has minimised the danger by ensuring that

- First, students choose their *own topics* – topics that they are personally interested in. It is only the text-type framework that is set and obligatory for each writing assignment.
- Second, the non-discipline-specific writing tasks are few, only three in fact, before students engage in genre writing. (This limitation, however, is not – I have to admit – due to pedagogical principles, but to budget restraints. I would personally have preferred at least one more non-discipline-specific writing task).
- Third, students are *free to choose* discipline-specific topics (as long as they stick to the text type), but very few do so. It would seem that they find coping with the new methodology (process writing) and basic textual analysis difficult enough at this stage.

With such precautions I believe that the course does not fall into the trap of what van Kruiningen and her colleagues in Groningen so wisely warn against in 'Schlüsselkompetenz Schreiben': 'the artificial division between isolated writing assignments and subject-specific writing assignments ...' (Visser, Kruiningen, Kramer & Nip 1999: 201). On the contrary, a distinction of the kind I am outlining here between the aims of a general writing course on the one hand and of a discipline-specific one on the other serves useful purposes in clarifying different typologies, and purposes, of academic writing. We are in international very good company in pursuing these principles, for top American universities, including such prestigious institutions as Harvard and M.I.T,[5] have a similar division between *introductory* and *discipline-specific* writing instruction.

Now, in view of the demands for *pure* or *focused* text types from the students, it is also reasonable to ask whether text types have any relevance outside a writing course, *i.e.,* do they exist in 'real life'? In addition to the connection referred to earlier between text types and basic language functions, there are more concrete manifestations. Newspaper articles, for instance, can often be identified as pure examples of the text types we deal with. One typical example comes to mind: an article entitled 'Why Hussein lost the Gulf War', published in a Swedish newspaper. The article was a pure causal analysis of the *causes* of Hussein's defeat. There was no celebration or condemnation of either side in the conflict – only an exploration of causes.[6]

---

[5] *Massachusetts Institute of Technology.*
[6] *I might add here, as a parenthesis that since this text was published as a newspaper article this makes it an example not only of a pure text type (causal analysis) but also of a genre (that is, newspaper article); in this case there is thus complete overlapping between text type and genre – but that does not make the purpose of the text, that is the text-type classification, less pure or focused. And here I am only concerned with this text's text-type features and not with its genre characteristics (which would call for a different perspective).*

Similarly, my experiences from in-service courses with teachers at the Chalmers University of Technology in Gothenburg testify to the existence of 'pure' text types in 'real-life' texts. These teachers from the most diverse departments – physics, architecture, injury prevention, mathematics – have assured me that distinct sections of their papers, reports and articles may be defined as pure text types: *i.e.,* the purpose of one section might clearly be to analyse the causes of something, another to solve a problem and a third to take a position for or against a proposition in previous research. The fact that teachers from such different disciplines find that these text types are common denominators in their own academic writing can be seen as strong support for the inter-disciplinary direction of this kind of *introductory* writing course.

The final, and bottom-line, general argument in favour of the initial focus on text types is that it seems to work well. Course evaluations have been very positive, and my experience is that, for instance, students internalise text-type features such as the ones listed above, reasonably quickly if the sample texts they study are not too complicated but clear and focused examples. And, students also manage to implement their textual consciousness in their own texts quite satisfactorily, if the writing tasks are not too difficult in the beginning of the course. Thus, for instance, last year after a workshop on the causal-analysis text type, I read about 150 (short) student texts and only five or six of them did not qualify as causal-analysis texts. This is not to say that the rest were excellent texts, but they displayed a clear overall purpose and included the basic features as outlined above.

Comparable support for the text-type focus has been provided by *graduate* students at the Chalmers University of Technology, who have taken a similar course. They have strongly indicated that the text-type component has clarified textual strategies and structures to them and raised their general language awareness. Course evaluations have contributed to the originally optional course having become obligatory.

Furthermore, once students have improved their text-type competence, I would claim, they are also better *readers* of expository texts. That is, they have improved their ability to identify the basic communicative purpose of a text – an ability that is crucial to academic studies in general. Again, student course evaluations support this claim.

Nevertheless, there is a final potentially problematic objection to my line of argument in this article. Is it not true, for instance, that the student text above is in fact an example of *genre* writing, of the traditional *essay genre*? It is, but not fully and exclusively for its *basic* text-type features would have been the same if taken from any other expository genre. As an 'underlying' linguistic structure (in Chatman's terminology), the text type is interdisciplinary and can emerge in any genre – in the essay, of course, but also, for instance, in the letter, report or review – *i.e.,* any genre that students are familiar with from their earlier schooling. The important pedagogical emphasis here can thus leave the genre characteristics aside and concentrate on the textual implementation of the *overriding communicative purpose* – the text type – in this case causal analysis.

But to focus on and teach text types is, it should be admitted, a challenge (as are so many other pedagogical endeavours). The main difficulty is perhaps that textual manifestations of text types are hardly ever completely *genre-free*. A pedagogical solution would therefore seem to be to work with examples – and production – of texts from, and in, contexts where specific genre characteristics are less prominent and conspicuous than they would be in strictly discipline-specific sources and contexts. Therefore, if I had to argue *for* genre writing in an introductory writing course, I would be reasonably comfortable arguing for the *essay*, although as Richard Andrews and Sally Mitchell remind us, there is often, especially in English Studies, a tendency to privilege and treat the essay 'as neutral and untouched by ideology.' (Andrews & Mitchell 2001). But perhaps the fact that the essay is a genre students have some familiarity with and therefore experience as rather 'neutral' or 'natural' offers a pedagogical opening: the specific *genre* requirements are *less* discipline-specific and therefore cause less concern [in a less than perfect (pedagogical) world, a relative stance seems appropriate]. My pedagogical emphasis would consequently still fall not on the genre characteristics but for reasons given earlier, on the *overriding communicative purpose* of each text, *i.e.,* on the characteristic text-type features.[7]

4   SUMMARY

To summarise, my overall proposition is that most beginning university students need to develop their *general textual consciousness* in order to improve their academic writing (and reading) ability. This development can be promoted, I have argued, by focusing on a few common expository text types, such as causal analysis, problem solving and argumentation. The justification for the initial emphasis on text types is two-fold: first, text types are less complicated areas of study than genres; second, text types are *not* discipline specific but can be seen as the basic building blocks of the genres that students will be writing within various disciplines and professions. Thus, to start with *pure* or *focused* examples of text types will, I have suggested, help students lay a foundation for the more advanced textual consciousness and writing ability needed for genre writing, which remains the core of academic writing and academic writing instruction.

---

[7] *At a writing conference in Munich,* Schreiben für die Hochshule *(21-23 March, 2002), Andrea Stadter made a strong case for the essay in her paper 'Der Essay als Instrument und Ziel geisteswissenschaftlicher Schreibdidaktik. Überlegungen zur Erweiterung des traditionellen Textsortenkanons.'*

TEACHING ACADEMIC WRITING TO INTERNA- TIONAL STUDENTS: INDIVIDUAL TUTORING AS A SUPPLEMENT TO WORKSHOPS

STELLA BÜKER

Department of German Studies of the Tokyo University of Foreign Studies, Japan

Abstract. In this chapter, the concept of the PunktUm-Project (Bielefeld University, Germany), which assists international students in academic writing, will be presented. Based on a compilation of relevant research findings on L2 writing, a scheme that categorises the students' individual problems analytically will be introduced. Then a practical example from a consultation sequence will demonstrate how extra-curricular writing assistance can react to the individual writing difficulties and for which of these it can be used as an effective tool. All in all, this contribution argues for a combined programme of individual tutoring and workshops.

Keywords: Culturally coined writing, German as a second language, German universities, International students, L2 writing, and Tutoring.

1   A WRITING PROJECT FOR INTERNATIONAL STUDENTS

Difficulties in academic writing do frequently occur; international as well as German students have to face them.[8] In the case of German students, this fact was hardly known and consequently caused some surprise, while for international stu-

---

[8] *The use of the binary terms 'German' and 'international' refers primarily to the nationality of the students. But it commonly also implies that a 'German' student received his primary and secondary education in Germany and has to be a native speaker of German, whereas an international student is believed to have a different cultural and linguistic background. However, in reality there are many more variations: A German student may be born in a foreign country and still hold a German passport, or a student with a foreign passport may have German as a native language. Even though the terms 'German' and 'international' are rather simplistic I will use them in this article for stylistic reasons: An explicit description of these terms would certainly be inconvenient for the reader.*

41

Büker, S. (2003). Teaching Academic Writing to International Students: Individual Tutoring as a Supplement to Workshops. In: G. Rijlaarsdam (Series ed.) & L. Björk, G. Bräuer, L. Rienecker & P. Stray Jörgensen (Volume Eds.), Studies in Writing, Volume 12, Teaching Academic Writing in European Higher Education, pp. 41-57.© 2003 Kluwer Academic Publishers. Printed in the Netherlands.

dents it was evident. Already in the 1970s, some studies[9] pointed to specific problems of international students during their studies: integration difficulties, isolation, trouble with authorities, and language deficits, which are also impinge on the writing process. However, only few initiatives were taken during the 70s and 80s which aimed at improving the students' writing skills. Overall the improvement of oral skills was given priority, *i.e.*, writing in the teaching of German as a Foreign Language (GFL) primarily served to test listening and reading comprehension and to a limited extent the competence in writing different text forms became an additional aim. This relation became more balanced in the late 80s and early 90s when a vivid interest in (academic) writing in a foreign language arose. There were several factors which favoured this development: In the USA the development of research in writing processes directed the attention to cognitive tasks that native speakers had to manage while writing. This had an impact on teaching methods in this field. At German universities the first writing labs were created, where not only local students asked for help, but international students as well. However, these institutions did not cater primarily for the foreign student's needs and in most cases teachers felt helpless. At the same time, L2[10]-writing processes were investigated, writing difficulties of international students were analysed in more detail, teaching methods were further reflected, and project initiatives were taken.[11] Particular emphasis was put on culturally coined[12] patterns of scholarly texts and the learners' foreign language difficulties, which impede the writing process. In addition, the current socio-political debate on the much-needed internationalisation of German universities gave new impetus to these initiatives.

As a consequence, we are now looking at a number of interesting research results and teaching conceptions in the area of writing training for international students. However, there is still much need of improvement in this field, for example in the research of writing processes, culturally-coined patterns in academic writing, the

---

[9] *See Grieswelle 1978, Skillen 1985, Projektgruppe Ausländerstudium 1987.*

[10] *L2 = Language 2; this abbreviation refers to the foreign language learnt, while the native language will be referred to as L1.*

[11] *In the year 2000 government funding for 'writing consultation and discipline-specific language training for foreign students' allowed the creation of project initiatives at ten North Rhine-Westfalian universities, which are aimed at supporting foreign student during their study of a discipline. Initiated by the PunktUm-Project of the University of Bielefeld, eight of these universities have formed a co-operation.*

[12] *The term 'culturally-coined' is my own translation of the term 'kulturelle Geprägtheit' which was introduced by Eßer (1997) to create an alternative to the common terms 'culturally-specific' and 'culturally-determined', which she regarded as problematic for the following reasons: Variations in text patterns easily tend to be described as culturally-specific, without explaining what it is in the culture that causes these text patterns. In contrast, the term 'culturally-coined' offers two advantages: Not all variations in text patterns must be exclusively explained by the culture concerned, which might also be a far too complex task. In addition, unlike 'culturally-specific' the term 'culturally-coined' does not trigger associations with a specific nationality.*

particular demands of German for academic purposes, and also in teaching conceptions and teaching material.

One of the initiatives, which arose throughout this development, is the 'Punkt-Um-Project: Language for Academic Purposes, Writing, and Communication. Individual tutoring and training for international students.' This project started as a pilot scheme in 1998 at the University of Bielefeld (Germany) and aims at providing support for international students during their study of a discipline and to enable them to complete their overseas studies more efficiently and successfully. The project's individual offers consist of consultation in language learning and academic writing, workshops on writing and oral skills, and language courses for discipline-specific and general academic purposes. As far as academic writing is concerned, we based the project on the concept of the successful approach of the university's Writing Lab,[13] which was modified and supplemented to meet the particular needs of international students.

From 1998 till 2002 I worked in this project and in this article I want to present the concept of its writing assistance: On the basis of a scheme that analytically demonstrates the difficulties involved while writing, I would like to delineate the essential features of our project and illustrate our way of teaching academic writing by a practical example. In doing so, I intend to demonstrate which insights had led us to combine individual tutoring, workshops, and language training for the area of writing assistance. In addition, it will become clear, what kind of general modifications had to be undertaken in order to adopt the approach of the university's Writing Lab.[14]

First, I would like to give an overview of research findings, which enables you to further comprehend our approach theoretically and to identify the specific practical aspects of our work.

2   THEORETICAL BASIS

Numerous studies and practical reports have, each with their own individual method, formulated answers to the following questions: Which are the problems that put a strain on international students' writing in Germany? Which are the individual difficulties that are faced by the reader / the writer respectively? How can teachers intervene? In this chapter, I want to present a survey of those studies which were relevant for our project.

Hayes and Flower (1980) have developed a model of writing processes for native speakers, which describes the activity of writing as a highly complex cognitive problem-solving process. The model explains how this activity may be subdivided into different sub processes the writer has to manage not in a linear order, but simultaneously and recursively. While writing, one tends to face a 'cognitive overload'. In addition to that, the act of writing has a knowledge-generating and knowl-

---

[13] *For further information see Frank/ Hollmann/ Ruhmann 1995, Ruhmann 1995 and the chapter by Frank et al. in this volume.*
[14] *This chapter can be seen as an extension of Büker 2001.*

edge-structuring function. Both of these qualities of academic writing – cognitive burden and heuristic function – suggest a specific writing strategy: the disentanglement of the processes involved, the step-by-step pursuit of partial aims. However, one needs to bear in mind, that the writing task plays an important role in the writing process: to produce an academic text is by far more complex than writing a shopping list (Eßer 1997:114).

Bereiter and Scardamalia (1987) investigated to what extent the writing processes of experienced and less experienced writers differ: The existing knowledge about ideas, language, aims, and text structures influence the quality of the written text.

Based on existing models of L1-writing processes, Krings (1992) and Börner (1987) developed models for the L2-writing process. Krings' model points out the comparatively high complexity of writing in L2 by adding a sub process defined as problem-solving of L2 deficits to the already existing processes of planning, linguistic realisation and revision. In addition, he demonstrates the potentially complex interplay between L1 and L2 in text production and concludes that the more the native language comes into play the more the writing process in L2 might be interrupted by translation problems. While translating, the writer is expected to find an appropriate L2 equivalent for an already formulated idea in L1. (See also Börner 1989a:60.). Indeed, it depends on the L2 competence of the writers to what extent they (have to) use their native language in the writing process, because for L2 writing there is often a discrepancy between the intention and the ability of expressing ideas (Börner 1989b:351). If the writer is unable to express in L2 what he wants to say, he can either use his L1, or he may draw on strategies of avoiding or compensating L2 deficits. My observation is, that particularly in academic contexts, writers with L2 deficits tend to formulate their ideas in their native language first because of fear of losing or not being able to develop their thoughts properly. In contrast to language classes, where the aim is L2 acquisition, writers of academic texts primarily have to explicate their knowledge.

Therefore, the command of L1 writing strategies can have a positive effect on the L2 writing process as well, *i.e.,* experienced writers (in L1) are likely to produce better texts in L2 than less experienced ones (Wolff 1992:122, Weissberg 2000), yet in writing L2 texts these writing strategies are not always accessible, for either L2 deficits interfere, or the writer lacks the ability to apply them on purpose.

Büker (1998) investigated the writing process of final exam papers from the students' perspective: Without intending to judge this negatively, the analysis revealed, that students rarely consciously use the heuristic function of writing, they often see their L2 deficits as the only source of their writing difficulties and they only have a superficial awareness of culturally-coined patterns in academic texts.

In addition to the analysis of writing processes, text-linguistic studies of scholar texts and students' writings offer a valuable methodical approach to the difficulties of international students. The research and teaching in German for specific purposes can look back on a long tradition in this field.[15] Since the 1960s, specialist vocabulary, terminologies, and morpho-syntactic and pragmatic properties of these discipline-specific languages haven been worked out and taught at some universities in courses before or during the study of a discipline. Ehlich (1995, 1999) observed that it is not only the discipline-specific language that creates problems for international students, but also the general academic language. He coined the term *alltägliche Wissenschaftssprache* (everyday academic language, [my translation]), which designates linguistic items that appear in certain combinations and have almost acquired an idiomatic quality. These linguistic structures also reveal conceptions of scholarly work, which can be traced back to the prevalent methodological understanding of scholarship during a certain period. Ehlich (1995:346) mentions the idiomatic expression *eine Erkenntnis setzt sich durch* (an idea wins the day, [my translation]) and points to the fact, that this linguistic structure is more than a random combination of noun and verb; it mirrors the methodological concept of competing findings to certain research questions.

On the basis of a text corpus, Graefen (1997, 1998) draws up corresponding vocabulary lists, and she is also particularly interested in the metaphorical quality and methodological implications of these expressions.

Another field of research is concerned with the culturally coined patterns of academic texts. The first contributions to this field were made by Kaplan (1966, 1987), the founder of contrastive rhetoric, the frequently quoted essay by Galtung (1983) on academic styles, and many more contrastively designed studies on text linguistics; for example, by Clyne (1984, 1987, 1991) on English and German scholarly texts. More recent studies, for example by Eßer (1997) and Hufeisen (2000), focus on texts written in German by international students: Eßer analyses term papers in linguistics and literature written by German and Mexican students. Hufeisen investigates reports, term papers and essays of students of German as a Foreign Language in Canada. Both studies conclude that the text products, which have been analysed, show culturally coined[16] patterns. Therefore, the teaching of text patterns should become an integral part of the GFL curriculum. Students need to know about the regular linkage between the function, content, structure, and style of a text and should be able to put this knowledge into practice; so that the text produced cannot be judged as – as Hufeisen puts it for the texts she analysed in her study: 'English thought in German idiom' [own translation] (Hufeisen 2000:17).

As a result, the studies under review show: Academic writing in L2 is not only difficult, because it is done in a foreign language, but also because of culturally-coined patterns in academic writing, a lack of understanding of the writing process, and the ignorance of process-related writing techniques and overall study techniques. It also became clear that successfully trained writing competence in L1 does not necessarily imply an equal competence in L2, even if the writer has a good command of the target language.

---

[15] *See for example Fluck 1998 and Möhn & Pelka 1984.*
[16] *See footnote 5.*

3   OUR ANALYTIC INSTRUMENT: A SCHEME OF DIFFERENT PROBLEM LEVELS

At the beginning of our project, we could not adopt an existing concept that was designed to assist international students in oral and written tasks in their individual subjects, for there weren't hardly any. By trial and error we drew from ideas of already existing approaches and, in doing so, we formed our own concept by evaluation and modification. The starting point was and is the problem analysis of our clients. In contrast to many other studies, which concentrate on a chosen aspect; we consider an overview of the different problems involved and their interaction as important to our work. This guarantees a comprehensive and therefore effective support.

On the basis of Büker's (1998) empirical study, some of the other studies just mentioned and first practical experiences in the project, we developed the following scheme, which categorises the students' individual problems analytically. This scheme proved to be a helpful tool for conceptualising our project's offers.

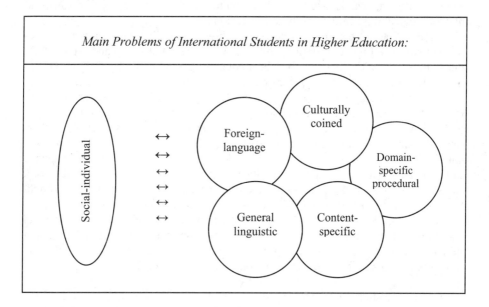

Figure 1. Main Problems of International Students in Higher Education.

All the problems international students face while performing oral or written academic tasks may be assigned to six different levels: the content-specific level, the domain-specific procedural level, the level of cultural coinage, the level of foreign language proficiency, the level of general linguistic competence, and the social-individual level.

Problems concerning the *social-individual* realm differ from those on the other levels in that they may complicate the student's performances, but cannot analytically be seen as problems directly linked with oral and written skills. The different levels may be characterised as follows.

The content-specific level refers to problems of content knowledge of the discipline, such as the correct understanding of the theory or an argument, the kind of methods applied in the discipline, its key literature, and so on.

Domains are socially established contexts of recurring task solving that are bound to certain institutions and organisations. In the field of writing, certain norms, conventions, and patterns of text production have become fixed and established for the solving of domain-specific tasks, which is also expressed in pre-formed structures and phrasing routines.[17] For writing an appropriate domain-specific text, one needs knowledge about the relevant production process and the specific text criteria. This knowledge can be designated as procedural knowledge in the form of enduring cognitive concepts (Baurmann & Weingarten 1995:14).

The problems faced by foreign students concerning processes and products of academic writing[18] and oral performances can therefore be described as *domain-specific procedural problems*. On this level the following questions arise: 'How can I discuss the chosen topic with my teacher?' 'How to produce and hold an oral report?' 'Which are the criteria for a term paper and how to go about it?' 'How can I participate in a discussion?' 'How to evaluate a scientific article?' *etc.*

Problems of cultural coinage take into account actual and assumed differences in the concepts of academic work done in Germany and the country of origin, which brings up the following questions: 'Is a term paper in Germany written like a term paper in the country of origin?' 'In my country this would have been an excellent term paper, why not here?' 'Can I deal with literature the same way as in my country?' *etc.*

Problems caused by improper use of foreign language belong to the *level of foreign language deficiency*. Difficulties may arise from specific (*e.g.,* use of tenses, sentence structure, word formation) to general questions and individual insecurities (*e.g.,* 'I have difficulties in understanding the text in this foreign language.' 'Does my German really express what I mean?'

---

[17] *According to this definition, difficulties on the domain-specific procedural level also contain an appropriate domain-specific language use. However, I attributed all problems which are caused by language use to 'foreign language' and 'general linguistic' problems, because in an individual case it is hard to decide whether a language difficulty should be characterised as 'domain-specific procedural' or 'general linguistic'. For example, the requirement 'to put things / facts precisely' is typical for the academic domain. Yet, the writer's inability to meet this requirement does not necessarily have to be the result of producing an academic text. The same difficulty may arise when he writes in other domains.*

[18] *Strictly speaking, the students' activities cannot be described as 'academic': During their studies, particularly designed assignments prepare the students to work in an academic context.*

The analytic distinction between foreign language proficiency and the *general level of linguistic competence* accounts for the fact that not all linguistic problems can be put down to the use of the foreign language. Difficulties in formulating precisely, in using specialist terminology appropriately, and in creating comprehensible sentences may not necessarily be attributed to foreign language deficiencies. These difficulties are also faced when writing in the native language.

Social-individual difficulties like loneliness, illness, or financial pressure may be additional obstacles.

The following conclusions can be drawn from the six levels of problems and their combination:
1. The special situation of international students can be described in terms of potential additional problems, which belong to the foreign language level and/or the level of cultural coinage. Local students might also face the problems of the remaining levels.
2. Sometimes the problems of the different levels merge, *e.g.,* many domain-specific procedural problems, which international students encounter, cannot be separated from culturally-coined styles of academic performance, just as general linguistic competence and foreign language proficiency are indissolubly connected.
3. On many occasions, problems which arise at one level may create problems on other levels: This is, for example, revealed by questions of how to speak freely in an oral report when foreign language difficulties occur, or how to deal with specialist literature that is too difficult to be understood.
4. Foreign students often face a variety of difficulties on different levels. According to Büker (1998), the complexity of the problems is usually hidden to the foreign student. The students themselves are usually aware of a foreign language difficulty, although there may also be problems on a social-individual, domain-specific procedural, cultural, or content-specific level.

On the basis of the problem-level scheme just outlined, the support in oral and written tasks was conceptualised as follows:
1. Massive problems primarily arise – and for the individual student often intricately intertwine – while completing a concrete assignment such as an oral report, a term paper *etc.* Therefore, it is advisable to offer direct assistance in completing these assignments.
2. Assistance can be provided most effectively by identifying the constellation of problems first. This situation is facilitated when the students are willing to talk about their situation openly. In order to achieve an atmosphere of confidence, the assistance takes place in a protected setting where the students don't fear to be assessed by their lecturers.
3. Then a strategy has to be introduced to solve the problems step by step. One has to bear in mind, that the more a strategy meets the individual problem constellation, the more efficient the support will be.

4. Our assistance has to be based on a careful distinction of the problem levels in-volved. This for example ensures that we only intervene in areas in which we are qualified.
5. The students have to be made aware of their particular situation. On the one hand, this awareness enhances their ability to actively participate in the prob-lem-solving process. On the other hand, it will also increase their motivation to face and remove deficits directly (see also Lonka's comments on 'diagnosing and activating' in this volume).

On top of these reflections, we decided to mainly offer support in training *basic academic skills*, which are to certain extent relevant to all disciplines. In doing so, we can offer support to a large number of students. Yet our experience showed, that in some cases we cannot do without a certain knowledge of the discipline in ques-tion. This particularly affects students from the faculties of law and natural sciences (see 5). However, it should be emphasised that we do *not offer support on the con-tent-specific level*: If problems on this level appear, we ask the students to seek ad-vice in their own discipline. Seen from this perspective, the dialogue between teach-ers and students is not substituted by our support, but often enhanced. If problems on the social-individual level are affecting the academic performance of students, we recommend them the Student Counselling Centre, which offers professional help, while we take care of the remaining questions.

For us it is important not only to point out the students' deficits, we also try to make them realise and take advantage of their *strengths and their resources*, which will aid them solving their problems (see Ruhmann 2000).

As far as this general didactic orientation of our project is concerned, we profited from the expertise of the university's Writing Lab.[19]

4   THE CONCRETE OFFERS: AN OVERVIEW OF THE PUNKT-UM-PROJECT

Before the project initiative was started on a limited financial scale in mid-1998, there was no support for the 1200 international students at the University of Biele-feld during their study of a discipline, except for one two-hour seminar on academic writing each term.[20] The PunktUm-Project can be seen as a response to this deficit. Due to its close proximity to content dealt with in the subject *German as a Foreign Language*; it is located in this department. Built on almost three years of experience and based on the analytic scheme of different problem levels, the following project structure was established (see figure 2).

---

[19] *For further information see Frank, Hollmann & Ruhmann, 1995, Ruhmann 1995.*
[20] *The regular support program offered by the university consists of a language course, which prepares the students for a compulsory language proficiency test (DSH-test). In order to take up the study of a discipline the students have to complete this test. The students' orientation and integration is alleviated by the International Office, and by a program called 'Brother-sister', which arranges tandems between international students and their German peers. However, there is no support for problems that arise during the study of a discipline.*

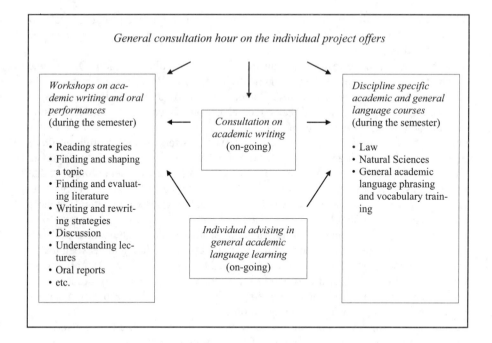

Figure 2. The PunktUm-Project structure

Our writing assistance mainly consists of two different offers: workshops and individual tutoring. L2 competence is additionally supported through language courses and consultation in language learning.

In the following, my first purpose is to illustrate our teaching method by presenting a practical example of our assistance in academic writing. I decided to choose a sequence from our writing consultation, because this allows pointing out the advantages of this form ofintervention. This will form the basis for my second purpose which is to argue for a combination of workshops, individual tutoring and language courses. Thirdly, it will be shown how we could design our writing assistance by profiting from the university's Writing Lab.

5   ASSISTANCE IN WRITING

As mentioned above, we adopted the approach of the university's Writing Lab for our writing assistance. The Lab offers product-oriented and process-oriented assistance: The students are not only supposed to know what a well-constructed text looks like, but also what necessary steps must be taken in order to achieve such a product. Therefore, they effectively have to handle the enormous complexity of the L2 writing process (see 1). For this purpose, the students are introduced to study techniques and procedures as well as to corresponding intermediate text products for each individual step. They learn how an intermediate text product is supposed to look like, that it does not impede the on-going working process, but rather facilitates it. The students get the opportunity to apply the suggested procedures and to receive feedback on their products. The individual working steps consist of finding and shaping a topic (research question), dealing with literature (reading strategies, evaluation, integrating literature into the text), writing and rewriting strategies *etc.* [21] The following text criteria have to be met: The research subject (topic, research question, objective) has to be described precisely enough to allow the reader to comprehend it and understand its use. The text must contain all the necessary information to enable the reader to verify the research findings.[22] The research method has to be demonstrated, the author's own ideas have to be separated from other sources and the language employed must be accurate.[23]

This concept of the Writing Lab was modified and supplemented successively to meet the particular needs of foreign students. As the scheme of the different problem levels suggests, modifications became necessary, due to additional difficulties caused by the foreign language and by problems that arise from the culturally coined level. What these particular modifications look like – especially for the support in academic writing – will be shown below.

Individual tutoring in academic writing
Three times a week we offer a general two-hour consultation, which the students can use without an appointment. Here they can explain their problems and we can discuss with them which of our offers suits their difficulties best; minor problems may be tackled instantly.

If the students express a difficulty with a particular writing assignment – usually a term paper – we advise them to use the individual tutoring or to participate in one of the workshops. The tutoring allows dealing with the concrete and individual situation more intensively; this option is usually taken whenever the problems expressed seem to make such an approach necessary.

What happens during a consultation session? The individual session usually takes one hour. While the student describes his difficulties, the advisor will ask further questions to the extent that appears necessary to solve the writing problem. The student's problem description is analysed by the advisor on the basis of his perception of work and writing processes in a foreign language. In order to develop a problem-solving strategy, the advisor tries to diagnose for himself which of the problems are putting a strain on the student at which stage of the writing process. Therefore, the advisor has to look at two levels: First, he has to decide whether the problems described fall into his area of competence (no primarily personal or content-specific

---

[21] *For further detail see Ruhmann 1996, 1997a, 1997b, 1999.*
[22] *In term and exam papers no new research findings have to be presented.*
[23] *These text criteria correspond to those which Rienecker and Jörgensen call the 'Anglo-American style' (see their chapter 'The (Im) Possibilities ...' in this volume). They are teachable, the students can employ them, and they also meet the requirements of the teachers as is proved by the markings.*

problems); otherwise he refers the student elsewhere. Second, if he locates several problems, he then has to decide which one needs to be tackled first; usually, this would be a problem at the very beginning of the work process, which usually affects all remaining tasks. For example, if the student complains about writing difficulties and it turns out that he has not properly assessed the chosen literature, the consultation must consequently start with guidance in the assessment of literature; the writing difficulties mentioned initially may then disappear by themselves. However, in some cases, there are problems, which acutely block the work process, and these have to be sorted out first. For example, an almost completed term paper is supposed to be handed in within a week, and it turns out that this paper does not at all meet the academic standards required. In this case, the due date of the term paper has to be extended first; only this allows an appropriate treatment of the remaining problems.

The following example will illustrate a consultation sequence:

A post-graduate German Studies student from Madagascar, who has a DAAD[24] scholarship, comes to the Writing Consultation and asks for advice. He expresses difficulties in writing his 'Diplome d'Études Approfondies', which can be seen as an equivalent to a doctor's thesis concerning the degree of difficulty, but requires a much reduced extent. His supervisor suggested him to consult the PunktUm-Project. The student explains that language deficits are the source of his problems, an opinion, he added, which was shared by his supervisor. The advisor offers him to read the introduction and a chapter of his paper and to provide feedback in the next session.

While reading, the advisor made the following observations: The student had clearly stated the aim of his thesis. His intention was to establish a canon of post-war literature for German Studies in Madagascar; for this purpose he wanted to answer the question: Which novels shall I choose? However, he did not shape his topic profoundly enough; he had not given enough thought to how he wanted to answer his research question in a way that would meet academic standards. Therefore, his chapter was characterised as a subjective and random compilation of information; the required argumentative passages were missing completely and the text reveals much of a style Bereiter & Scardamalia (1987) call 'knowledge-telling'. In addition, there was not enough literature integrated into the text, direct and indirect quotes were not sufficiently marked, and parts of one chapter were taken from a lexicon with no references made. From the linguistic point of view, there was a lack of general academic vocabulary and a number of colloquialisms in his text. Yet, there were only a few grammar mistakes, which could be marked easily.

In the next session, the supervisor gave the student feedback on his text. He explained his corrections in detail and warily indicated that the paper mirrored a general difficulty to work academically. This feedback was hardly surprising to the student, it rather caused a sudden insight: up to this point, he had not really understood

---

[24] *'DAAD' is the German abbreviation for 'German Academic Exchange Service.'*

what the German supervisor asked for when she said that he would have to rework his text apart from language deficits. The reason is, that in his point of view he had actually done well – especially because he had read over fifty German novels for his thesis. So the only problems he had been expecting were foreign language deficits. Understanding now the comments of the advisor made him also understand the comments of his German supervisor. A decisive communication difficulty between the student and his German supervisor was revealed.

During a longer conversation it also turned out that the student had two supervisors, one in Germany and one in Madagascar; both of which had different expectations. The Madagascan supervisor was rather interested in a comprehensive compilation of information, while the German supervisor, as it became now clear to the student, criticised the missing arguments. Consequently, the student became insecure as to what extent he should provide arguments or simply list information. The advisor decided not to judge these different views or to add another opinion. Instead, he commented that different supervisors could hold different views, particularly if the supervisors differ culturally in their academic traditions. Therefore, the student may decide himself – but always in consultation with his supervisors – to what extent he wants to follow their individual suggestions. Finally, the advisor and the student decided that he would have to talk again to his supervisors. However, as far as the extensive borrowing from the lexicon was concerned, the advisor expressed his clear opinion that this could not be tolerated.

In the next session, the student brought some annotations by his German supervisor; she had marked a missing explanation and provided three references on which he could base his argument. On this basis, the advisor and the student worked out the explanatory and argumentative text passages for this chapter. For this purpose, the student had to read the relevant literature in advance, and during the consultation, he was asked to develop an argument by means of clustering.[25] The student also met the expectation of his Madagascan supervisor by providing a broad source of information; in addition, he minded the clear distinction between his own thoughts and ideas taken from other sources in his text.

During the next five consultation sessions the student applied the same procedure to the remaining chapters of his thesis: He worked out the value of his research question, he gave arguments for the chosen criteria in selecting the individual novels, he provided a solid evaluation of the novels, and finally argued for a number of novels worthwhile to be adopted in a canon.

The succeeding linguistic revision of his thesis proved to be comparatively easy. The advisor did some exercises with him that were aimed at understanding the distinction between colloquial and academic language. For the thesis, the student finally obtained the second highest grade from his German supervisor and was highly contented. According to the assessment, the highest mark would have been possible if there had been more argumentative passages in his text.

---

[25] 'Clustering' is a technique developed by Rico (1984).

In my view, this case illustrates the following: For the student's individual difficulties the writing consultation was the best option, because in contrast to workshops or seminars the assistance is particularly designed to meet individual needs, which were in his case as follows:

- a communication difficulty between the German supervisor and the student,
- the student himself assumes that only foreign language deficits reduce the quality of his text,
- he has a tendency to orientate towards academic norms of the country of origin without being aware of it,[26]
- limited time frame,
- and finally, having almost completed his entire thesis, he is now in need of a feedback and instructions of how to revise his text.

The writing consultation enabled us to meet him where he was in his writing process, to give him detailed feedback (on his text), to prompt a reflective process of culturally-coined text norms, to initiate text revision step by step, based on the local criteria of academic text products, and finally to correct his assessment of his foreign language deficits. The interaction between himself and his supervisors was also intensified. The student attained a different self-assessment throughout the consultation process. His obstructed view on his deficits gave way to a more positive assessment. As a result of the consultation, he was able to appreciate the fact that he knows two methods of treating a topic academically: he knows how to fulfil German and Madagascan text norms. In addition, his foreign language deficits finally appeared to him less extensive than he had previously thought.

Regarding the different problem levels mentioned earlier, the following conclusions could be drawn for this example: domain-specific procedural and culturally-coined problems overlapped. With help of the consultation, the student became aware of these difficulties, which enabled him to solve them and finally achieve his aim, a completed thesis. The foreign language deficits were diagnosed and by means of a small exercise – colloquial vs. academic language – the student was made aware of these deficits and could start solving them by himself.

As the example above suggests, the adoption of concepts of the Writing Lab can be successful for individual tutoring – and also for workshops, which had not been treated here – if the following modifications and supplements are taken into account:

1. Problems which arise from culturally coined different conceptions of academic work can be solved easily during a consultation sequence for a concrete assignment; in our workshops this aspect can only be introduced and exemplified,

---

[26] *Just as Rienecker and Stray Jörgensen put it in their chapter, 'The (Im)Possibilities ...' in this volume, it is 'an eye-opening experience' for students to realise that text patterns can display cultural coinage. Particularly for international students who already went to university in their native country this realisation can be rather difficult. In contrast to first year students (cf. Kruse in this volume) they consider themselves capable of writing appropriate academic texts, because they have already proved it in their first-degree course.*

but it is not possible to treat the individual student's difficulties thoroughly. So problems emerging from this particular difficulty may be solved in the offers provided and do not necessarily demand the creation of an additional offer.

2. The situation is different when it comes to foreign language deficits: In most cases they cannot be treated profoundly during a consultation sequence. These deficits may only be diagnosed, made aware to the student, and some exercises may be applied. As a result, the students develop an awareness of their linguistic deficits and show more motivation to work on them. In a workshop, we can demonstrate the linguistic necessities, which are required for the fulfilment of concrete tasks, *e.g.,* we demonstrate the link between the conjunctive form and certain lexical items, which should be used when quoting indirectly. We conduct small exercises and in doing so we give the students an incentive to reflect on their individual language competence.

3. The foreign language level of the writing problems, therefore, calls for a particularly designed offer. Consequently, the Punkt-Um Project offers a language learning consultation, courses, and workshops on general and discipline-specific academic language.

4. No matter whether in workshops or in individual tutoring, we always have to keep the additional needs of international students in mind, which result from the use of the foreign language and cultural differences. This sometimes demands different instruction methods when introducing working techniques and procedures. For instance, the technique of clustering – mentioned in the example above – is usually carried out as follows: If the students apply this method – the aim of it is to activate previous knowledge and to generate ideas – they are instructed to use the foreign language only as long as they can do it without effort. If they are not able to express their thoughts instantly in the foreign language, they are encouraged to use their native language. Therefore, the stream of associations is not blocked by translation difficulties. In contrast to applying this technique in language learning contexts, the focus is put on content, and not on activating foreign language vocabulary.

6   MERITS AND DRAWBACKS OF OUR WAY OF TEACHING ACADEMIC WRITING

The writing assistance offered by the PunktUm-Project consists of individual tutoring and workshops on academic writing, and complementary offers in the training of academic language. In conclusion, I want to argue for this combination of workshops and individual consultation sessions, because – as far as the training in writing for international students is concerned – German universities tend to provide courses only.

What would the Madagascan student have done, if writing consultation hadn't been offered? In his case, a language course would probably have shown him that his language deficits were not as problematic as he thought. It is unlikely that he would have attended a course on text patterns, for he was not aware of this deficit.

Had he participated in such a course, he certainly would have obtained a global knowledge in text patterns and their cultural-coinage. However, it would still have been a challenging task for him to apply this knowledge to an almost completed thesis in order to identify the difficulties in his text and to develop a revision strategy. Also our workshop on academic writing, which combines product and process oriented aspects of academic writing, would not have been designed appropriately enough to meet his specific individual needs. It is true that he would have gained procedural knowledge, he may even have been able to detect the basic difficulty in his paper – the lack of academic standards – but most likely he would not have been able to make the necessary revision by himself. None of these offers (language courses, courses on text patterns, and workshops on academic writing) would have met his particular situation in its entirety: two supervisors of different cultural background, limited time frame, the text produced so far, his own perception of his difficulties. However, this had to be taken into account in order to provide assistance effectively.

The Writing Consultation can therefore be seen as an instrument which allows us to react to individual writing difficulties. The intertwined problems can be disentangled through the analytic scheme of problem levels (see above) and solved step by step during a consultation sequence. The consultation also provides a forum for feedback to written text passages, which is what many international students ask for. I would like to emphasise that we do not offer any content-specific assistance; we can only direct the student's attention to content-specific difficulties and suggest seeking further advice in the appropriate discipline. We also do not revise the students' texts. We rather teach them a procedural model of how to complete their assignments step by step, taking into account their individual difficulties.

Additionally, on a research level writing consultation also allows deeper insights into students' problem constellations, their work and problem-solving strategies and the efficacy of the writing techniques and procedures taught in workshops and the consultation itself.

In our project writing consultation has become a key intervention form besides workshops in academic writing. Workshops are usually designed for students who report problems that do not seem to be too complex, students who just started writing a paper, students who have received poor results in their previous term paper, or students who have a general interest in improving their writing skills. Workshops offer great advantages, too: the students experience that writing problems are widespread and the group functions as a resource to develop problem-solving strategies (see Rienecker & Stray Jörgensen 'The Genre in Focus, not the Writer ...' this volume).

In my experience, the co-existence of these two different forms of support plus an additional offer for language learning has been proven successful and can therefore be recommended, even though individual tutoring is a highly costly intervention form and does not correspond to financial bottlenecks of higher education. Therefore, individual tutoring is used only in cases, in which we cannot do without its benefits. In addition, we are planning to integrate students of GFL (German as a

Foreign Language) into the project's activities by training them in giving feedback on texts. The benefit is threefold: it helps to extend our limited financial and time resources, it improves the GFL-students' writing skills and prepares them for their future jobs.[27]

A further need of improvement lies in our aim to offer appropriate support for the different disciplines: *i.e.,* that our offers should take into account the discipline's specific procedures of how to produce research results as well as the discipline's specific text criteria. Experience has shown that this particularly accounts for the faculties of law and natural sciences. However, one has to bear in mind that the consideration of discipline-specific criteria of academic writing does not necessarily imply for us to teach the discipline-specific language. The training of discipline-specific language – considered as lexis and morpho-syntactical structures – is indeed useful, however, in our own experience, the linguistic structures which Ehlich and Graefen term *alltägliche Wissenschaftssprache* [*everyday academic language*; my translation] represent most difficulties.

Throughout our project experience we have reduced the number of courses on discipline-specific language and have introduced workshops and courses on general academic language instead. On the basis of the actually perceived linguistic difficulties, we have developed teaching units, which proceed from concrete difficulties in the text and illustrate the problem through exercises. The particular needs of participants are the decisive factor to what extent we direct our attention to relevant grammatical and lexical items. The teaching units deal with the following content: too overcomplicated nominal style or sentence structure, simplified verbal style, monotonous sentence structure, lack of linguistic tools to produce a coherent text, writing style is too impersonal or subjective, facts are described not precisely, paraphrasing in a foreign language shows difficulties, one's own point of view is not expressed academically enough, colloquial expressions are used.

Studies on general academic language, as conducted by Graefen (1997, 1998), and on cultural-coinage of academic work, which take a particular look at different cultures, represent a solid foundation for our work.

Further research, concepts and teaching materials are necessary until we can say with certainty, in which combination intervention forms and intervention procedures become efficient support for international students during their study of a discipline in Germany. The efficacy of the support measures will largely depend on how well they meet the complex problems of international students – as described by the scheme of the different problem levels.

---

[27] *See the multiplier-program by Ruhmann (2000), which she developed for the writing assistance at the University of Bochum.*

THE GENRE IN FOCUS, NOT THE WRITER: USING MODEL EXAMPLES IN LARGE-CLASS WORKSHOPS

LOTTE RIENECKER & PETER STRAY JÖRGENSEN

Academic Writing Center, University of Copenhagen, Denmark

Abstract. Nearly 16.000 students, 25 departments at the Faculty of Humanities, University of Copenhagen, and 2½ writing consultants, no tutors – what are the pedagogic options available? In order to reach out to as many students as possible we choose to spend a good part of our limited resources on teaching academic writing in large-class writing workshops. In this chapter we present, exemplify and explain one of our favourite teaching strategies: Using the in-class analysis of model-examples of excerpts from term papers and theses, as a basis for teaching the desirable genre-qualities of term papers and theses at the university. The aim of commenting on model examples is to help students internalise the features of the overarching academic genre: the research paper and its quality criteria, and the aim of teaching large classes is to offer teaching within the constraints inferred by political and economical conditions that are imposed on most modern mass universities in Europe – including the University of Copenhagen. Firstly, we describe the problems we encounter and the context our centre functions within. Secondly, we account for our pedagogical use of model examples in our teaching of the scientific paper genre and its quality criteria, and thirdly, we point out what we consider the advantages of this approach as well as some problems we encounter.[28]

Keywords: Academic genre, Large-class, Model examples, Problem oriented writing, Research question, Rhetoric of science, and Scientific writing.

1   TEACHING WRITING AT THE MASS-UNIVERSITY

Activities aimed at a broad audience are an absolute necessity at a mass-university, given the numbers of students, and the acceptance into university of students with seemingly fewer skills and abilities than university teachers hope for, the lack of clearly formulated criteria and expectations in regard to student writing, the political stress on swift completion of studies and low drop-out percentages. All in all, we

---

[28] *The main content of this chapter was first presented at The Writing Lab Conference in Bloomington, Indiana, USA (April 1999).*

Rienecker, L. & Stray Jörgensen, P. (2003). The Genre in Focus, not the Writer: Using Model Examples in Large-class Workshops. In: G. Rijlaarsdam (Series ed.) & L. Björk, G. Bräuer, L. Rienecker & P. Stray Jörgensen (Volume Eds.), Studies in Writing, Volume 12, Teaching Academic Writing in European Higher Education, pp. 59-74. © 2003 Kluwer Academic Publishers. Printed in the Netherlands.

have to negotiate the huge need for, and student interest in, writing courses on the one hand and our limited resources on the other.

There are no institutionalised writing activities such as Writing Across the Curriculum or general composition-courses in Danish universities, though a number of individual university teachers develop their own writing instructional material and introductions to term-paper writing for their courses. Still, most university disciplines require extensive essay and term-paper writing, and as a final prerequisite for graduating, a 50-100-page thesis. Teachers function as advisors on a largely reactive basis, this is the well-known trial-and-error pedagogy as regards academic writing. Thus, the Writing Center at the Faculty of Humanities at the University of Copenhagen offers the only institutionalised and continuous opportunity for students to take a longer university writing course. In teaching and working with students' ongoing writing we have chosen to do a number of very large-class how-to-do-it workshops with as much dialogue and text-commenting (and on-the-spot writing, which we will not discuss) as possible with an audience of up to 180 participants at each session. The students do not get credit for attending, yet they flock to our 3-hour workshop courses, each featuring one aspect of academic writing.

1.1   Main topics in The Basic Course (7x3 hours)

The main topics of the basic course are listed below. The content of the courses is what we consider basic knowledge and skills for an academic writer:
1.   Criteria: What is a good research paper?
2.   Get started: Ideas for the writing process
3.   The research question as the organizing point of the research paper
4.   The research paper as one argument
5.   Sources, theories and methods and how to handle them
6.   Structure and elements of the research paper
7.   Academic language, editing and physical format.
Every 3-hour session has elements of both lecturing and workshop. Participants are university students representing all levels from first year to PhD, from all of the 25 departments of the faculty.

2   OUR WRITING CENTRE ACTIVITIES

One solution to the problem of addressing large numbers of students is of course to distribute instructional material on writing: textbooks, pamphlets, (online) handouts and writing software. A second possibility is to work with teachers as proliferators, as described elsewhere in this volume (Frank *et al.*, Kramer *et al.*). Publishing instructional material has a top priority for us, alongside teaching activities. We also do a number of writing consultations (up to 150 per year), but we reserve such tutorials for students with individual writing problems.

But even in the best of all worlds, we would not change our large-class courses for a high number of writing consultations, for we believe that transmission of both the traditions and transformations of academic writing benefits from the multiple exemplifications and the following discussions with the students which the presence of a big audience and the analysis of text-examples allow: Our procedure aims at developing the students' metacognition about academic, scientific writing, and at demonstrating common 'rules' applying to the writing of a term paper/thesis: focusing and structuring the paper, building a solid argumentation, citing sources, and developing an appropriate academic language. Most of all, the key message we want our students to take home is that the most important rules for scientific writing as practised at the university – even first-year writing – are or should be determined by the demands of Science itself (and with a capital S!), and reinforced by the rhetorical rules for the well-functioning text in the genre of the research paper (see section 6 of this chapter).

3   THE GENRE IN FOCUS, NOT THE WRITER

We presuppose here that there is an overarching scientific genre – the research paper – which is the umbrella-genre for many (all?) other sub-genres of writing done at university. The research paper has the investigation of one problem as its all-important aim, and any paper can be seen as a piece of argumentation to solve the problem. Sub genres are variations and derivations of this, and the formulations of these sub genres depend on discipline-specific criteria, which are subordinated to the over- all genre-criteria. The overriding aim of our teaching academic writing is to exemplify the genre and its local sub genres at the Faculty of Humanities.

The better part of our teaching has the *analysis of texts* in focus: Examples from papers already handed in and graded, or from papers still in the writing process are analysed by the students and by us during the large-class workshops. We choose examples from student papers given to us, or from a small term-paper-database on the university home page. Of interest, are mainly good and very good papers, which may serve as examples to be studied, discussed and emulated, though they may still leave room for improvement.

Our present focus represents a 10-year development of an earlier investment in teaching the writing process and encouraging much exploratory writing (taking Peter Elbow (1973, 1981) as the most important inspirational source), to a gradual realisation that the students need to understand in some detail the workings of a good university paper in order to determine steps in a purposeful writing process. As a result of that, we now introduces what the good paper might be and what qualities, it displays before we talk about writing processes – which (hopefully) shall lead to a good paper. In our experience, 'The Good Paper' (the title of our popular textbook for students on writing at the university (1997, 2000)), cannot be reduced to a matter of the mastering of conventions in local discourse communities or to a matter of communicative, rhetorical skills either. The qualities of 'The Good Paper' are not haphazard, and teachers (even across continents) are likely to agree on criteria to a large extent. Criteria can be explained, exemplified, emulated (and hopefully expanded!) by those who understand the underlying principles.

The shift in our overriding focus from process and writers to product, texts, genre, and quality criteria, has been gradual and spurred on more by contacts with students than anything else.

Although a text and genre oriented approach to teaching academic writing is not the most prominent in the literature, we find it represented for example by Lennart Björk (in this volume; and Björk & Räisänen 1997) and by John Swales (1990; Swales & Feak 2000). A study on 9th grade students by Schoonen & de Glopper (1996) shows that knowledge about writing improves the writing performance. And directly focused on writing research texts, Rubin (1996) argues, 'Writing courses should [...] include genre-related instructional materials and tasks.' A prominent US writing pedagogue, John Bean (1996), refers to the approach of teaching genre through using model examples, an approach which we will describe in detail in the following, as a 'norming session' in which students and teacher establish norms for what good student writing is.

Our 'norming sessions' take place on our Basic Course, and on the Writing Centers' thesis-writer's workshop, in which 50 % of the thesis-writers of the department of Humanities (approx. 100 per semester) participate, without getting any credit for it. In this chapter, we demonstrate our teaching practice on two excerpts from bachelor-level papers. We have used these two examples on our basic course.

4   TWO MODEL EXAMPLES REPRESENTING THE RESEARCH PAPER GENRE

We will exemplify the use of models, in this case used for discussing the qualities of a good research question. We wish to focus both on what good academic writing is and on our teaching strategy. The aim is to demonstrate for the students – and make them articulate – what they think works well in academic writing.

The following two examples see table 1 and 2, of students' research questions are shown to workshop participants on transparencies. The excerpts are taken from two 'bachelor projects': A 25 page research paper, written in all university disciplines in the fourth semester. We invite participants to comment on:

* Which of the following two research questions would you rather base a paper on?
* What are the academic qualities, or lack of same, represented in the way these two research questions are posed?

When we use these examples in class, our students are not in doubt: the second example shown (b) comes in as a clear winner, no one opts for (a). The students find that the second question poses a better opening with its problematisation of previous understandings and its promise of a new, independent inquiry into a hitherto overlooked topic from a theoretical angle. These two young second-year students are aiming high: they want to make a contribution to their field. (We find that students frequently aim to make a contribution and in fact conduct research, though naturally on a small scale). Students in the audience always recognise the wording of example (b) as promising a high quality paper.

Table 1. Research question, model example (a).

Research Question for a paper titled: 'Communication in Network'
Film, Bachelor project

It is the cultural importance of computer-mediated network communication I will discuss in this paper. I will examine the characteristics of the computer network and its potential as a new type of media. In the paper, I will analyse the general characteristics of network technology and describe a series of ways in which networks are used at the present.

After the preliminary methodical deliberations, I will reveal how theories about mass media research have problems characterising the forms of communication in computer networks. Instead will be mentioned a series of newer theories about computer-mediated communication. After that, a pragmatic perspective on networks will be constructed, and a number of concepts that can be used in the analysis of social organisations within computer networks will be presented. Finally, system development is touched upon, which is perceived as a cultural process during which the structure of the computer network takes shape.

Table 2. Research question, model example (b).

Research Question for a paper titled: 'The Computer Game'
Film/Psychology, Bachelor level

It is our impression that the debate about computer games rests upon a series of problematic premises. Prejudices and faulty logic also characterise parts of the research, the very purpose of which ought to be to eliminate the worst of the wrong conclusions. One particularly hardy but unfortunate perception of the relation between players and games presumes that an unambiguous causal link exists between theme and reception. Accordingly, one overlooks the child's media skills as well as the fact that the computer game cannot in any meaningful sense be considered in boxes, but is a dynamic, reflective play-culture.

We seek to establish an understanding of the games as a cultural phenomenon with a particularly close link to the central narrative of post-modern society. This is done by answering the following main questions:

How can the computer game be described as a medium? What is the special appeal of computer games? How can the relationship between players, computer games and post-modern society be described?

After hearing and discussing the students' comments, we always offer our evaluations (and possible corrections). Our evaluations most often serve to systematise and appraise the students' statements so that they may experience their ability to formulate quality criteria for and principles of academic writing, in this case criteria for how to formulate a good, workable research question. These are our prepared comments to these two specific texts:

Table 3. Our comments to the research question (a) 'Communication in Network'.

'Communication in Network'

- We cannot identify the problem? What is it?
- The question rests on an observation ('problems with the theories'), but the observation is not highlighted
- Much paraphrasing will be necessary in order to cover this piece of theoretical ground
- The question is broad and seems to contain several diverse theories and concepts
- The subject gets lost and the theories and concepts remain
- Relations between the parts are unclear (how is the 'system development process' related to 'the cultural importance of computer-mediated network communication')
- The words lack precision ('theories have problems', 'a series of newer theories', 'a number of concepts')
- Words such as 'mentioned', 'presented' and 'touched upon' do not give the impression of in-depth treatment
- There is some resemblance to a knowledge-telling strategy (Bereiter & Scardamalia 1987)[29]

Table 4. Our comments to the research question (b) 'The Computer Game'.

'The Computer Game'

The text has
- An observation: 'one overlooks the child's media skills as well as the fact that ...'
- A focus and a problem
- A departure from the point of: 'something has been overlooked' – and the students will now set things straight
- (Seemingly) thorough knowledge of the state-of-the-art
- The promise of a new theoretical understanding
- Clear relations between parts
- Good integration of the subjects of film and psychology
- A knowledge-transforming strategy, *i.e.,* this paper will demonstrate the purposeful use of selected items of knowledge for the investigation (solution) of a problem.

---

[29] *Bereiter and Scardamalia (1987: 183-4) distinguish between knowledge-telling and knowledge-transforming writing strategies. See section 5 in the following.*

These young writers demonstrate that they write well within a genre where 'over-arching characteristics' are movements from the general to the specific, and from problem to solution (Swales & Feak 1994: 6).

'The Computer Game' (b) earned the highest possible grade (and later the students went on to publish a much appraised book on the subject), and 'Communication in Network' (a) earned an above average grade. You may say that the first one represents a problem-oriented approach, whereas the latter represents a more source-driven stance in a term paper. It is a question of what it is that primarily steers the paper-the problem or the sources?

During the workshop, we will hear the reactions, first the students', then ours, to the specific texts, and then we will give some characteristics of what *generally* makes a good research question, to be discussed, reacted to, further exemplified *etc.*, thus moving from the specific example to more general guidelines for how a worth-while research question for a term paper may be posed. We go through this heuristic on a transparency:

Table 5. Checklist for research questions.

Check Out Your Research Question

Questions to the content:
- Is there a problem within the field (an anomaly, a lack of knowledge)?
- Do you have a clear main focus?
- Are you transforming knowledge?
- How high on Bloom's taxonomy (see below) is the main content?
- Will your paper constitute one argument?
- Have you narrowed the topic down sufficiently?
- Are you using/reflecting upon relevant concepts/theories/methods?

Questions to the wording:
- Are questions open (*i.e.,* not either/or, yes/no)?
- Is the research question
  - Precisely worded?
  - Indicated clearly?
  - As short as possible?
- If several questions:
  - Is one focal point singled out?
  - Are relations between questions clear or explained?

We teach students to look for focus, problem-orientation, argumentation and knowledge-transforming and to be conscious of this taxonomy of learning goals: know/use/evaluate, according to Benjamin Bloom (1974, orig. 1959). We will return to Bloom in the following.

When using examples of student writing in a workshop context, we observe the following guidelines:

- The more examples, the better. We find that in order to give a nuanced picture of the varied possibilities in appropriate and workable scientific writing, the use of only one or two examples might give the students the impression of only one stereotyped solution. Using a number of examples (of research questions, structures, citing, analysing, criticising sources *etc.*) gives us the opportunity of depicting various formats of scientific writing, which can be employed in different discipline-specific ways.

- Examples of good academic writing are generally more instructive than examples of bad academic writing. It is important that the teacher highlights the important features of the example and also any positive qualities of the texts.

- The teacher should give guidelines for positive and constructive comments. Students often tend to perceive negative criticism as 'the name of the game' and devalue even papers which we find excellent and which we also know have obtained a high grade. Thus, we have learned to formulate our instruction before students' comment thus:

This is an excerpt from a good paper. What contributes to making it good?

5   THE RATIONALE BEHIND:
RELATING THE SPECIFIC EXAMPLES TO THE GENERAL PRINCIPLES

We back up our teaching strategy from two angles: the quality criteria for academic texts, and a pedagogical rationale.[30]

5.1 Text Qualities

The general principles are those on which evaluations are based. We find the criteria and principles laid out in the grading scale in use. The grading scale consists of numbers and for each grade a rationale, written by the Ministry of Education. An example: To obtain the highest grade, it is specified that the student should 'demonstrate' a 'broad knowledge' of facts, concepts and methods, and an ability to 'select',

---

[30] *Notice that our teaching practice and our criteria are embedded in an Anglo-American approach to scientific writing. We discuss the challenges we meet when teaching writing to students writing in a continental tradition in Rienecker & Stray Jörgensen ' The (Im)Possibilities in Teaching University Writing in the Anglo-American Tradition when Dealing with Continental Student Writers' this volume).*

and to 'give a rationale' for the selection of facts, concepts and methods, to 'compare' and 'combine', 'evaluate' and 'generalise', and lastly to 'use' knowledge and skills in investigating known and unknown 'problems' and to 'combine' existing principles in order to seek 'solutions to problems' (Danish Ministry of Education, 1995). We find this text very helpful in explaining to students what their graders have in the back of their minds as the qualities they look for in all written and oral exams. We find another helpful source of knowledge about quality criteria in actual use in the university teachers' criteria for the good paper – as far as we know them at the Writing Centre! We collect teachers' individual and collective brainstorms and other utterances about what they perceive as desirable qualities in student papers. We perceive this as teachers' actual transformations and translations of criteria and how they are weighted, and we have compiled them in long lists of very concrete do's and don'ts from teachers. Students can obtain them on handouts and in our textbook 'The Good Paper' (Rienecker & Stray Jörgensen 2000).

Very importantly, criteria for the good research paper should stem from the demands which science itself puts on writing, and the suggestions coming from the angle of the rhetoric of science, *i.e.,* the rules and conventions for writing about research among scientists and scholars in the academic society.

5.2 Knowledge-transforming

We have already mentioned that a very important underlying principle for a research paper is that it be knowledge-transforming, *i.e.,* selectively using parts of knowledge from a discipline/discourse to investigate (and possibly solve) problems in a purposeful, reader-oriented manner, rather than knowledge-telling, *i.e.,* regurgitating knowledge pertaining to a topic, *i.e.,* not primarily a problem, in a more writer-based manner, meaning not purposefully aimed at (the right) audience (Bereiter & Scardamalia 1987). The vast majority of papers we have seen which earned an above average grade (not solely at our faculty but at all other further education institutions from where we have seen examples) have been clearly knowledge-transforming: Knowledge-transforming is exactly what scientific endeavours are or should be about, namely to use and expand the knowledge of the field to address new challenges. Thus, we find the concepts of knowledge telling and knowledge-transforming immensely useful in teaching the ground-rules of the overarching scientific genre. The words themselves are new to students and teachers alike, but they accurately conceptualise an experience that many students and teachers already have made and they easily recognise that this in fact is one clear dividing line between the good and the bad research paper. It is of course not enough that a paper may be labelled knowledge-transforming, but it is an important step towards the good paper – which again is important in so far as the good paper communicates investigations of problems within fields, and displays that a student has learned how to do academic research, and has learned how to communicate their scientific work.

Hence, we see an important pedagogical tool in the concept of knowledge- transforming for the writing instructor who is teaching the genre: we need to focus on how to make knowledge-transformation happen, and we need to show how texts representing knowledge transforming is written – process and product. Here we see the research question as the pivotal point. Many textual concerns such as which sources to cite and how much space to allow each one of them, which text-types (see below) to write in, structure, language and much more, derive from (lack of) decisions about the papers' research question. Much of this will fall into place easier if the point of departure is sound. Vice versa we often consult with students who are writing a paper based on a question which leads to a knowledge-telling writing strategy (such as: 'What are recent developments in x?') and these writers pose any number of questions about what 'rules' should guide every decision concerning their text.

5.3 Bloom's Taxonomy

Another important dividing line is Bloom's taxonomy of educational objectives (Bloom 1974, orig. 1959 – see appendix). In the appendix, you can see that the steps in Bloom's taxonomy roughly correspond to the text-types used in factual prose, *i.e.,* all texts within the genre of the research paper. Thus genre is the unitary concept at the top of the hierarchy, and every good paper consists of parts which may be defined as text types within the genre: parts of any paper is summary, then often analysis, discussion, evaluation *etc.* (See also Björk in this volume.)

In actual evaluation practice, we observe that a good paper at least reaches a level of analysis, and includes more discussion or evaluative material (often in the form of evaluation of sources), signifying that the writer goes all the way with the material: that is to evaluate, and where possible to design courses of action, based on analysis, interpretation and argumentation.

Bloom's taxonomy underlies the grading scale employed in Denmark, as we have seen from the formulations accompanying the number grades. The formulations express which abilities should be trained and tested in the educational system, according to the Ministry.

Bloom's taxonomy is new to most university teachers in our courses even though they recognise that their own evaluations follow the taxonomy.

Pedagogically, the consequence of Bloom's taxonomy is to advice students to write as much as possible in the text-types corresponding to the higher steps of this ladder.

5.4 Teacher's Criteria of Quality

When we collect criteria from teachers and students, we tend to get long lists of the criteria, which we might label the rules from the rhetoric of science, such as listed in table 6. The rhetorical criteria for good scientific writing (which teachers on our teachers courses focus strongly on), we find are very important features of (teaching) university writing as well. The lists are understandably popular among students, since they show what their actual audience expects and wants. The lists can thus serve as identifications of aims during drafting and as tools during the revision process.

Table 6. Criteria of quality.

A Good Paper is

- Clearly focused
- An argument
- Well structured
- Has a proper mix of generalization and exemplification
- Linguistically correct and well formulated
- Reader-oriented
- et cetera.

5.5 Scientific Demands

We believe that the students should see writing at the university as emerging from the studying and practising of serious scientific endeavours. This is more compelling for teaching academic writing at the graduate/Ph.D. level, but it should be introduced from the very beginning. The students write papers not only to demonstrate knowledge and methodological abilities, but also as a means to learn how to present their knowledge and methodological abilities in scientific writing. We therefore put up scientific ideals as objectives for the writing (see table 7).

Table 7. Scientific ideals as objectives for the writing.

A Scientific Text Should

- Investigate (solve) a question/problem within the field
- Use concepts, theories, systematisations and methods of the field in question
- Include relevant, current and academically acceptable documentation
- Respect norms for citing sources
- Use acceptable and controllable methods, reasoning and argumentation
- Demonstrate awareness of the state of the art
- Strive for a minimum of – or explain – contradictions
- Strive for conceptual and linguistic precision, consistency and unambiguity.

When studying a model example, we will in many cases eventually point to scientific criteria to determine what good writing is in a university context: 'If you agree that precision should be an ideal to strive for in university writing, what better wording could you suggest for this passage?' Teaching writing at the university means to make these connections between writing and ideal science, while of course trying not to lose the writer out of sight.

Thus, we go from the specific examples to the general principles for scientific writing.

5.6 The Pedagogical Approach: Inductive Learning and Metacognition

Why do we find this simple teaching sequence such a useful teaching strategy? We have some good reasons. The first reason is that it entails analysis rather than description of texts and textual features. We are not just telling the students how to do it, but they are actually learning by doing and learning concretely. It is analogous to how one might teach other subjects such as for instance literary analysis, namely by doing and demonstrating it on texts in class, not just by lecturing on the principles.

Secondly, it forces the students to metacommunicate about the examples, and thereby strengthens the students' awareness of and metacognition about their writing.

Thirdly, we will expect the student to internalise academic standards and criteria more fully by voicing their own comments out loud in class.

Finally, the presence of an audience makes it possible to experience reactions from peers: objections and discussions of the wordings of the texts as well as of the underlying principles of the writing of the individual participants.

6   DISCUSSION

By our Writing Centre practise, we take a stance in discussions about teaching academic writing. We are certainly aware of other attitudes than ours, as discussed in the introduction to this volume (see chart in the introduction to this volume on different approaches to teaching writing).

6.1 The genre in focus, not (just) the writer

As the title of this chapter indicates, what we believe is most important is whether the teacher of (academic) writing takes the writer or the text and the genre as his or her didactic 'centre of gravity'. Especially in the American writing literature we see the writer as an individual placed in focus of the pedagogy, as in the famous article by Steven North: 'The Idea of a Writing Centre':

> 'In axiom form it goes like this: our job is to produce better writers, not better writing.'
> (North 1995: 76, orig.1984)

We do not focus on the development of the individual student's writing abilities with the primary aim of evolving specific individual rhetorical abilities. Our primary point of departure in teaching is not the student as a person, but the scientific genre that all students have to write – and the processes that lead to a quality product within that genre (whereas in our individual tutorials the focus is on the meeting between writer and text). Academic writing should not be taught in the same ways as expressive writing. Ideally, academic writing can take on as much personal meaning as more expressive forms of writing – and this is often a topic we discuss with students in one-to-one tutorials as well as on courses – but *the ways* of expressing any given content are bound by the ideals of science and the rules of the overarching scientific genre. Thus, our axiom is that we set out to teach how to write better academic *texts*.

6.2 The Science, not Just the Rhetoric

When consulting a great many writer's manuals for students and writing centre home pages, what you will find is university writing seen from a rhetorical angle, whereas the angle of science and the demands placed on any students' writing by the rules of scientific writing is often downplayed. In other words: much advice to students on writing pertains more to the form and the presentation (see for instance the Norwegians Dysthe, Hertzberg, and Hoel (2000), and many US Online Writing Labs: A search can start at Purdue University: http://owl.english.purdue.edu/. It is interesting to see that many resources on university writing contain no separate entries on how to write about theories and methods which certainly in the humanities and social sciences is such an important aspect of university writing. Rhetoric is an important issue for writing centres and programs, but at the heart of how especially university students should write lie the scientific demands on university texts.

6.3 The Large-class, not Just the One-to-one Tutorials

The counselling given in a tutorial by one teacher or one student tutor, can be experienced by the tutored as one individual's idiosyncratic way of seeing writing or a local writing centres' choice of a set of to-do-lists for process and product. The one-to-one tutorial concentrates on one single specific text, and the advice may not be communicated or it might not be heard as general and generalisable, when in fact much advice on academic writing is general. We hear ourselves repeating the same kind of advice over and over, and having surprisingly similar conversations with students, on largely the same topics, year in and year out and across disciplines! And we wonder if students who only come to tutorials, but do not read the manuals or attend workshops, realise what general challenges all academic writers face, and get a broader picture of possible options. Courses like those described above and the pedagogical use of model examples, will demonstrate that there are common agreements about the genre in the academic society – on the courses the students themselves and the teacher represent the academic society. The students discover that as a group they know the rules and are able to express them and often name them. Furthermore, they see the rules applied to not one (their own) but several texts of the same kind. And they hear not one, but several individuals express the rules.

If a student who has attended the Basic Course later signs up for a one-to-one tutorial, we have a common frame of reference and the student will much more easily anchor the conversation about his own paper in his awareness of general challenges and general principles.

7   ADVANTAGES OF USING MODEL EXAMPLES IN LARGE-CLASS WORKSHOPS

To sum up: We are convinced that the large-class workshop involving analysis and comments on model texts is a teaching strategy with a number of advantages, in pedagogical and financial terms (see also Björk and Hegelund & Kock in this volume).

7.1 Pedagogy

Most importantly, the students experience how not just one writing consultant or one teacher, but a general academic audience of their peers prefer to see academic problems examined and presented. There is a lot of inspiration and concrete ideas for the students on how to handle their own text, even if their specific text has not been discussed. It is training in metacognition, and that is what (some of) the students need if they are to perform that crucial skill. And it is the consciousness and verbalisation of criteria they will need to be able to evaluate the writing of others and indeed their own writing.

Furthermore, an overwhelming majority of the participants likes to hear examples analysed and discussed. In the students' written evaluations of our courses, a recurrent comment is that they can hardly get enough concrete examples, and even if we have discussed 20, some will request even more examples.

7.2 Economy

We are able to address a large number of students at a time. And this is not only an economical advantage, but also a necessity at the mass-university. We save precious time and money by limiting costly one-to-one tutoring to those students who claim to have special and individual problems. Furthermore, it is easier to help students with special problems when they know the general principles of academic writing from our large-class courses.

7.3 Applicability

Teaching academic writing involving model examples is easy to implement and usable on all levels, in every discipline irrespective of the number of attending students and without the teacher having specific knowledge in the field.

7.4 Visibility

Our courses are well spoken of around campus due to the fact that the non-obligatory classes each easily draws a crowd of over 100 participants. So if the problem is raising money to get the centre running, large classes is a way writing centres can be seen clearly in the landscape of the university.

7.5 Some problems

Finding and renewing appropriate examples is a time-consuming task: The collection of suitable examples is a constantly on-going concern, and our endless search would hardly be possible without help from students and teachers.

It is a pedagogical challenge that some students find it hard to make analogies from an example to their own writing. These students write on evaluation sheets that they would prefer all writing instruction to be held in their disciplines, but this is rarely offered in the disciplines. With 2 ½ writing consultants and 25 disciplines in the Faculty of Humanities, we can rarely find time to co-teach with subject teachers.

Over the years, we have read hundreds of term papers from the 25 disciplines, and we find the similarities in for instance the elements that a good paper will contain more striking than the differences. Yet, some disciplines represent different cultures of writing, most clearly philosophy, literary science and to some extent history, and students from these disciplines tend to gain less from our writing courses. These special writing cultures at (perhaps especially European?) universities, we address in 'The (Im)Possibilities in Teaching University Writing in the Anglo-American Tradition when Dealing with Continental Student Writers.' (This volume).

APPENDIX

Table 8. The correspondence between text-types within the genre of the research paper and educational objectives in Bloom's taxonomy.

Bloom's Taxonomy of Educational Objectives	Text-types
Evaluation	Evaluation
Synthesis	Argumentation
	Discussion
	Interpretation
Analysis	Analysis
Application	Comparison
Comprehension	
Knowledge	Paraphrase
	Description
	Summary
	Quotation

A GOOD PAPER MAKES A CASE: TEACHING ACADEMIC WRITING THE MACRO-TOULMIN WAY

SIGNE HEGELUND & CHRISTIAN KOCK

Academic Writing Center and Department of Education, Philosophy and Rhetoric, University of Copenhagen

Abstract. In this paper, we contend that students' problems with genre and task definition in the writing of academic papers may be helped if we adapt Toulmin's argument model to explain what the genre requirements of the academic paper are, as opposed to everyday argumentation. The student should be encouraged to apply the model as an assessment criterion and, at the same time, as a heuristic tool during her work on the paper. This involves a 'macroscopic' or 'top-down' approach to the evolving draft, not a 'microscopic' analysis of individual passages. The paper suggests a number of class activities that will help students apply a 'Macro-Toulmin' view to their own work.

Keywords: Academic Paper, Academic Writing, Argument Model, Genre, Task Interpretation, and Toulmin & Writing Pedagogy.

1 THE TOULMIN MODEL OF ARGUMENTATION IN HIGHER EDUCATION

Faculty across all departments, perhaps especially in the liberal arts subjects, have trouble teaching students what an academic paper is, and how to write it. Central to the problem is students' difficulty with 'task definition' (Flower *et al.* 1990), *i.e.*, in making the appropriate 'task interpretation' (Nelson 1990). Another way of saying this is that what many students lack is not the motivation or even the ability to write good academic discourse, but an understanding of the *genre* of the academic paper. They fail to understand one or more of the following: the overall *purpose* of the academic paper, its components, and how the components contribute to the overall purpose. This is frustrating for teachers, but it is even more frustrating for students. Often they find themselves lavishing high hopes and hard work, only to receive the dampening response that they are trying to do the wrong thing.

Hegelund, S. & Kock, C. (2003). A Good Paper Makes a Case: Teaching Academic Writing the Macro-Toulmin Way. In: G. Rijlaarsdam (Series ed.) & L. Björk, G. Bräuer, L. Rienecker & P. Stray Jörgensen (Volume Eds.), Studies in Writing, Volume 12, Teaching Academic Writing in European Higher Education, pp. 75-85. © 2003 Kluwer Academic Publishers. Printed in the Netherlands.

We suggest that Toulmin's argument model (1958), in a particular interpretation, is a significant help against this frustration, for teachers and students alike. To argumentation scholars, there is nothing new in using the Toulmin model for pedagogical purposes; however, its use in general argumentation courses is, in many people's experience, very debatable – a view also taken in Fulkerson's comprehensive discussion (1996), with which we tend to agree. But what we shall suggest in this paper is that the model, while not particularly successful in general argumentation pedagogy, is highly useful precisely when it comes to teaching academic writing.

In our view, the main problem with the Toulmin model in relation to general argumentation from everyday life is that it sends students searching for warrants in texts where the warrant, ever so often, is simply not there. Instead, such texts often contain multiple grounds or data for the claim they support. Armed with Toulmin's model, students tend arbitrarily to label some of these 'warrants' and others 'data', but they often realize that there is no real difference in status between the elements thus labelled – and confusion ensues.

A better approach, but still a problematic one, is to point out that everyday argumentation is often based on tacit 'assumptions' of a general kind. Toulmin's model may then be invoked, with 'warrant' serving as a synonym for such assumptions. This is the approach taken in one of the better argumentation textbooks, John Gage's 'The Shape of Reason' (1991). However, the explicit formulation of other people's tacit assumptions – what many argumentation theorists call 'reconstructing' the argument – is, we believe, a questionable practice, especially when it amounts to formulating those unstated premises that will make the argument deductively 'valid' (cf. van Eemeren *et al.*1993).

But the typical absence of stated warrants in everyday argumentation is precisely one of the major features that separate it from argumentation as it is supposed to be in academic papers. Thus, what amounts to a weakness in the Toulmin model when applied to the analysis of ordinary argument is a strength when we use it as a tool in teaching the academic paper. We contend that students' problems with genre and task definition in the writing of academic papers may be significantly helped if we adapt the model to explain what the genre requirements of the academic paper are.

2   MACRO-TOULMIN

The adaptation implies that we use the model in a *macroscopic* way – hence our neologism, 'Macro-Toulmin'. We suggest that we should use the model to attack the difficulties of the academic paper top-down, saying to students, 'The overall purpose, components, and inner functioning of an academic paper *as a whole* can be better understood by means of this model.'

What this means in practice is that the student is encouraged to apply the model as an assessment criterion and, at the same time, as a heuristic tool during her work on the paper. The idea is not to use it microscopically, looking at individual sentences in her text and checking for data or warrants for claims that occur (or do not occur) in them. This is the way the model is often used in attempts to adapt it to the analysis of everyday argumentative texts. Instead, we suggest that the student should learn to apply the model to her evolving draft in a top-down manner, asking herself, 'Does my draft contain material that will fit into each of the six categories represented by the model?' As a rule, we suggest that a 'default' good academic paper contains material representing each of the six categories. The following graph will illustrate how.

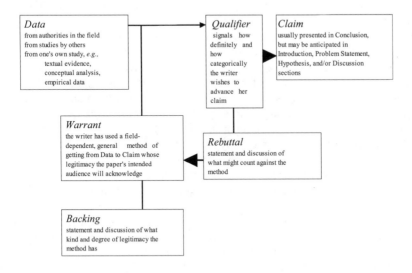

Figure 1. The Macro-Toulmin model.

As the figure suggests, the *Claim* in a typical academic paper is something that will often be located in the conclusion. This feature, incidentally, is one that often annoys non-academic readers, who (understandably) expect to be told or at least warned from the outset what the drift of the paper is going to be. Wise instructors, especially in academic sub-genres that come close to non-academic writing, such as literary criticism, comply with this expectation by asking students to offer the reader some pre-understanding of their line of argument in the Introduction. But in many academic papers, perhaps most, the claim cannot be located to one or two single passages. Even so, a good paper does make a claim. It should not merely be the kind of paper that many students write, and which some are even required to write, titled 'An Analysis of...' Such a paper is not a valid instantiation of what academic research is about; rather, it can be seen as an exercise that sharpens a skill necessary for doing 'real' papers, *i.e.*, real research work. A good paper is not merely an 'analysis' of something; it may use analysis as a tool, but its end is to make a point or claim.

There are a many criteria that the claim in an academic paper should live up to, more than can be discussed here; but the first criterion is simply that the claim should be there. The student should have something to say – she should make a statement that is hers, not just reiterate or summarize statements made by the scholars she has studied.

The second category is, of course, *Data*. It usually constitutes the body of the paper. Basic criteria for the data include: 1) Data should support the claim. 2) Data that are irrelevant to the claim should be omitted. 3) Data that the student can be expected to know, and which might serve to undermine or qualify the claim, should be discussed.

Data may be of at least three kinds; what a specific paper, including the present one, has to present by way of data is often a combination of all three types:

1. Theoretical data, *i.e.*, theories, concepts, definitions drawn from authorities, either esteemed individuals (for example, 'Habermas says ...') or current paradigms (for example, 'it is generally assumed in Generative Grammar ...'). Such general assumptions belonging to a current paradigm that the writer subscribes to are often presupposed rather than stated.
2. Specific data, drawn from studies by others.
3. Specific data, drawn from one's own study.

Specific data may include, according to field: textual evidence, conceptual analysis, examples, qualitative or quantitative empirical data, and many more.

The *Warrant* category: One of the defining features, perhaps the constitutive feature, of academic writing is that the writer should carefully discuss the warrant for the data she presents. Debaters in practical argument are generally not required to do so, and rarely do it – which is part of the reason why we find it so hard to teach the proper understanding of warrant in practical, extended argument. What happens when students try to apply the Toulmin model to instances of practical argument is often that they arbitrarily label some of the statements in the text 'data' and others 'warrant', while other students analysing the same text may have applied these labels the other way around.

In academic writing, as opposed to practical argument, the notion of warrant has much more meaning. This will be clear when we specify that what we propose to call warrant in academic writing is what academics often refer to as *method*. The method in a piece of research can be defined as its manner of collecting, selecting, and interpreting data. A given academic field allows and makes possible the use of certain types of data, and it prescribes ways these data may or may not be interpreted.

In some fields the methods are few, strictly defined and rigorously adhered to. In other fields, it is common that new studies give methodology a slightly new twist, *e.g.*, by suggesting new types of data (as, for example, a new type of qualitative interview). In such cases it is essential that the paper clearly explain how these data are collected, selected, and interpreted. It may be that the method is drawn or at least inspired by studies in a neighbouring field; the method may also be a combination of traditional features, borrowed or adapted features, and new features. By codifying how to interpret data methods constitute the bridge between data and claim; and this is why warrant is really another word for method.

Like warrants, methods are field-dependent. In fact, warrants or methods are not only field-dependent; they are actually constitutive of fields. The mastery of the codes we call method or warrant is at the heart of what constitutes professional competence in any academic field. Bazerman (1981) presents an instructive study of how professional competence in three highly separate academic fields is largely constituted by differing norms as to what counts as warrants in the respective fields.

Backing, according to Toulmin, is what we come up with if we are asked, 'why *in general* this warrant should be accepted as having authority' (Toumin 1958: 103). That is, the 'backing' category should be represented by statements about how and why we are justified in adducing and interpreting the data we offer in support of our claim. And that implies discussing and defending not only this way of interpreting, but also the way we collect and select our data. Here again we have various options. We may refer to authority, either 'authority figures' (here again, Habermas may be our example) or a current paradigm that sanctions such an interpretation; or we may point to parallel studies where a similar or related method has borne fruitful and reliable results. The synonym generally used for what the model labels backing is *theory*.

Rebuttal indicates 'circumstances in which the general authority of the warrant would have to be set aside' (Toulmin 1958: 101). The criterion that there has to be something in the rebuttal category means that the paper must show awareness of what counts against allowing the step from data to claim. Hence the rebuttal category is connected to the warrant category; notice that rebuttal in this sense does not include data that seems to count against the claim; such data should be discussed in the paper as well, but belong in the data category, as mentioned above.

Rebuttal may take many forms, according to field. On a very general level, a specific study might lead into the kind of fundamental problems of theory or paradigm known to many fields, for example as to whether the study of human phenomena is better or worse off by limiting itself to the observation of behaviour, or whether introspection is allowable or preferable, and the like. In other situations, there might be specific questions, of either a theoretical, a practical or even an ethical nature, which might be raised to question the warrant of the data used.

What we see generally is that awareness of what might count in rebuttal of one's method of interpreting is central not only to the merit of an individual paper, but also to the professional competence and identity of the writer.

Taken together, the three elements Warrant, Backing and Rebuttal constitute what we might call a full-blown statement and discussion of Method. Depending on how known and accepted that method is by the intended audience, the categories Backing and Rebuttal may be represented by more or less material. The liminal case is research papers written so squarely within a paradigm accepted by the intended audience that the warrant might be taken for granted. This may be so, for example, in certain schools of literary criticism where the use of biographical data in the interpretation of texts by a given writer is seen as a matter of course (whereas other schools, as is well known, do not take that view at all). Here we may in fact see papers consisting exclusively of data and claim – and perhaps some instantiation of the last of the six elements in the model: the qualifier.

The *Qualifier,* in Toulmin's own words, indicates 'the strength conferred by the warrant' on the step from data to claim. For the academic paper, this means that the student should discuss or at least signal how definitely and how categorically she wishes to advance her claim. There need not be any separate passage that can be labelled 'qualifier'; more often a certain amount of qualification is indicated along the way by means of phrases like 'this rather strongly suggests' or 'a plausible interpretation would be.'

3   TEACHING MACRO-TOULMIN

We believe that the Toulmin model, thus interpreted, may not only help students understand the task definition of that problematic genre, the academic paper; it may also be a procedural help to them in producing such papers: While work on the paper is in progress, the student may use the model as a criterion for assessing material already in the draft, as well as a heuristic for inventing material still missing – by asking, 'What have I got in this draft to fit into each of the categories represented in the model?' Thus, the model may help giving an awareness of the overall function of the genre, as well as of its component parts. Also, just as it may help in assessing one's own writing-in-progress, it may also help students read and assess academic writing by others.

In our experience, the main pedagogical advantage of using the Toulmin model as a macroscopic layout of the academic paper is that it increases the student's sense of the paper as one focused or functional unity. Students get a better understanding of what intimidating words like data, method, and theory refer to if they understand more clearly what these elements *do.* This in turn helps them tie the components of their paper together. This is also true on the verbal level, where we may see an increased and more discriminating use of metadiscourse – signposts telling the reader how the parts of the text work together.

On the level of substance, students may, for instance, suddenly realise how theories may supply the Backing that legitimises or even prescribes a certain methodological choice; this again may help them collect, select, and interpret the material that constitutes their data. They may realise the various functions that theory may have in academic discourse, which may in turn help them generate theoretical ideas of their own and give them a critical understanding of what goes on in professional debates within a field. A functional awareness of Backing and Rebuttal may help them make a Claim that is no taller than their data will plausibly permit, and with the appropriate degree of qualification. Students realise how important it is for the plausibility of their claim that Method is made explicit (Warrant), legitimised (Backing) and scrutinised (Rebuttal). Essentially, students may learn to assess critically the merit of their own work – a skill high in the Bloom hierarchy of educational goals. (See appendix in Rienecker and Stray Jörgensen 'The Text In Focus ...' in this volume). This in turn may help them assess strengths and weakness in the work of others, either their peers or established authorities in their field.

Many students have difficulty applying theories in a critical and constructive way. This, we believe, is especially so in those fields in the humanities where methodological considerations are usually implicit rather than explicit, *e.g.*, literary criticism. Student papers in these fields often leave the impression that theories are adduced, not in order to strengthen the writer's argument, but in order to please the instructor. Students whose papers seem to use theories in this way may benefit from seeing how theories function in an overall argumentative plan; they may realise that theories matter to method, both as legitimisation and as criticism. And they may see that theories themselves may be subject to analysis in terms of argument structure.

Finally, approaching the academic paper as one argument may benefit students by heightening their awareness of the uses of metadiscourse to signal the overall plan of a paper. As noted by, among others, Prosser & Webb (1994), the presence of meaningful metadiscourse significantly makes for higher grades; Hyland (1998) has shown how metadiscourse in academic writing functions not only as a help for the reader to understand the intended structural relations within the paper, but also text-externally, by alluding to presupposed disciplinary assumptions and by helping the reader construct appropriate contexts.

Admittedly, the approach to the paper as one and just one argument is a pedagogical simplification. Many academic papers can better be described as making several claims, either parallel or hierarchically arranged (or a combination of both). Still, the model has the pedagogical advantage of facilitating novices' overall understanding of the genre, as well as of the specific paper they are working on. In our experience, the model does not inhibit creativity; instead, the overview of the paper's constituent parts that the model affords often allows students to improve further on its design.

We have used the model in teaching academic writing in a variety of formats. In the most basic version, it is possible, in a one-hour period, to introduce the model and offer a few examples of its elements with reference to excerpts or projects contributed by students in the class. A more spacious format is a seminar of two separate three-hour sessions. This allows for more elaborate presentation of the model, more extensive exemplification from students' papers in progress with class discussion, and some exercise activities, of which we will describe a few.

3.1 Activity: Early Claim Formulation

This is the instruction given to the class for this activity:
- Freewrite for 8-10 minutes on 'the essence of my papers is...'
- Boil the essence of your paper down to one sentence – either a statement or a question.
- Based on this sentence, state the claim of your paper. To help you do this, ask yourself the following question: 'If I were to hand in this paper tomorrow, what would my conclusion be?'
- Read aloud – let us all hear what claims in research papers may sound like.
- (Optional question to the class:) Which of these claims would you choose to base a paper on?

3.2 Activity: Analysis of Model Examples

We generally use fairly short excerpts from selected student papers (max. 3 pages, preferably with line numbers). These papers are not by participants, but it is still important to use student papers so as to encourage the response 'What they can do, I can do.' After silent in-class reading, everyone is instructed to locate claims, data, warrant, rebuttal, backing, and qualifiers. The aim is to teach students to identify the various elements, which are not always separate or neatly marked off, and assess the balance in the argument as a whole – *e.g.*, will this set of data support a claim as large as this, is there enough backing, shouldn't the qualifiers be stronger? This activity is a useful exercise before analysing the participants' own papers-in-progress.

3.3 Activity: The Devil's Advocate – Critical Assessment of Argumentation in Others

The class looks closely at the argumentation in a paper and discusses whether each element is sound in itself, and whether the elements are in harmony. As an aid in this discussion, a checklist with these questions is handed out:

- What is the main claim? Given the argumentation presented in the paper, is it reasonable to make this claim?
- From where is data drawn to support the claim? Is the data credible and sufficient?
- What is the warrant, *i.e.*, what method is used? Has the method been used in a sound way?
- What problems are there in connection with this method? What possible rebuttals are there?
- Why is the method applicable? What backing is there that may eliminate or minimise the effect of the rebuttals?
- How certain may we be of the soundness of the claim when we consider rebuttals and backing? In other words, what kind of qualification is called for?

3.4 Activity: Apply the Model to Your Own Paper-in-Progress

This activity plays a large role in our seminars. We have developed the following rubric, see figure 2 below, which we ask students to fill in with answers relating to their own paper-in-progress. If they are able to fill in all the slots and find that the elements are in reasonable balance, then the paper is probably on the right course. We find that this rubric has a capacity to get many students going. Some realise that they have a great deal more material in the right places than they thought, while others are confronted with holes that should be filled, or with a claim that needs modification, *etc.*

Questions on the overall argument in my paper (model examples, drawn from an archaeology paper, are given in *italics*):

Claim
"What is my claim at this point in the writing process?"
Model example: The ancient city of X has directly influenced the architecture of city Y. Hence, there must have been a migration from X to Y.
My paper:

_____

_____

Data
"What will I use as data for this claim?"
Model example: The bricks used in X and Y are identical to the millimetre.
My paper:

_____

_____

Warrant
"What is my warrant (what method will I employ)?
Model example: Description of how I will proceed as to selection of samples, measurement, number of bricks selected, etc.
My paper:

_____

_____

Rebuttal
"What may be said in rebuttal of this method (what makes it problematic)?"
Model example: Only one parameter is used. The identity, rather than suggesting an influence, could be a coincidence.
My paper:

_____

_____

Backing
"What supports the warrant (the use of this method), in spite of rebuttal(s)?"
Model example: It is extremely unlikely that such a similarity could be a coincidence, hence an influence must have taken place: the bricks must come from he same mould.
My paper:

_____

_____

Qualifier
"Given the rebuttal and backing cited above, I expect to make my claim with the following qualifier."
Model example: It is highly probable that a migration has taken place from X to Y, but...
My paper:

_____

_____

Figure 2. Paper-in-Progress model by Signe Hegelund & Lotte Rienecker.
An elaborated version of the model in Rienecker (1999: 105)

In our experience, students benefit particularly from analysis and assessment of argumentation in model excerpts drawn from papers in the top third of the grading scale. In one and the same process, students are trained in applying the model, recognising well-made academic argumentation, and making critical but constructive assessment of each other's work. Thus, this activity may be used in the early part of a course, and it may be help even for novice writers of academic papers.

Special non-credit courses, featuring activities such as those described above, are not the only way to heighten students' awareness of the academic paper as a genre. In 'content' courses, especially on the more advanced levels, there will be frequent opportunities to apply the model to heighten students' awareness of the demands of the genre.

For example, it is customary in such courses to include excerpts from scholarly books, papers from journals, *etc.*, as required reading in course packs or the like. As a rule, such readings are discussed only for the content, *i.e.*, the results, theories, or ideas that they present. However, the instructor may also make a point of discussing such readings with regard to how they relate to the argument model.

For example, in history courses where actual historical studies in the form of journal articles or book chapters are studied, it will be relevant to dwell on passages where the writers discuss the validity of their sources. Such passages, in which some of the key skills that constitute 'historical method' are called for, usually represent the 'warrant' category. The sources used are, of course, the data. The claim is the historical interpretation derived from the sources.

In papers reporting empirical studies, it will generally be easy to locate passages where the elements of the model are in evidence. Often there is a separate 'Method' section, which will usually contain most of the 'Warrant' material in the paper. The theory underpinning the study, *i.e.*, the Backing, may often be found in the introductory section, and/or under the discussion of Method. The Claim may be found near the beginning in the form of a hypothesis, and in the 'Discussion' section in the form of an actual claim. Often, the Discussion will also contain elements of Rebuttal, as well as material that may be identified as Qualifier. As an example, chosen at random, we may cite this passage from a journal article on advertising (McQuarrie & Mick 1999). In the subsection 'Limitations and Future Research' (under 'General Discussion') we read:

> 'We did not demonstrate that replacing, say, the visual pun in the almond ad with a verbal pun conveying the same brand attitude would, in turn, produce the same impact on consumer response. This limits our ability to assert that, for instance, a pun is a pun, whether visual or verbal, with the same characteristic impact' (McQuarrie & Mick 1999: 52).

A propos a discussion of the points the writers are trying to make about visual effects in advertising, the teacher may also point out to students that such a passage constitutes a Qualifier, and that its presence (together with several others) increase the credibility of the article as a whole. If it is part of the course requirement to write a research paper, we think the teacher should go out of his way to point out that the use of appropriate qualifiers, like this one, is one of the criteria by which these papers will be graded.

More generally, in any content course there will be numerous opportunities for the teacher to make statements or initiate discussions on the functions and merits of specific passages in the course materials. This practice is a modern version of what ancient rhetoricians called 'imitatio': We read important writers not just in order to learn what they have to say, but also in order to learn from them how to say what *we* have to say.

An important part of this kind of reading is to be as critical as we are when reading papers or drafts by our peers. Here, too, the teacher will probably have to show the way. Statements by the teacher like: 'This is an interesting study, but I think part of the data is irrelevant, and the writer ought to have discussed the following obvious objection to his method ...' may be eye opening to students. They will realise that published research by esteemed scholars is not necessarily beyond reproach; that the merits of such research is not a black-or-white matter, but one in which there may be pros and cons; and that the criteria the teacher will apply in assessing the students' own papers include these, by which he finds others to fall short.

Even when only textbooks are being used (as opposed to actual research papers), it is still possible for the teacher to make observations like this: 'What the textbook does here is something you should never try to do in a research paper. These are two different genres. It carefully introduces and explains Habermas' theory of the public sphere, but does not supply backing for its application to talk shows on TV; in your paper it should be the other way around.'

To sum up, we suggest that there is indeed a use for the Toulmin model, despite much frustration with it in the teaching of general argument analysis among faculty and students alike. Coming as it does from a philosopher and ex-scientist, it is perhaps not surprising that more than anything it models the ideal case of *academic* argument. Moreover, we suggest that its real usefulness is only brought out when we give up applying Toulmin's labels microscopically to individual sentences and phrases in existing texts – and turn it upside down, as a tool for searching a text top down for material representing each of the categories. Finally, what we propose is using the model as an aid in production rather than in analysis, *i.e.*, as a set of criteria to guide the tentative unfolding of a paper-in-progress. What is does in that capacity, judging by the responses of the hundreds of students who have attended our non-credit seminars, is to furnish them with an understanding of the academic paper as one purpose-driven speech act.

RETHINKING FEEDBACK:
ASYMMETRY IN DISGUISE

MARY SCOTT* & KELLY COATE**

*Centre for Academic and Professional Literacy Studies at the Institute of Education.
University of London, UK,
**Centre for Higher Educational Studies Institute of Education,
University of London, UK

Abstract. On many postgraduate courses in the humanities and social sciences in the UK, the traditional three-hour examination has been largely replaced by 'coursework' in the form of written assignments. The feedback that subject tutors give students on the drafts of their assignments thus has an important pedagogic role to play. It is against this background that we describe the initial stages of an ongoing research project into feedback within our own institution, a postgraduate college within the Federal University of London. While we concentrate on feedback to postgraduate students, we would argue that our focus is relevant at the undergraduate level, too.

Our primary aim in this paper is to highlight an aspect of feedback that has been neglected in the research into feedback in the UK, viz., the relation between teacher and student as realized in samples of written feedback. This is an unexplored field that we regard as especially important in view of the increasing number of students with a widening diversity of past learning experience and, consequently, of assumptions regarding the roles of teachers and students. We would thus suggest that discussions of examples of feedback such as we examine in this paper should form the substance not only of seminars with students but also of staff development sessions, to which writing teachers now contribute in many UK universities.

Keywords: Feedback, Pedagogic relation, and Postgraduate education.

1   CHANGES IN HIGHER EDUCATION IN THE UK

Higher education in the UK has been the site of huge changes in recent years. The changes can be broadly characterized as representing a move away from a highly exclusive system, in which the participation rate of 18-20-year-olds was still only 15 per cent in the mid-eighties, to a more open system in which over 30 per cent of that age cohort had gained access by the mid-nineties (Scott 1995). It can thus be said that, broadly speaking, higher education in Britain has undergone a transformation.

Scott, M. & Coate, K. (2003). Rethinking Feedback: Asymmetry in Disguise. In: G. Rijlaarsdam (Series ed.) & L. Björk, G. Bräuer, L. Rienecker & P. Stray Jörgensen (Volume Eds.), Studies in Writing, Volume 12, Teaching Academic Writing in European Higher Education, pp. 87-99. © 2003 Kluwer Academic Publishers. Printed in the Netherlands.

The process of transformation is not yet complete, however. The current government would have the participation rate of 18-20 year-olds leap to 50 per cent in the near future.

The transformation of higher education has not been confined to participation rates at the undergraduate level. The number of postgraduate students is now almost double the number of undergraduates in the 1960s (in 1960 there were 270,000 undergraduate students in the UK, and by 1998 there were 403,000 postgraduates (HESA 2000). The postgraduate student population represents diversity of several kinds. Some students are, for example, following courses that are not directly related to their undergraduate fields of study; others are returning to study after a long absence, in which case their academic skills tend to be rusty or outdated.

A consequence of these changes in the composition of the student population at undergraduate and postgraduate levels is that teachers in higher education can no longer assume that their students will arrive with the kinds of academic 'know how' that could be taken for granted in the past. Within this context, student writing is receiving particular attention since students' success or failure on most higher education courses depends to a very large extent on the quality of the students' written coursework, dissertations or theses. There is thus a growing body of research that seeks to address the need for teachers in higher education to help their students to 'move on' as academic writers. This general concern to help student writers is the context framing the ongoing research project on issues of feedback in the institution where we teach.

2   OUR DATA

Although we recognize that feedback on student essays can come in many forms, which inter-relate in complex ways (Low 1996), we have concentrated on written feedback. The reason for our decision to delimit the object of our research in this way is that our students attach primary importance to the written comments they receive from their tutors on individual pieces of work. As an MA student put it: 'unlike oral feedback, the written has permanence. We can take it away and think about it; we can refer back to it when we have to write the next assignment.'

We initially collected two kinds of data: (i) comments obtained in the initial phase of our ongoing research project when we conducted a preliminary survey by means of a short questionnaire about teachers' own practices regarding feedback, and (ii) samples of written feedback on drafts of student essays. We are now in the stage of the research in which we are interviewing a sample of teachers and their students. Both are asked, individually, to discuss a particular piece of written work for which the teacher has provided some form of written feedback. Although we have only just begun this stage of the research, we are already seeing signs of gaps in communication between teachers and students that relate to different perceptions of the teacher-student relation as realized in the feedback.

3 EXISTING RESEARCH INTO FEEDBACK IN UK UNIVERSITIES

Surprisingly, in spite of the increasing concern to help students 'move on' as learners, to which we referred above, there is a dearth of research in the UK into written formative feedback on students' written assignments (Higgins *et al.* 2002). The primary trend within the existing literature of the field is to emphasize the failure of students to understand teachers' comments on their written work. This was first pointed out by Hounsell (1987). His large-scale investigation of undergraduate conceptions of the essay provided evidence of a mismatch between student understandings and teacher meanings. Thirteen years later Lea and Street (2000) produced a similar finding. Their research in two UK universities revealed that typical feedback discourse (*e.g.,* references to 'structure' and 'argument') tended to be 'rather elusive' to students.

More recent studies in the UK have also explored problems with feedback (Ivanic, Clark & Rimmershaw 2000; Higgins *et al.* 2001; Lillis & Turner 2001). In these, as in earlier instances, the investigation of feedback practices is largely driven by a concern that students are not receiving the kinds of feedback that will help them improve their writing. Underpinning such criticisms is the unexamined, idealised conception of feedback as a process in which teacher comments should be precisely mirrored in student comprehension and use. In other words, as Higgins *et al.* (2002) point out, there are complexities that are not addressed since important aspects of feedback have been left largely unexplored in the UK. These aspects include the relation realized in the feedback between teacher-writer and student-reader, which must surely play a significant part in the extent to which students are able to put feedback to use.

The existing research referred to above focuses on feedback at the undergraduate level. However, we would argue that studies of feedback at the postgraduate level could make a contribution to teaching and learning at all levels in the university since any complexities in the teacher-student relation in written feedback are likely to be writ large at the postgraduate level. Our ongoing research project thus focuses on written feedback to students following postgraduate and post-experience degree courses in our institution. Since our primary aim is to unveil complexity, the examples we offer below represent a selection of instances that we regard as telling.

4 THEORETICAL PERSPECTIVE

We approach feedback as an example of a social practice. From this perspective, samples of written feedback are examples of documents which, to borrow Bazerman's (1981) words, 'serve specific functions within historical and social situations'. We find an amplification of this focus in the concept of 'communities of practice' (Lave & Wenger 1991). Lave and Wenger write:

> 'Through textual practices writers and readers convey to one another the beliefs and value systems of the disciplinary cultures in which they participate.' (Lave & Wenger 1991).

This emphasis on practice as socially and historically situated and as incorporating the values and beliefs of a particular community has led us to treat samples of written formative feedback as shaped to a large extent by the teacher's perception of the social relation between teacher-writer and student-reader, and by the meanings and values (discourses) of the university.

The concept of the 'pedagogic relation' (Bernstein 1990, 1999), broadly interpreted, gives specificity to this perspective. We use the 'pedagogic relation' as the lens through which to examine the samples of written feedback that we have collected. The 'pedagogic relation', *i.e.,* the relation between teacher and taught in terms of authority, is a concept that carves out a rather different object of attention from any that we have come across in the growing number of published papers about feedback. It seemed to us to be particularly appropriate to a discussion of feedback given to postgraduate and post-experience students. In such a pedagogic context the boundaries between teacher and taught are not clear-cut and the relation between tutor and student may need to be very carefully negotiated. Although analyses or discussions of feedback at the undergraduate level inevitably touch on the relation between teachers and students (Hounsell 1987; Ivanic, Clark & Rimmershaw 2000; Lea & Street 2000), the problems and complexities surrounding the teacher's role and authority do not fall within the authors' remit.

Bernstein's conception of the pedagogic relation draws attention to such complexities. Bernstein treats the relation between teacher and taught as essentially and intrinsically asymmetrical. Its realisation is, however, often very complex since strategies may be used for disguising, masking, and hiding the asymmetry. One of the most important points about this asymmetry, Bernstein suggests, is that the power and authority of tutors over their students is always there, even if it is 'hidden'. The tutor has the power to (in Bernstein's language) 'frame' the pedagogic messages they send to students. Weakly framed 'messages' – such as feedback – do not convey a strong, authoritarian, didactic relationship. So, although, on the surface, a more equal relationship may be interpreted, the power of the tutor has been concealed.

In our research project, we have examined the samples of written feedback that we have collected for evidence of 'disguising, masking, and hiding'. What we have found adds subtleties and ambiguities to the portrayal of the teacher-student relation that emerges from our other data, viz., the comments teachers made in response to our preliminary questions about their practices concerning feedback.

5   TEACHERS RESPONSES TO OUR PRELIMENARY QUESTIONS

In view of our interest in the 'pedagogic relation', the most significant questions in our survey are those that required respondents to state what they considered the purpose of feedback to be and, in particular, what they regarded as the value students derive from feedback. Responses as to the purpose of feedback can be summarized as generally depicting the teacher as a helpful guide, whose comments would enable the students to improve their essays and to identify with disciplinary cultures – or, as one tutor described the purpose of feedback, to 'deepen their understanding and immersion into the academic community of practice'. Students were thus primarily portrayed as apprentices with knowledgeable and helpful teachers anxious to share their expertise so that the students might become junior members of the discipline. In the responses to the question about the value that students derive from feedback there is, however, a shift of emphasis with the responses focusing mainly on the students' psychological needs. Feedback is invested with the power to 'motivate' and 'encourage'.

This emphasis on the importance of the positive in feedback echoes much of the advice given in staff development programmes. Drawing on Open University practice, Baume & Baume (1996), for example, recommend the 'feedback sandwich' in their advice to the novice teacher on how to give feedback:

- First the good news

- Then the bad news (constructively!) and how to overcome it

- And finally a note of high encouragement

(Baume & Baume 1996: 10)

This sandwich unequivocally ascribes to teachers the knowledge and authority to separate the good from the bad. However, it also echoes the literature about learning that stresses the importance of not discouraging students. Teachers must be 'kind', by being 'constructive' and by 'rounding off the feedback with a high note and encouragement.' (Baume & Baume 1996). The many samples of feedback we have collected often follow this sandwich type of format within a fairly weak framing. However, as we shall finally demonstrate the 'sandwich' can mask considerable complexity.

6   SAMPLES OF FEEDBACK

The pedagogic relation that has emerged from our discussion so far represents a marked asymmetry between teacher and taught. It is, however, a benignly intended asymmetry that would avoid discouraging the student. Our examination of samples of written feedback does not destroy this emphasis on encouragement and motivation, but does complicate this apparently clear picture. The feedback samples we analysed bring to light the ambiguities and dilemmas that tutors negotiate, part consciously and part intuitively no doubt, when writing feedback. This is particularly apparent in samples where the teachers may be attempting to engage in a supportive dialogue with their postgraduate students. We have selected three samples for discussion. Each represents a different way of 'disguising, masking, hiding' the pedagogic relation.

Example 1
This example of feedback was typed on a slip of paper that was stapled to the first page of the essay draft:

(1)   You have targeted the question and given a very full and interesting
           answer. How heavily have you relied on your sources?

The opening sentence offers a positive and emphatic judgment ('You have targeted...)', 'you have given...'. It begins with a reference to a familiar assessment
criterion: students should always address the questions given. The sentence continues in the assessment mode, calling the essay 'full and interesting'. The asymmetry
between teacher and student is obvious. The fact that the feedback is attached to the
top of the first page of the essay emphasises the asymmetry. The feedback functions
rather like an abstract, summarising what is to come and, by its position on top of
the student's text, visually representing the hierarchical relation between teacher and
student. However, a paradox emerges at this point, as the teacher gives no examples
from the student's text to substantiate or illustrate her judgment.

    As so often with feedback (see Ivanic, Clark, & Rimmershaw 2000), this lack of
specificity implies the existence of a set of norms that transcends the personal and is
possessed by both teacher and student. This is perhaps most clearly evident in the
teacher's choice of the epithet, 'interesting'. Although 'interesting' suggests 'interesting to me the teacher', the epithet here takes on the status of a norm independent
of the teacher. Thus it is that the asymmetry between teacher and student is simultaneously both asserted and hedged by being depersonalised. A further assumption
follows from this implicit claim that the student also owns such normative metadiscourse. The student is assumed to be able to relate the teacher's comments to what
she has done in her essay, so giving particularity to 'you have targeted the question'
and 'a full and interesting answer'.

    The second sentence, *i.e.,* the question 'How heavily have you relied on your
sources?' represents a shift to the negative, and it is potentially a negative of huge
import. Behind it lies the spectre of plagiarism, regarded as a serious offence in UK
universities. Student handbooks tend to carry heavy warnings about plagiarism. For
example, the student to whom the question is addressed would have earlier been
provided with a handbook containing the following statement:

> 'Plagiarism, that is the unacknowledged presentation of another person's thoughts or
> words as though they were your own, must be avoided. Direct quotation from the pub-
> lished or unpublished works of others (including internet sources) must always be
> clearly identified as such...and a full reference to their source must be provided in the
> proper form. Remember that a series of short quotations from several different sources,
> if not clearly identified as such, constitutes plagiarism.... Equally if you summarise an-
> other person's ideas or judgements, you must refer to that person in your text and in-
> clude the work to which you have referred in your bibliography. Failure to observe
> these rules may result in an allegation of cheating ...' [31]

It is beyond the scope of this paper to discuss the complexities around the concept of
plagiarism, which, for all such attempts at explicitness, remains highly problematic
(See Angelil-Carter 2000). What is significant in relation to the 'pedagogic relation'
is the contrast between the 'musts' of the quotation above and the tutor's apparent

---

[31] *From the* Student Handbook*; Registry, University of London Institute of Education 2002:*
31.

tentativeness. The question form overtly masks the tutor's authority as a representative of the institution's rules. It can thus be read as a coded warning in which the teacher avoids the adversarial by refraining from making a direct accusation. She is signalling to the student, albeit in a non-threatening and weakly framed way, what she regards as a serious issue.

Example 2
This example of feedback was provided by e-mail:

(2) Dear A.

You have made a number of very good points in your discussion of the two passages. As you said yourself, what could be improved is the organization of the content rather than the content itself.
Here are some comments that I hope you will find helpful:

1. Your introduction
It is not necessary to define lexical, syntactical and organizational. The meanings are not open to debate in this context. [It is always difficult to know to what extent one can assume that the meaning of a term is so well known generally that there is no need to explain it].

2. It might help you to organize your points if you began with a brief reference to the different conditions under which passages like those given (*i.e.,* informal spoken and formal written language) are produced. You have included a number of points (speech is face-to-face; the speaker is composing at the moment of utterance; writing: audience at a distance, unknown; time to compose and revise). What you have not said is that these differences result in the differences in the characteristics of speech and writing that you refer to in another part of the essay *e.g.,* more informal vocabulary (lexis) in informal speech; fillers-to give the speaker thinking time; pauses; appeals to the listener).

3. The following points refer to statements in your text that I have asterisked.
*1.There are no sentences in speech, sentences with capital letters and full stops are features of writing. Speech has units of information and pauses. See Kress & Halliday on your reading list.
*2. In the literature about spoken and written language, speech is described as sequential; co-ordinating conjunctions (and, but) are common. Formal written language is hierarchical-main clauses with subordinate clauses. Look at the organization of the written passage. What is the function of the sentences? Is there a generalization; elaboration; examples, conclusion...?
*3. What do you think the intonation pattern of the spoken excerpt might be?

I will be happy to answer any queries you have about the comments above either at the tutorial or by e-mail in advance of the tutorial.

Best wishes
B.

_____

The asymmetry between teacher and student is again marked but in a different way. The teacher offers detailed comments on the content and organization of the essay draft and obviously has a clear conception of how the essay could be improved. She mostly makes that explicit, pointing to omissions and irrelevancies and giving instructions. For example: 'What you have not said is that...', 'It is not necessary to define...', 'There is no need to give long general accounts of spoken and written language. Tie the comments...' There is, in fact, only one instance of the use of a modal verbal form that overtly reduces the asymmetry between tutor and student, viz., 'It might help you to organize your points if you....'.

There are, however, several other ways in which the teacher also seeks to mask the asymmetry between herself and the student. She presents the feedback in the form of a friendly letter that begins with 'dear' and concludes with 'best wishes'. She begins by acknowledging the student's self assessment of the draft. She implies that she shares a problem with the student: 'It is always difficult to know to what extent one can assume....'. She also reduces her own authority in relation to the topic of the student's essay by appealing to the authority of published authors. In other words, she acts as an intermediary presenting not her own ideas but rather drawing the student's attention to those of the experts.

It is, however, the teacher who decides which of the experts are relevant. Although she gives credit where she can to the student's points, and attempts to show, rather than simply state in general terms, how the essay might be improved, she is clearly guided by her conception of the 'good' answer on this particular topic. Whereas the teacher who provided sample (1) can be said to represent the authority of the academy in general, the teacher in sample (2) represents authority in relation to a particular area of knowledge; an authority which rests finally on her knowledge of the literature of the field.

Example 3
This sample was hand-written:

(3) Dear C

*Thanks so much for sharing your draft with me. We agreed that you shld try to let me have this draft when you did even though it may not be as polished as you wd wish. Please, therefore see my remarks as being offered in a supportive spirit, to help you to take it forward
    *May I offer you some general comments on your approach to academic writing? It comes across as a rather disconnected set of generalisations. Try to develop and substantiate your points more, *e.g.,* by referring to the literature more, by offering data or other evidence, and (here) by quoting from the reports in question

Specific suggestions for developing your argumentation would include
*Avoid single sentence paragraphs; develop each point

*Aim for 2-3 paragraph breaks per page
*Adopt a 12-point typeface and always put your text into a double-line spacing format
*Avoid single paragraph sections-aim for sections, say, of 2-3 pages

Particular points on this essay
Do you answer the question (*e.g.,* around the respective visions of the 3 reports)?
Do you develop a definite account of the learning society? Are the different interpretations compatible?

Try to ensure your conclusion draws the threads together specifically in relation to the title. Please do not be alarmed by all my comments and please keep going!

D

This sample brings to mind a comment made by a teacher in our initial survey on feedback: 'Not enough time for dialogue with them all – often rely on written feedback – a gift – rather than conversation, a loop!' The perceived benefits of engaging in a dialogue with students were reinforced by Ivanic, Clark and Rimmershaw (2000), who nevertheless found that feedback written as an ongoing 'dialogue' between students and tutors was rare in their sample. Both our samples (1) and (2) opened up the possibility of 'dialogue'. However, in sample (1) the tutor posed a question that disguised the potential seriousness of the issue that might be discussed viz., plagiarism. In sample (2), the tutor issued an explicit invitation to dialogue, but a dialogue that would enable the student to have any misunderstandings clarified. In each instance the 'dialogues' would thus be likely to be characterized, albeit in different ways, by a marked difference in authority between tutor and student; in other words, the student would finally be 'put right' on certain matters.

Sample (3) appears at first reading to encourage dialogue on almost equal terms. It clearly sets out to narrow the gap between teacher and student and to engage in a (written) conversation. This is indicated by the informality of contractions such as 'shld', 'wld', and by the colloquialism of 'thanks so much', and by the fact that, as in sample (2), the feedback begins in personal letter mode ('Dear C'). The teacher refers to previous communication between himself and the student and his comments are thus obviously intended to be part of an ongoing dialogue with the student. However, if we consider the sample in relation to the description of written feedback as a 'gift', what we find here is not so much a dialogue as an exchange of gifts. The teacher begins by thanking the student for the 'gift' of their draft: 'Thanks so much for sharing your draft with me.' Having thus constructed the essay as a 'gift' given to him, the teacher then offers his comments in exchange, and overtly narrows the gap between himself and the student still further by referring to an agreement reached earlier: 'We agreed that you shld try to let me have this draft when you did even though it may not be as polished as you wd wish. Please, therefore see my remarks as being offered in a supportive spirit, to help you to take it forward.'

What is glossed over in these opening sentences is the difference in the kind and value of the 'gifts' to be exchanged. The 'gift' that is being given by the teacher is, in fact, complex. On first reading, the opening comments sound positive and encouraging. However, the feedback does not begin in the style of the typical 'feedback sandwich' by pointing out what is good in the essay. Instead, the initial sentences serve as a sugaring of the potentially unpleasant pill that is actually the main 'gift' being offered by the teacher. This impression is strengthened when the teacher asks (rhetorically) for permission to continue ('May I ...'), as if about to cross into dangerous territory.

The asymmetry of the teacher-student relationship is, however, less masked in the attempt to make explicit the purpose of the feedback (to help the student improve). The comments then become quite specific as the teacher moves into his position of authority in order to show the students how they can improve their work. Although the comments continue with the reference to a 'gift' being given ('May I offer you ...'), what is then offered indicates that the essay needs much revision and has not yet conformed to the academic conventions required. In fact, the statements 'May I offer you some general comments on your approach to academic writing? It comes across as a rather disconnected set of generalisations', begin to point to serious weaknesses in the student's work. The most direct and serious criticisms are perhaps the 'particular points' which are left to last: 'Do you answer the question?', 'Do you develop a definite account of the learning society?' and 'Try to ensure...'.

However, these criticisms are framed by attempts to lessen the teacher's power. In his final comment ('Please do not be alarmed by my comments and please keep going') the teacher returns to an encouraging note but it is in a different key from his opening sentences. There he explicitly ceded power to the student before claiming the authority to make specific comments about the student's work. Here he acknowledges that the 'gift' may have been hard to accept and (successfully?) lessens its force.

Our comments on the three samples above are not intended as criticisms of the teachers who wrote the feedback. We cannot tell precisely why the pedagogic relation is masked in each case or the extent to which the teachers may be shaping their feedback in the light of a personal knowledge of the particular student and her likely response to criticism. Nevertheless, viewing feedback from the perspective of the 'pedagogic relation' has led us to see that the 'feedback sandwich' hides complexity from sight. In fact, if there are serious issues to be raised, as in Samples (1) and (3), providing written feedback can be an uncomfortable, even risky, task. This is almost certain to be so when the students are like those in our sample: postgraduates with professional experience. Such students are almost our colleagues but not quite.

Taking a wider view we would, however, suggest that an analysis of the pedagogic relation could be valuable at the undergraduate level, too. The expansion in undergraduate enrolments includes an increasing number of mature students who question institutional authority patterns (see Lillis 2001). Are these students contributing to a change in the pedagogic relation at that level, with tutors less likely to adopt an explicit and clear-cut position of authority-with-kindness such as is expressed in the 'feedback sandwich'?

7   FURTHER COMPLEXITIES: TEACHER AND STUDENT MEANINGS

As stated earlier, we are currently interviewing pairs of individuals, each pair comprising a teacher and a student, about the written feedback the teacher had given the student on a particular assignment. Although this phase of the research is at an early stage, it adds emphasis to the importance of the pedagogic relation as realized in written feedback. In fact, we would now argue that attempts to provide feedback that students can use are likely to fail if attention is given only to trying to make concepts such as 'argument' or 'structure' transparent'. In other words, our interview data add further complexity to the 'sandwich' view of feedback and lead us to claim that how students interpret feedback is strongly connected to how they perceive the teacher-student relation. To give one illustrative example: when interviewed, an MA student stressed the importance of the encouragement she felt her teacher had given her through the written feedback on her essay. She was confident that she had grasped what the teacher's comments meant. That this was not, in fact, the case became very clear when the student was asked how she felt about the comment that her 'critical review of the literature' was adequate. The student replied:

> 'I wasn't 100% sure that I was being critical enough but apparently I was....I wasn't sure if I would be asked to be a bit more critical or not, but apparently it was fine ...'

In this response, the student is equating an adequate 'critical review' with offering a large enough number of criticisms. However, the teacher, who was also interviewed, meant that the student had shown some insight into the major issues relating to the topic of the essay. We would argue that this mismatch in meaning rests finally on a particular perception of the teacher-student relation. The student's quantitative notion of criticism assumes that the teacher's role is that of an assessor awarding points on some kind of right-wrong scale. For the student the asymmetry between teacher and student is thus marked with the student seeing her role as requiring conformity to expectations relating to quantifiable criteria. From this student perspective, the teacher's role in giving feedback is to ensure that the student has scored enough points on the particular topic. The teacher, however, related being critical to epistemological understandings and intellectual development within the disciplinary field. She saw herself as a representative of the field of study, and as a guide and mentor rather than as an assessor. In brief, she saw feedback as a means of inducting the student into a particular 'community of practice' (Lave & Wenger 1991).

What the feedback did achieve in this instance was a boosting of the student's confidence – a purpose recommended in descriptions of the 'feedback sandwich': the student now feels she can write at the appropriate level. The student has, however, been left with misperceptions that are likely to put her at a disadvantage further on in the course.

The example above is typical of a dominant theme that is emerging from our interview data in that it graphically illustrates how perceptions of the function and meaning of feedback are rooted in perceptions of the pedagogic relation. This has important implications for classroom practice especially in view of the 'internationalisation' and 'massification' of universities in the UK and elsewhere since students now bring with them markedly different past experiences and expectations of the 'pedagogic relation'.

8   IMPLICATIONS FOR THE CLASSROOM

Our suggestions for classroom practice are based on our conclusion that if students cannot act on the written feedback they have received it may be that they have not appreciated, or are questioning or rejecting, the particular ways in which the asymmetry of the pedagogic relation is realized in the feedback. It is thus important that as teachers we consider feedback not simply as an assessment of the student's work but also as one of the primary forms of interaction between our students and us.

It is here that writing teachers could make a significant contribution in collaboration with subject teachers. We would recommend awareness-raising staff development sessions at which subject and writing teachers would discuss the teacher-student relation in samples of feedback, so identifying the complexities and reflecting on their own practices and assumptions as givers of feedback. We have in mind a productive dialogue that would represent a sharing of expertise. Writing teachers would bring their linguistic skills and experience in analysing genres and discourse; subject teachers their discipline-specific aims. Each group would have understandings of students' backgrounds and responses to share.

We would also recommend the discussion of samples of feedback as an extension of a common practice in higher education classrooms in the UK where students are given samples of student essays to comment on and are asked to identify what the teachers saw as positive or negative features. In discussing the kind of relation between the teacher-writer and the student-reader that may be realized in the samples of feedback students would be able to articulate their own assumptions about what it means to be a student and about how their teachers are trying to communicate with them in their role as teachers. The development of this kind of awareness could be particularly important for the students (and valuably informative for their teachers) in view of the changes in the participation rates in higher education that we referred to earlier. It could foster a continuing conversation between teachers and students in which the essential asymmetry between teacher and taught would, of course, continue to exist but would be a matter for discussion and debate.

Finally, what we have reported is intended to be tentative and to prompt enquiries in others' classrooms. Among the questions, which our survey and the samples of feedback raise are: at what stage should formative feedback be given to students; *i.e.,* at what point is it most valuable to the students? It would seem that Sample 3 was given at an early stage (when the student was reluctant to let the tutor see the essay). Was the student able to use the feedback or did she feel crushed by it – in spite of the tutor's very good intentions? These are the kinds of essential but under-researched questions that both writing and subject teachers could pursue in relation to their own students.

9   CONCLUSION

What we have presented in this paper are only snapshots from an ongoing research project. We have concentrated on an unexplored aspect of feedback – the pedagogic relation as realized in written feedback. In so doing we have sought to uncover complexities, which are hidden by advice to teachers such as is contained in the recommendation that their feedback should conform to the 'feedback sandwich'. We have thus aimed not at closure but at stimulating debate and agenda for further reflection and enquiry.

THE (IM)POSSIBILITIES IN TEACHING UNIVERSITY WRITING IN THE ANGLO-AMERICAN TRADITION WHEN DEALING WITH CONTINENTAL STUDENT WRITERS

LOTTE RIENECKER & PETER STRAY JÖRGENSEN

Academic Writing Center, University of Copenhagen, Denmark

Abstract. Writing centres and writing tutors are an American invention. For us Europeans it is a case of cultural importation. If we import American manuals, handouts, even on-line tutoring services on academic writing, it may collide with continental ways of writing and of teaching and tutoring writing at the university. We see the diversity in the European traditions and styles of writing as one of the major challenges to writing centres and their staff outside the US. The development from elite universities to mass universities adds to the problem, and we believe that at the modern mass university it is almost impossible to teach and tutor our students to write in a traditional continental way. This article lines up the problems with teaching academic writing to continental writers and sketches out the historical, economical, cultural and pedagogical background, and we put forward some suggestions for advising and tutoring the continental writers, and how and when to place the continental writing within studies at the modern mass universities.

Keywords: Academic genres, Anglo-American tradition/writing, Continental tradition/writing, Problem oriented writing, Scientific writing, and Topic oriented writing.

1   THE PROBLEM

A German Ph.D. student approached us at a seminar and told us that she had studied both in Germany and at a US university, and she found the ways of writing she had been taught at odds with one another. She gave us an article by an Australian, Michael Clyne (1987) who has researched the national differences in student and scholarly writing in a number of countries, concentrating on the observable differences in Anglo-American and German scientific and scholarly articles and student term papers. (Other observers on this matter are Anna Duszak (1997) and Susan Peck MacDonald (1987, 1994)). Clyne's article finally verbalised an observation we

Rienecker, L. & Stray Jörgensen, P. (2003). The (Im)Possibilities in Teaching University Writing in the Anglo-American Tradition when Dealing with Continental Student Writers. In: G. Rijlaarsdam (Series Ed.) & L. Björk, G. Bräuer, L. Rienecker & P. Stray Jörgensen (Volume Eds.), Studies in Writing, Volume 12, Teaching Academic Writing in European Higher Education, pp. 101-112. © 2003 Kluwer Academic Publishers. Printed in the Netherlands.

had done before: We notice two different kinds of writing from the students who use our tutoring service.

2   THE ANGLO-AMERICAN MODE OF WRITING

A large body of students study and write in an Anglo-American tradition of doing and writing research. The typical features of studies within the Anglo-American tradition are that they are often empirical, based on real-world objects, people and events, problem-based, methodologically oriented, systematic, argumentatively written, in a clear, concise, unmistakable and often quite impersonal language. The subject matter is in the foreground, not the scholars who wrote the studies – sometimes you scarcely remember their names. We are thinking of all the empirical works and surveys so prominent in post-war social, historical, linguistic and psychological studies. This Anglo-American tradition springs from the natural and social sciences, but is now very common in the humanities where we teach, as well.

3   THE CONTINENTAL MODE OF WRITING

On the Continent especially there is another prominent mode of research and academic writing: University departments of for instance Theology and other subjects in the Humanities such as Philosophy, Arts and Literature have a strong tradition of writing focused on interpretations of the great European thinkers such as Barthes, Bourdieu, Buber, Derrida, Eco, Freud, Heidegger, Jaspers, Kierkegaard, Lacan, Marx, (to mention just a few). There are of course also Anglo-American representatives, but we want to stress the continental angle. Furthermore, we are not saying that writing about a continental thinker classifies a text as 'continental'. It clearly does not; it is the form and the approach to the text – not the topic –, which may define it as written in an Anglo-American or a continental tradition.

   The studies and the term papers on the continental thinkers and written in the continental mode are often interpretative, hermeneutical and epistemological in nature, as this research question from a term paper in Philosophy exemplifies: 'The concept of freedom is fundamental in existentialism. This paper focuses on Jean-Paul Sartre's concept of freedom and its meaning for human existence'. What makes this formulation a continental one in our view is firstly the absence of an explicit problem in the research question, secondly the focus is on the interpretation of a concept linked to a particular thinker (as opposed to: as observed empirically), and thirdly, the broadness of the parameter: 'the meaning of human existence' has a scope often seen in continental writing. Another example: a continentalist stronghold of teachers in the Psychology Department in an internal manual advise their students to use (and recycle!) the research question: 'What is (... any concept from the realm of emotion/cognition/volition) really?' In this paper, it is required that the student includes a high number of theoretical psychological thinkers 'as knights around the Round Table' (as expressed by a subject teacher). Over the years, this highly theoretical continental paper placed in the 4th semester has spurred the highest number of contacts to the Academic Writing Centre than any other single assignment in the department. Besides being concept-laden and theoretically heavy, the continental texts are sometimes ripe with metaphors typical of literary texts, and always linguistically demanding.

Although the writing we are thinking of here is theoretical, there also seems to be a continental way of doing empirical studies. Its features may be comprehensiveness, all-inclusiveness pertaining to the topic, and topic-based rather than problem-based exposition. An example from a master's thesis research question: 'What are the prefixes of the field names on the Faroe Islands?' We observe that continental research questions often begin with 'what' or 'who', whilst Anglo-American research questions more often use 'why' and 'how'. Of course, styles of writing and reporting scientific endeavours know no boundaries; we are referring to tendencies, probably more discipline-specific than national. At Danish universities, we see both cultures represented, very often present within the same institute, but it seems to us that the Anglo-American tradition is the most widespread culture. It is also the dominant culture, in step with the economical possibilities and the current political climate, for instance the political demand for internationalisation of research.

We sum up the main characteristics of the two important traditions of scientific writing at European universities in table 1.

Table 1. The Continental and the Anglo-American Scientific Writing.

← A continuum →

Continental (German-Romanic) tradition	Anglo-American (British-American) tradition
• 'Think'-texts (see below)	• Problem solving texts
• Sources in the foreground	• Problems in the foreground
• Philosophy, the history of ideas, epistemology, culture, spirit and mind, arts and aesthetics	• Facts, realities, observable matters, empiricism
• Emphasis on concepts and theories (methods)	• Emphasis on methods (concepts, theories)
• Interpretation (preservation) of traditional culture	• New understandings, evaluations and actions
• Contingent epistemology	• Controlled, purposeful epistemology
• Numerous points, claims, conclusions, around the subject	• One point, one claim, one conclusion
• Often a non-linear, discursive structure	• Linear structure, digressions discouraged
• ('Exkurse'), digressions allowed	
• Academic writing as art and inborn abilities	• Academic writing as learned craftsmanship

Examples of text-genres typical of the continental writing are: The interpretive/reflective philosophical essay, the textbook, the biography, and the monograph. Examples of text-genres typical of Anglo-American writing are: The empirically based study, and the systematically and up-to-date literature-based research paper.

We acknowledge of course that our picture is simplifying, and that we are indicating tendencies only, and that there is a good deal of overlapping.

Note that the genre we have in mind is the scientific research paper (and genres of graduate education derived from this such as theses and dissertations). We do not address other genres written in college and at university for training purposes, for instance essays, for which the rules and demands may be much broader.

4   THINKING AND PROBLEM SOLVING

These different modes in academic writing spring from fundamentally different perceptions of the nature of science: The continental tradition emphasises science as thinking, whilst the Anglo-American tradition emphasises science as investigation and problem solving. Nevertheless, there is no necessary contradiction here. The following quotations of what we consider authoritative sources evidently demonstrate the difference:

> 'Science and scientific thinking begin where I am prepared to believe in my own thoughts, make them explicit, relates them to the opinions of others and enters the results of my thinking into the scientific discourse. (Our italics).
>   Science has, according to this definition, nothing to do with scientific method, with abstraction, formal language, objectivity *etc.* Science is primarily a social activity: Precisely stated, it begins with the publication of our thoughts – in that particular moment when we do not consider the thoughts as a private matter, but as a social contribution to epistemology' (our translation). (Kruse 1997b: 72).[32]

> 'Research is simply *gathering the information you need to answer a question and thereby help you solve a problem.*' (Booth, Colomb & Williams 1995: 6).

Text-features, which distinguish continental university writing from that of Anglo-American university writing, are listed in table 2.

Along these lines, according to empirical studies carried out by Michael Clyne, a key-difference between Anglo-American and especially German writing in higher education is that while *structure* is a primary concern in the Anglo-American tradition of writing in academe, *content* is all-important in the continental tradition. Anglo-American teachers will comment on and punish the *inclusion* of material which is subject-relevant, but which clutters the overall structure and argumentative pur-

---

[32]*The original German text:*
'Wissenschaft und wissenschaftliches Denken beginnen dort, wo ich bereit bin, meinen eigenen Denken zu trauen, es zu explizieren, auf die Meinungen andere zu beziehen und seine Resultate in den wissenschaftlichen Diskurs einzubringen.
Wissenschaftlichkeit hat, dieser Bestimmung entsprechend, primär nichts mit wissenschaftlicher Methode, mit Abstraktion, formaler Sprache, Objektivität usw. zu tun. Wissenschaft ist primär eine soziale Handlung: Genau gesagt beginnt sie mit der Veröffentlichung unsere Denkens, mit dem Moment also, an dem wir das Denken nicht mehr als Privatsache ansehen, sondern als soziale Aufgabe der Erkenntnisgewinnung.'

pose of the text. Continental teachers will be more likely to comment on *omissions* of content, which could be seen as subject-relevant, thus promoting breadth of information even at the cost of focus and a clear structure. (At our writing centre, we have heard Ph.D. students from Southern European universities complain that the worst thing that could possibly happen is to overlook some obscure article, which the professor happens to know. 'They expect that no stone is left un-turned'). As one senior lecturer at our university observed the difference: 'All you have to do is read both German and American articles, and you will notice a vast difference in breadth and detail of information, level of theorising and abstraction, even sentence-length.' As we see it, Anglo-American, and especially American university writing, and the teaching of it, is heavily influenced by rhetoric and rhetorical text-concerns such as purpose, aim, reader, focus, structure and argumentation. (The ironic part of it is that classical rhetoric is very much a European 'invention'. Rhetoric seems to have been almost forgotten in continental European academic writing, while American and British teachers of writing have reintroduced the classical rhetoricians).

Table 2. Text-features in Continental Writing.

Text features in Continental Writing

- Frequent research questions:
  - What is the inherent content of...
  - What did X really mean?
  - What lies behind...
  - The development of X's thoughts
  - Who influenced whom and by what?
  - What are the similarities/contrasts/contradictions between X an Y?
- Structures which do not necessarily follow fixed patterns
- Excursions, digressions and associations
- Short introductions, little metacommunication, little reader-information
- Long paragraphs, few sub-headers
- High number of abstract concepts
- Linguistic complexity and abstraction
- Varied language, reformulations, varied use of concepts
- In student papers: often source-influenced language
- Reflections of the writer's personality (and possibly originality) in reasoning, thoughts, conclusions as well as in style.

5   THE VIRTUES AND THE DIFFICULTIES OF THE CONTINENTAL TRADITION

We acknowledge that many very interesting (also students') contributions of the humanities come from the continental writers of for instance reflective essays – think of Barthes, Eco and Giddens (though the latter is not from the continent), and great biographies of historical persons. All of this is writing that helps us view and interpret people and culture in thought-provoking ways. And is this not what the Humanities are supposed to do? Are we always really all that interested in systematic, methodological, intersubjectively controllable empirical studies, which just hand us the facts? Does not every lecturer in the humanities think that the best thing that could happen for his or her university would be for the next Heidegger to walk out of the university gates? At our faculty of humanities, many of the successful and prestigious young researchers adhere to the continental tradition, they are reflective philosophers and cultural theoreticians with a very broad scope of knowledge and association to draw on and cite (and name-drop!) They are not merely out to 'investigate a (one!) problem' in a linear fashion, rendered in a pre-fabricated argumentative format from a textbook (see for instance Neman 1995, Booth *et al.* 1995) or on a handout from the writing centre, the kind you can obtain in most Online Writing Labs (see for instance Purdue University!).

But are these kinds of writing teachable, even at the university level? (And another disturbing question is: Do they represent science? A number of the continental primary texts are published as books, and have never been intended as or handed in to be judged at any university on their scientific merit, and are thus very confusing to students. Good questions are: 'If Lacan tried to hand this book in as a Ph.D. project at my university, would he even pass? Am I supposed to write *like* Lacan, or *about* him, but in a very different style?' The flip side of the coin is all the writing problems that get piled up where the continental writing is most prominent in higher education: It is exactly at those departments where the continental writing is in vogue (such as Philosophy, Theology and Literary Science) that students and public surveys carried out by the Ministry of Education report and criticise the great number of drop-outs, prolonged studies, 'thesis-swamp' and problems with even minor written assignments, and it is also often from these departments we hear the most student complaints about the lack of instruction, and where we see some really poor writing and total misunderstanding of the task. It is here we often hear students and teachers speak of 'the art of writing a thesis' – and not the craft! In fact, if it were not for the writing problems of the Humanities and the bad-will it has generated among politicians and the general public, there would not be a writing centre at our university in the first place. It is no coincidence that the need first arises in the humanities departments, and not in the natural or social sciences. You may argue that the need for writing centre facilities is reinforced where continental ways of researching and writing are strong.

6   PROBLEMS FOR THE CONTINENTAL WRITERS

The continental students' writing problems as we see them, consist of difficulties with
- Living up to their demanding and difficult literary idols
- Finding and maintaining a focus
- Selecting, sorting, using, transforming and acknowledging sources
- Understanding and decoding difficult primary sources

- Getting beyond mere restatement and reformulations of the thoughts of others
- Writing in too little or too much of the writer's own 'voice'
- Quoting too much and writing conceptually and linguistically too close to sources.

Thus, there are extreme quality polarisations in continental writing. It can be very good, and it can be terribly bad. Likewise, some students become very successful in their endeavours, but many drop out, or fall behind with their term papers, which are written with great difficulty. On the other hand it is relatively easier in the Anglo-American teaching research and academic writing tradition to help a great number of students write good papers, pass their exams and graduate.

What do our students make of it? And what do we, the writing centre staff, do? Teach different traditions of writing as separate sets of guidelines? We do not, for a number of reasons. Firstly, we do not see the continental way of writing as an appropriate training mode for new (young) students. We stick to teaching and tutoring the Anglo-American way of writing, and to teaching those features of academic writing, which may be common ground (examples are: How to handle sources, formalities and many aspects of writing process). And besides: In fact we are not able to provide the continental writers with *continental concrete and operational* criteria for The Good Paper, formats of structures *etc.*, because to some extent such criteria cannot be generalised: They are specific to their discourse communities and to the individual teacher.

7   THE TWO WRITING TRADITIONS AND THEIR WRITING PEDAGOGIES

We believe that the way you teach writing springs from your understanding of the genre you teach and that genre's criterion of quality (see Rienecker and Jörgensen elsewhere in this volume). All American manuals for college writing include basic structures and lists of criteria and heuristics for the existing types of papers. The Anglo-American tradition makes it possible to teach writing in large classes, or from books, manuals and handouts on for instance how to write a research question, how to use methods to collect and analyse data, how to criticise the use of methods, how to structure a paper, what to include in an introduction and a conclusion *etc.*, because it is expected to be done in conventionalised ways. Thus, the Anglo-American writing style has a complementary pedagogy, which can be used in writing courses, workshops and writing centres, as well as for on-line help services, writing software *etc.* The instruction can be taken care of by writing tutors (who may even be students and can relatively easily be instructed on what to tell the young writers, see for instance Ryan: 'The Bedford Guide for Writing Tutors', 1994). Essential in the Anglo-American teaching of writing is the use of heuristics. Heuristics for writing (parts of) papers are on most Writing Lab home pages.

But how do you teach how to write a bachelor project focusing on how to understand Lacan, Popper, Kierkegaard or Bourdieu without juxtaposing the thinker in question with other thinkers or empirical phenomena or cases? It seems very hard to put forward general guidelines, instructions, concrete criteria of qualities, because continental ways of writing are bound by more or less tacit rules that are specific to certain teachers and certain circles and not to commonly accepted rules and are not at the moment suitable for any on-line handout service – except maybe if written by those very same subject teachers. The features and formats of continental texts are closely connected with the author and his/her discourse community. As one continental philosophy-teacher put it: 'We do not instruct before writing, our students are supposed to sit at the feet of their masters and absorb their writing themes and styles'.

8   DECLINE OF THE ELITE UNIVERSITY

In the 'old fashioned' universities, the students did just that. This was the time when you found – in the opinion of some – Heaven on university campuses; it was an era with fewer, more able and independent students; more time for teacher-student contact; narrower fields of knowledge, and longer studies with little time pressure.

The current pedagogical challenges in higher education are the results of the changing status of universities during the last three or four decades. In the fifties and sixties, the universities were elite institutions. It was easier then to uphold the notion that writing instruction was solely the task of the school system. Up through the seventies and eighties most universities in Europe changed from elite to mass universities with much broader intakes of students, and no longer just the 'best' 5-10 percent. Some of the problems are connected with the fact that universities no longer are 'what they used to be.' This development has subsequently altered the conditions of the pedagogy in general, and consequently the ways of teaching students how to write in particular. It is not possible for the teacher to take care of every single one of 'his' students. To write well in a difficult genre such as 'the knowledgeable cultural essay' takes time, reflection, courage and often personal guidance, and for this time is scarce. The students are too many and there is not enough room at the feet of the masters for all of them. What we see is that the traditional university pedagogy of the apprenticeship (German: 'Meisterlehre') is threatened, the masses are moving in, but pedagogy for the masses does not fit the task or the variety of text-subgenres required.

The continentalists have lost their prime pedagogy with the change in student-teacher ratio, whereas the Anglo-Americans in higher education have identified genres and text types needed and a corresponding pedagogy for the needs of the mass university. So the Anglo-American-influenced writing programs and centres have a hard time offering instruction and tutoring within the many varieties of continental discourse – just as individuality, originality and personality of expression may well be considered unteachable per definition or at least impossible to formalise.

Continentalist teachers as a general rule do not believe in instructional materials, or any kind of instruction before or during writing other than one-on-one dialogue, and many teachers do not even believe in or practice more thesis-advising than the minimum required by their department. (Several of our older philosophy teachers pride themselves of keeping advising to a minimum, thus leaving the writing of perhaps the most difficult of all university papers up to the students themselves.) Interestingly, we cannot find instructional materials, books *etc.* for students of the continental tradition (the only possible exception being Umberto Eco's book on thesis-writing which has continental elements). Thus they are left with much less instruction in and dialogue about their writing than the students of Anglo-American scientific cultures, although the continental writers face much greater challenges with regard to writing because they have no concrete rules or formats to guide them.

9   OUR WRITING CENTRE'S ANGLO-AMERICAN WAY OF TEACHING ACADEMIC WRITING

In our teaching, a most prominent and important activity is the demonstration and discussion of model examples from student writing (see Rienecker and Stray Jörgensen: 'The Genre in Focus, not the Writer...' this volume). This kind of teaching is only possible because we and a majority of the students present have – or are just beginning to acknowledge – criteria and text formats that are so widespread that they can be shared and reinforced.

What we do is schooling in 'How to do it the Anglo-American way.' We will focus strongly on the research question and make sure every paper does in fact investigate a problem, that the structure of the paper reflects the problem-investigation, that methods can be stated explicitly, that university papers are in fact an argument, that (student) research is written so that it may be labelled 'intersubjectively controllable', and that research papers are written in a clear and unambiguous language.

This we see as in keeping with the political intentions behind establishing writing centres: We are supposed to limit research tasks to a manageable level so that more students will feel able and confident to do it, and to understand the workings of and evaluate the academic writing of others. It is our role to be the 'simplifiers', not the 'complicators', yet we must not oversimplify matters.

Where are the continental students at those sessions and what do they say? Precious little. We have the impression that they do not often attend the writing centre activities because they know full well that what they must do is to stick closely to their subject teachers.

10   HOW CAN THE ANGLO-AMERICAN WRITING CENTRE ADRESS THE CONTINENTAL WRITERS?

One problem that we frequently encounter is a complaint from students that what they have been told about writing has been contradictory and sometimes not consistent with what we say at the writing centre workshops. The different writing traditions have not been made explicit to them. When we verbalise the different modes and different ideals of the two traditions, it is often a startling eye-opening experience. The consciousness of the existing traditions and your own possible choices between and within them is one of our goals in the teaching of writing.

10.1 Anglo-Americanise Papers as Much as Possible

When it comes to the individual writer's handling of her/his own text, we will bear in mind that those who consult us are experiencing problems with their paper, and we will try to suggest that the writer:

- Narrow the focus of the text, make a point, and organise documentation within an argumentation structure.
- Look for a problem to investigate.
- Exemplify more concretely.
- Include analysis of empirical material.
- Pay attention to questions of methodology, both as to methods used by the sources and methods the writer might want to use in his or her own writing.
- Write in a language that shows that the writer has absorbed the content and not just the jargon of his sources.

All of these might be considered typical Anglo-American features of university writing. We will in fact examine the individual writer's possibilities of writing within a continental discourse community in a more Anglo-American way, thus making the paper more manageable.

10.2 Use the Teachers as Much as Possible

No matter how our tutoring is received, we will always encourage especially continental students to ask their teachers for guidance and advice on how to write, and to study the writing styles of their individual teachers, rather than relying on general advice, in order to get as close to the ideal continental writing apprenticeship situation as possible.

10.3 Keep a Distance from the Sources

It is important too to tell the continental university writers that to write their papers in the same genre as those works of the great names they are writing about – books which may contain speculative and hypothetical constructions of ideas are difficult, even risky business and requires the support of the subject teacher. Often these important and weighty works would not get through the eye of the needle of science because of lack of documentation, evidence, methodology, clarity – although these works are indispensable sources of inspiration, valuable points of departure for further research or theoretical tools for explaining data.

10.4 Continental Writing is Best Suited for Advanced Levels

On an *institutional* level, we are of the opinion that the reflecting, philosophical essay is not an appropriate kind of training text at early levels of studying. University writing at introductory levels, we suggest, can best be taught within the Anglo-American formats and criteria.

Continental writing as a study activity is a challenge for those who master the basics of academic writing and are already very knowledgeable in the field, have an overview (In German: 'Überblick') which allows them to acknowledge the aspects, the different points of view and conflicts, the significance and the intricacies of the continental thinkers and their discourse communities. Therefore, we find that writing in the continental tradition – if necessary or desirable at all – should not take place at least until the later stages of study, when some sort of apprenticeship relation between teacher and student is a realistic possibility.

Consequently we would propose to planners of education in continental surroundings a *progression* in the teaching of writing from the more manageable Anglo-American approaches, with emphasis on focused problem investigation towards a more comprehensive, hermeneutical treatment of the subjects in their entirety – a continental approach.

11   REACTIONS FROM CONTINENTAL STUDENTS AND TEACHERS

We have many – unsystematic – experiences with tutoring students writing in a continental tradition. We often find them taking our advice and benefiting from them in terms of completion and higher grades. We have often heard the remark: 'My teacher is sceptical of the Writing Centre, yet when I took your advice he approved of my paper.' We believe that Anglo-American modes of writing are widely recognised as acceptable modes of academic writing far beyond where they are practised. But when we address the two university cultures openly, the issue invites conflict, more than what seems productive. At a meeting of 60 faculty members titled 'The Continental and the Anglo-American Writing at the University – a Discussion of Pedagogies' in which we attempted a debate, mutual withdrawal was the result. An invited speaker known to be a good representative of continental writing took a defensive stance, titled his speech 'We Are Already Dead', and lamented Anglo-American influence on university writing.

We hear from several disciplines that their institutes are torn in two rather irreconcilable parts. As one teacher told us: 'At a teachers meeting, we all tried to read sample papers and justify our evaluations. I don't think we will ever repeat the experience, we are just too far apart.' Experiences like these show how necessary it is for student writers to be aware of cultures of writing. Discipline-specific writing is not nearly enough to guarantee adequacy, there are strong sub-cultures within (some) disciplines.

12   THE CRAFT, NOT THE ART

The continental way works for some students, whereas Anglo-American writing instruction in higher education works for most.

As writing centre staff we should be conscious of possible limitations in our own knowledge of text genres and conventions which are used in our institutions, and hence in our relevance to some of the discourse communities present within them. We can teach and tutor the general and common principles, but not all the discourse-

specific features of university sub-genres, and not the individual and original presentations and wordings. We can teach students the craft, but not the art of writing.

HELPING DOCTORAL STUDENTS TO FINISH THEIR THESES

KIRSTI LONKA

University of Helsinki, Finland and Karolinska Institutet, Stockholm

Abstract. The context of this chapter is a competitive and high-achieving environment, namely, a medical school in Finland. A concrete process-writing course is described with Ph.D. candidates in medicine, psychology, and dentistry as participants.

The approach is a combination of courses in cognitive strategies with generative writing and shared revision, whereas practical advice on stylistic rules and grammar are not emphasised. The aim of the intervention is to reveal and then revise practices and ideas of writing that usually remain tacit. The theories and methods are applied by Bereiter and Scardamalia (1987), Olson (1994), Björk & Räisänen (1996), Boice (1993), Tynjälä, Mason, & Lonka (2001), and Lonka & Ahola (1995). The idea is to put these theories in action in a very demanding real life situation.

The means included doing focused free-writing exercises, using multiple drafts, training peer-feedback strategies, revealing the myths and revising mental models of writing (for instance, by sharing research evidence on writing), analysing different text types and therefore increasing metalinguistic awareness, making tacit knowledge overt to discussion, and reflecting on the participants' own writing practices.

Keywords: Academic writing, Activating instruction, Dissertation, Higher education, Medical education, PhD students, Postgraduate studies, Process writing, Scientific writing, Supervising, Writer's block, and Writing program.

1   THE TACIT KNOWLEDGE OF WRITING

The central problem in the teaching of academic writing is that important tacit knowledge, silent and procedural in nature, has generally been left untaught. Boice (1993) presented the estimation, for instance, that of graduate students in the U.S. who qualify to write dissertations but never finish them is as high as 50 percent. Why is not more done to help these students? According to Boice, part of the problem is that university professors prefer demonstrations of brilliance rather than the acquisition of it, and this preference denies many students the chance to become

Lonka, K. (2003). Helping Doctoral Students to Finish their Theses. In: G. Rijlaarsdam (Series Ed.) & L. Björk, G. Bräuer, L. Rienecker & P. Stray Jörgensen (Volume Eds.), Studies in Writing, Volume 12, Teaching Academic Writing in European Higher Education, pp. 113-131. © 2003 Kluwer Academic Publishers. Printed in the Netherlands.

successful writers. One reason for this is that tacit knowledge is, by definition, hard to teach and difficult to find in written and substantive form.

Another problem is that writing is not seen as a form of learning, but rather, it merely serves as a tool of assessment (Björk & Räisänen 1996; Hounsell 1984). Students seldom have the chance truly to learn about the process of writing because the academic world prefers to concentrate on assessing, grading, and their written products.

The context of the present chapter is a competitive and high-achieving environment, namely, a medical school. The intention is to describe how process writing, previously applied at the Department of Psychology, is applied with Ph.D. candidates in medicine, psychology, and dentistry. In Finland, previous experience shows that process writing is a promising approach in the training of psychology students (Lonka & Ahola 1995). But how can this technique work in medical school?

The aim is to reveal and then revise practices and ideas of writing that usually remain tacit. For this purpose, theoretical insights are presented by Bereiter and Scardamalia (1987), Scardamalia and Bereiter (1991); Olson (1994); Björk & Räisänen (1996); Boice (1993); Tynjälä, Mason, & Lonka (2001), and Lonka & Ahola (1995). A writing course for doctoral students is described where different techniques are applied. The exercises are based on those introduced by Björk (1997), Boice (1990), Healy (1986), as well as Lonka and Ahola (1995).

2   THEORETICAL BACKGROUND

A tradition of studies from Vygotsky to Olson argues that the acquisition and use of writing are powerful factors in the development of thinking (Tynjälä, Mason, & Lonka 2001). David R. Olson (1994) addressed the question of the impact of writing on thinking in his book, 'The World on Paper: The Conceptual and Cognitive Implications of Writing and Reading'. The power of writing lies in bringing into consciousness those aspects of spoken language that turn language into an object of reflection, analysis, and design (Olson 1994: 258). Without written language, it would be impossible to deal with such concepts as 'assumption', 'inference', or 'conclusion'.

Once a written expression has influenced our common thought (and spoken expressions) it is extremely difficult to unthink that model and see how someone not acculturated into the same way of thinking would perceive language and the world it describes. Writing forces us to think about our own thinking in terms of what is actually claimed and what is the evidence – the basic distinction in scientific thinking (Kuhn 1989). Literacy is not only functionally oriented but, also, a social condition: 'in reading and writing texts one participates in a 'textual community', a group of readers (and writers and auditors) who share a way of reading and interpreting a body of texts.' (Olson 1994: 273).

Olson's notion comes close to the movement of 'New Literacy Studies', which sees literacies as social practices with their own conventions. From the student point of view the dominant challenge is to switch practices between one setting and another, to deploy a repertoire of appropriate linguistic practices, and to handle the social meanings and identities that each evokes (Lea & Street 1998).

When students take part in the practices of a scientific community, it is crucial that they learn the conventions and ways of thinking that are typical of that specific literary tradition. The idea is to see the act of writing as a participation in the scientific culture, rather than as mere reporting of what one knows. It follows that conceptions of learning, knowledge, and philosophy of science cannot be avoided in the teaching of academic writing.

Thus, writing a thesis requires not only the ability to organise an extensive amount of content, but also knowledge about the discourse conventions of the academic community for whom the thesis is being directed (Torrance, Thomas, & Robinson 1993). Olga Dysthe's (2000; see also this volume) theoretical framework of writing-to-learn is heavily based on Vygotsky and Bakhtin (1895-1975). She emphasises the sociocultural view, on which her four key tenets are based: First, knowledge and understanding are constructed in social interaction. Second, language is the key cultural tool, which mediates learning. Third, learning takes place in 'a community of practice', this also includes well functioning group processes. Fourth, because knowledge is always situated, motivation to learn is largely dependent on the learning culture, which is created in a particular classroom.

2.1 On Literate Expertise

Scardamalia and Bereiter (1991) presented a more cognitive account. They called 'literate expertise' the academic skills connected with expertise in various domains, and they described two approaches to reading and writing: knowledge-telling and knowledge-transforming (see also Bereiter and Scardamalia 1987). The former refers to an activity that minimises the cognitive load, whereas the latter engages the learner in effortful and reflective, dialectic processes. Research on skilled writers shows the critical importance of various cognitive strategies, such as building deep-level mental representation of the task, engaging in more active and reflective problem-solving, relating the nature of the task, the anticipated audience (*e.g.*, Hildyard 1996).

Literate expertise is related to domain expertise (see also Lea & Street 1998). Scardamalia and Bereiter's (1991) conception of expertise in reading draws on the van Dijk and Kintsch's (1983) theory, which assumes two mental representations that are constructed during comprehension: a *text-base*, in which a coherent representation of the text is formed, and a *situation model*, in which the text content is integrated into the comprehender's knowledge system. The text base reflects the coherent relations between the propositions in the text and their organisation, whereas the situation model is a mental representation of the situation described by the text.

Scardamalia and Bereiter (1991) pointed out that the construction of both the text base and the situation model during reading depends on domain knowledge, but also that a process is involved, similar to knowledge-transforming in writing. Problem solving during reading is typical of expert readers, whereas inexpert readers tend to reveal a process such as knowledge telling by interpreting each statement immediately and not in the light of subsequent information. Scardamalia and Bereiter (1991) conclude that the text base is a representation of the text as a particular case, whereas the situation model is part of domain knowledge relevant from the point of view of the text. They find that the text base may be too much emphasised in instruction, at the cost of students' difficulties in applying information in real-world situations. Scientific thinking would be impossible without being able to go 'beyond the information given' (Bruner 1973), that is, to distance oneself with the actual text at hand and to look at the phenomenon described in the text or presented by the teacher. This calls for integrating new knowledge with previous knowledge, and the skill to differentiate between what is said and what is previously known.

The text base and situation model may also be considered in the light of Olson's exciting redefinition of literacy: 'Learning to read is a matter of learning to recognise the aspects represented graphically and to infer those aspects of meaning which are not represented graphically at all.' (Olson 1994: 272). Learning to read is therefore learning to cope with the unexpressed; using what is known as the illocutionary force of language. This force of language comes from the ability to form a situation model, to go beyond the text, and to differentiate between what is intended and what is actually written. This also calls for taking into account the point of view of both the potential reader and the scientific conventions, which often remain tacit.

Our own research on note-taking shows that it is quite difficult even for university applicants to write answers to questions that call for going beyond a given text, especially if the writer is too much attached to her literal notes. In order to be successful in tasks that call for building a situation model, it is useful to reformulate knowledge, for instance, by drawing concept maps or by writing notes in one's own words (Lonka et al. 1994; Lahtinen et al. 1997; Slotte & Lonka 1998; 1999ab; Slotte & Lonka 2001). Any activity that increases the student's own constructive efforts may enhance learning from text.

The art of scientific writing obviously calls for various skills: domain expertise, knowledge-transformation, and well-developed literate skills. These do not take place in a vacuum, but in the context of social practices and academic literacy (see also Dysthe, this volume). However, literate and cognitive reasons are not sufficient in explaining why writing may become difficult.

2.2 Maladaptive Ideas of Writing

There are many doctoral candidates with highly developed domain-specific and literate expertise who still fail to finish their thesis. This has a lot to do with teachers' and students' different ideas about what makes a good text (Lea & Street 1998). However, Boice's (1993) review of the so called writing blocks sheds light on the question at the psychological level: why do people sometimes fail in written productivity, although there is nothing wrong with their intellectual capacity? Boice presents reasons that are mainly emotional and motivational. They are related to beliefs about oneself as a writer.

Boice (1993) discusses the most often mentioned reasons for blocks: internal censors, fears of failure, perfectionism, early negative experiences, procrastination, and poor mental health. He concludes that blocking seldom has a single cause, and that many different maladaptive thoughts and emotions may be related. He points out that cognitions of writing are crucial in avoiding blocking. That is, ideas of writing are crucial in controlling related emotions. Writers need to engage in active metacognition about writing that will help them to talk about problems and strategies, in order to monitor effectively their writing, and to develop a variety of writing strategies.

It is quite likely that those students whose thoughts about writing are maladaptive in nature are likely to see writing as an act of simple knowledge telling. In previous research, surface approach to learning was related to anxiety in students (Entwistle & Ramsden 1983). It is thus possible that this kind of approach to learning is related to anxious feelings and maladaptive thoughts about writing.

Boice (1993) ends up in a list of different methods aimed at curing the problem. First, oldest and best known are variations on *automaticity*, referring to writing with reduced awareness of what is being written. The most widely used strategy of the mildly dissociate strategies is free writing, where the writer lets the text flow without being critical. It has proven helpful for inducing temporary momentum in formerly blocked academic writers. Second, Boice gives the practical advice on regular writing, namely, *regimen*. This includes, for instance, constitutive strategies that help induce lasting changes in fluency. Writers who work in regimen of regular writing, regardless of readiness or mood, produce more writing and more creative ideas than do writers who wait for inspiration before beginning. Third, *cognitions of writing* are crucial in avoiding blocking. Writers need to engage in active metacognitions about writing that will help them to talk about problems and strategies, to effectively monitor their writing, and to develop a variety of writing strategies. This is closely related to the fourth treatment: need for external pressures and *social supports* to make writing efficient and effective.

2.3 Process-oriented Instruction

In many cases, academic environment is far from optimal when it comes to social support. It only provides deadlines, but not tools to meet them. Many professors possess tacit knowledge that they are not able to share (Boice 1993; Lea & Street 1998). The act of writing remains a lonely journey, when it could be an act of participating in a scientific community.

Process-oriented approaches have little by little become quite popular in writing instruction (Applebee 1986). Process-oriented teaching of writing is by far the most effective writing instruction available (Björk & Räisänen 1996). This development is based on research, which has since the 1970s and 1980s emphasised the thinking strategies underlying the writing process (*e.g.,* Flower & Hayes 1981; Bereiter & Scardamalia 1987). Process-oriented writing instruction has been designed to help students think through and organise their ideas before writing and also, to revise, reflect and rethink during their writing (Healy 1981). According to Applebee (1986), typical learning-by-writing activities include, for instance, brainstorming, journal writing, free writing, small-group activities, and emphasis on multiple drafts. He suggests that 'properly implemented process approaches are more effective in fostering good writing and breadth of form, and also encouraging more reasoned and disciplined thinking about the topics themselves' (Applebee 1986: 97).

Learning-by-writing activities have also been applied in many colleges and universities (Tynjälä, Mason, & Lonka 2001). For example, McGovern and Hogshead (1990) state the following goals: (1) to assess students, (2) to promote students' learning, (3) to develop students' writing skills, and (4) to facilitate analytic and creative thinking. They describe their own reconceptualisation of writing from thinking of writing as a noun towards thinking of writing as a verb. Thus, writing is not only a text produced by the student, but rather, 'writing is an action, a process of thinking and learning, which is inextricably tied to our students' cognitive development in our particular courses and in their college careers in general' (McGovern & Hogshead 1990: 5).

It is obvious that process-oriented instruction may be helpful in academic writing, because it lowers the threshold for writing and enhances automaticity, provides social support and regimen, and helps the writers to revise their cognitions and beliefs about writing. It may also relieve blocks, anxiety, and procrastination, which are, according to Boice (1993), so common among academic writers.

2.4 Activating Instruction in Training Doctoral Students

Lonka and Ahola (1995) presented the model of activating instruction in higher education. In writing, this approach has ambitious goals. The central idea is to enable students to view the act of writing as an aid to their learning, a tool to be used in acquiring mastery over new information, and a means of revealing their present understanding of a given subject (Healy 1981). It is intended to support the process of writing with the help of peer groups. Second, our learning-by-writing exercises are based on the idea that not just any writing fosters study and thinking skills: exercises that are aimed at enhancing knowledge-transforming (Bereiter & Scardamalia 1987) are the means that may best help the development, when carried out in meaningful social interaction (see also Rienecker & Stray Jörgensen 'The Genre in Focus ...' in this volume).

The framework of activating instruction is a synthesis of various theoretical ideas. It is based on three general principles that can be derived from the points presented above:

1. Diagnosing and activating: It is important to diagnose the quality and level of students' (mis)conceptions in the beginning of instruction. Some exercises that make diagnosing possible like focused free writing; also help students to activate their previous knowledge. In training doctoral students, writing instructions starts by diagnosing their ideas of the writing process. After these ideas are

made overt to reflection and discussion, students may start the process of revising their beliefs.

2. Fostering the learning process and reflective thinking: It is essential to make students' strategies and knowledge open to discussion and reflection during the course. Students' reflection and metacognition may be enhanced, for example, by using learning logs (or journals), small group discussions, and some special forms of focused free writing. Peer groups are an excellent means for reflection of one's writing process.

3. Giving feedback and challenging misconceptions: It is important that students get feedback from both their peers and from the trainer. After the course is over, it is important to make clear what has been the basis of evaluation and how the student might enhance her writing habits and approaches in order to make the performance better in the future.

Lonka and Ahola (1995) reported a six-year follow-up study on activating instruction as compared to traditional teaching at the department of psychology. They found that those who participated in activating instruction curriculum proceeded in their studies more slowly in the beginning of their undergraduate years but had fewer problems in thesis writing and finishing their studies. The possibility was discussed that those who participated in activating instruction slowed up their pace in the beginning of the studies but enhanced their later studies, because the students had thoroughly internalised some important study skills. Those who survived the first college years with surface strategies scored high credit points in the beginning, but found thesis writing and final exam more difficult. On the basis of questionnaires and evaluation forms, students clearly appreciated activating instruction. They thought it made studying more interesting, fostered understanding, and developed study skills, especially literate skills. As in process-oriented instruction in general (Applebee 1986), the effect of activating instruction was experienced more significantly in procedural than in declarative learning.

The most important lesson we can learn of the present small case study is that effects of instructional innovations may emerge after a long period of time. Had we looked at the follow-up data after a three-year period, it would have been very discouraging. Only after five years were we able to see something about the quantitative and qualitative outcomes of the instructional procedures.

Complex skills of expertise take a long time to develop – what appears to be 'inefficient' within a short period of time, may be truly effective in the long run. Therefore, it is quite unlikely to expect straightforward outcomes of a one-term intervention such as the one reported here. However, the main criticism toward basic experimental 'comparison group' designs in academic writing have been that they tend to be theoretically naïve and to use simplistic outcome measures (Torrance, Thomas, & Robinson 1993). I have tried to avoid these problems here.

The intention of this chapter is not to provide 'objective' outcomes of a course, but rather, to present one conceptualisation of writing that may prove helpful for doctoral students. I describe how activating instruction may be realised in the concrete setting of a one-semester course for doctoral candidates. The main idea of the course was to apply the theories and methods described above and to put those theories into action in a very demanding real-life situation.

3   OBJECTIVES OF THE INTERVENTION

The means of the course were activating instruction and process writing. The course was based on free-writing exercises, multiple drafts, constructive feedback strategies, revealing the myths and revising mental models of writing (for instance, by sharing research evidence on writing), rearranging the writing environment and rearranging writing habits, analysing different text types and therefore increasing metalinguistic awareness, making tacit knowledge overt to discussion, and reflecting on the participants' own writing practices. The main objectives of the course were:

1. Analysing oneself as a writer: What are my ideas? Are they adaptive and positive?
2. Understanding the process of scientific writing: Knowledge-telling and knowledge transforming. What is process writing?
3. Recognising obstacles for productive writing and tools for minimizing them.
4. Acquiring awareness of different text types: How to build an argument (see Björk, this volume).
5. Engaging in collaborative learning: Using a peer group to enhance productivity. How to apply constructive feedback strategies.

4 · PARTICIPANTS

A total of 11 medical, psychology, and dental doctoral candidates attended. They were all volunteers, at different phases of writing their Ph.D. theses. The form of the intended doctoral dissertation varied: Some candidates were writing their first drafts, some others were already writing summaries of already published articles. The topics varied from natural scientific microbiology, bacteriology, and genetic domains to less clearly defined domains, such as child psychiatry and the psychology of learning.

Supervisors were also invited to attend, but only one of them finished the course. The main reasons for supervisors for not attending the course was that they (a) 'already knew what academic writing includes', and (b) 'did not have time' (this claim is based on oral communication with the supervisors and on the reports of the students).

5   CONTENT, MATERIALS AND DESIGN

5.1 Content

The main contents of the course are summarized in Table 1. However, the intention was not to simply deliver this knowledge, but to use experiential learning methods and different exercises in order to make this knowledge useful for the participants. Some mini-lectures were included, but the method mainly consisted of activating instruction (as defined above), free-writing exercises, and discussions.

Table 1. Some central theoretical ideas introduced at the course.

Content of the course

Maladaptive Thoughts of Writing (Boice 1993)
- Blocks – the feeling that I am not able to write
- Negative Thoughts – writing is not enjoyable, I do not feel good about it
- Procrastination – I cannot get started!
- Perfectionism – I cannot stop revising!

Adaptive Thoughts of Writing
- Productivity – the feeling that I am able to produce
- Positive Thoughts – writing is enjoyable, I feel good about it!
- Creativity – I see writing as an act of creation

How to cure blocks? (Boice 1990)
- Automatisation – getting rid of the 'internal critics', setting the threshold lower for writing.
- Regimen – constant writing regardless of mood, time, and space
- Social support – peer groups *etc.*
- Adaptive cognitions about writing – useful beliefs about oneself and writing.

Eight misconceptions about writing a psychology paper (Sternberg 1988)
1. Writing the paper is the most routine, least creative aspect of the scientific enterprise, requiring much time but little imagination.
2. The important thing is what you say, not how you say it.
3. Longer papers are better papers, and more papers are better yet.
4. The main purpose of a paper is the presentation of facts, whether newly established or well established.
5. The distinction between scientific writing on the one hand and advertising and propaganda on the other is that the purpose of scientific writing is to inform whereas the purpose of advertising or propaganda is to persuade.
6. A good way to gain acceptance of your theory is by refuting someone else's theory.
7. Negative results that fail to support the researcher's hypothesis are every bit as valuable as positive results that do support the researcher's hypothesis.
8. The logical development of ideas in a paper reflects the historical development of ideas in the researcher's head.

Constructive feedback strategies (Healy 1986)
- Start with careful reading and listening: what the author wants to say?
- Present strong and positive aspects about the text
- Present specific questions about the text, *e.g.,* 'what do you mean by saying x on page 5?'
- Do not comment on the writer or writer's abilities
- The author is not supposed to answer orally; but to underline the strong points of the text and to write down the questions – it is her task to think through the comments and decide what to take into account.

Two modes of thinking about writing (Bereiter & Scardamalia 1987)
- *Knowledge-telling*: Writing is simply listing what you already know – minimising the cognitive load
- *Knowledge-transforming*: Writing is an effortful and reflective problem-solving process

Some Text types (Björk & Räisänen 1996; Björk 1997)
- Causal Analysis: To analyse the causes of something
- Problem Solving: To identify a problem and to propose solutions to the problem
- Argumentation (pure): Argumentation for and against; to take a position on an issue

Genres (Björk & Räisänen 1996; Björk 1997)
- Academic papers, articles, or books. In psychology, linguistics, literature, philosophy, physics, architecture, mathematics *etc.*

Boice's (1990) practical guide to productive writing gives tools for putting his theory in action. He goes through the typical problems of academics and gives hints about how to avoid them. Typical obstacles and difficult situations were related to either procrastination or perfectionism. Boice's ideas were very useful in designing a course for doctoral students. His practical, almost 'behaviourist' advice for stimulus control for rearranging the writing environment and rearranging writing habits were explicitly dealt with (Boice 1990: 76-79). They were copied to and discussed with the participants.

It was also useful to identify various text types and on that basis increase the writer's awareness of different ways of building an argument (Björk 1997; this volume). The participants were even introduced to eight typical misconceptions about writing scientific papers (Sternberg 1988, see Table 1). Although these were originally intended for psychologists, it was fruitful to discuss how they would apply in medicine and natural sciences.

5.2 Materials

The materials that were collected during the course consisted of:

1. The Writing Process Questionnaire (Lonka 1996). The students used this as a self-assessment instrument. Everybody filled in the Writing Process questionnaire during the first introductory session and analysed their results in their writing logs in terms of scales: Blocks, Negative thoughts, Perfectionism, Procrastination, Creativity, Positive thoughts, Productivity, Knowledge-telling, and Knowledge-transforming.
2. Writing logs, where the participants analysed their writing profiles (on the basis of their experiences and as they emerged in the questionnaire)
3. Produced texts: Every student had to bring in a draft for an article, conference paper, or a chapter of his or her thesis. The intention was to work on this piece, essential for the student's thesis, and to finish it during the course.
4. Assignments: These included small group exercises, such as constructive feedback strategies for commenting on each other's drafts. An interesting exercise to increase text-type awareness was to ask the participants to analyse a simple text written by an American college student on 'The Deer Problem of Moraga' (Björk & Räisänen 1996, Appendix). This text demonstrated the so-called problem-solving text type, where the author intends to define a problem and to propose solutions for solving it. After the participants had analysed the structure of this text, they were given the assignment to write a popular text for a newspaper, which would convince the reader about the dangers of cholesterol.
5. Feedback forms were filled in immediately after the course. Everybody answered three open-ended questions: What helped your learning? What hindered your learning? How would you develop this course?
6. Four months after the course was completed, the students were e-mailed a short questionnaire about the outcomes of the course. They were asked: (1) How do

you see yourself as a writer at the moment? Did the course change your conceptions – if yes, how? (2) Did the course provide concrete help for writing? If yes, what kind of help was it? (3) What kind of support, encouragement, or training do you think you will need in the future? (4) What was the use of peer feedback? (5) Have you still met with your small group? (6) What are the biggest challenges in writing for you at the moment? Can you meet them? (7) What kinds of emotions do you relate to writing? Have they changed? (Eight participants replied to the questionnaire.)

The main intention was not, however, to collect research material, but to focus on materials that would enhance the writing process and the productivity of the participants.

5.3 Design

The design of the course was as simple as possible. It was a one-term intervention (October–January) with four three-hour workshops, peer sessions, and written assignments (Table 2). The idea was to have few sessions together with the whole group, and to divide it into small groups of three to four participants. The plan was that all small groups would get together and comment on each other's drafts between the workshops.

Table 2. The structure of the course.

First Session (October 8, 1999, 3 hours)
- CONTENTS: Self-assessment: My own ideas about writing? The Writing Process Questionnaire. Forming peer groups. The idea of a writing log. A feedback exercise. Knowledge-telling vs. transforming. Writing blocks.
- ASSIGNMENTS: Setting up peer group meetings. Choosing a text to be worked on. Practicing constructive feedback. Analysing a given text. The writing log: Analyse yourself as a writer. E-mail feedback to the trainer.

Second Session (October 22, 1999, 3 hours)
- CONTENTS: Self-assessment. 8 misconceptions about academic writing. How are the peer groups functioning? The writing log? An exercise: The Deer Problem of Moraga text – what did the writers do? Text types and genres. Discussion.
- ASSIGNMENTS: Write a convincing text about the dangers of cholesterol. Writing log. Working on your own text. Peer meetings.

Third Session (December 3, 1999, 3 hours)
- CONTENTS: How is my text handled in the peer group? Writing logs. Analysing the exercise: the cholesterol text. Feedback strategies – discussion. How to prevent burnout in the academic world.
- ASSIGNMENTS: Peer group meetings. Working on one's own text. Writing log. E-mail feedback.

Fourth Session (January 28, 2000, 3 hours)
- CONTENTS: What has happened? How to write a grant proposal. Specific features of writing in natural sciences. What helped me during the course?
- ASSIGNMENTS: The future of the peer groups? Scheduling my own writing & rearranging my writing habits. Feedback after the course is over. Peer meetings, assignments, e-mail feedback, working on one's own text.

What has happened? (E-mail inquiry in May, 2000)

---

6   OUTCOMES AND SOME REFLECTIONS

The participants found the Writing Process Questionnaire to be a useful tool for their self-assessment and reflection. For example, they analysed their scores on the Knowledge-transforming scale:

> 'I got very high scores (21) on the scale Knowledge-transforming. Therefore, I am ready to get feedback and to revise my text. I think that should be self-evident for a novice like me, I shouldn't think that I know things as well as those who have been working in this area for years! Moreover, when I modify my text for several months, I may become blind to its fallacies. The text changes but one can't notice some obvious inconsistencies. I know what I want to say, but am I able to express it?'

Torrance, Thomas, & Robinson (1993) differentiated three approaches to training in thesis writing: a product-centred course which taught grammatical and stylistic rules; a cognitive strategies course which provided heuristics for generating and organising thesis content; and a generative writing and shared revision course which entailed the production of a draft followed by extensive revision on the basis of reviewing by the peers. All these courses were short, lasting for only two days, and they were well received by the students.

The aims of the course were mainly rhetorical and psychological, and it was a combination of approaches introduced by Torrance, Thomas, & Robinson (1993). Unlike the short courses they described, the intention of the present course was to provide a one-term process with working on true pieces of a doctoral dissertation. The approach was a combination of courses in cognitive strategies with generative writing and shared revision, whereas practical advice on stylistic rules and grammar were not emphasised. The approach was close to that of 'academic literacies' (Lea & Street 1998) which views student writing and learning as issues of social practices, epistemologies, and identities (see also Kruse, this volume and Dysthe, this volume). The academic literacies perspective takes into account study skills but includes them in the broader context of the acculturation process.

Not all participants were at ease with the psychological and philosophical approach of the course. Epistemological differences reflecting conceptions of scientific knowledge as well as approaches to academic writing emerged between medicine and psychology, similar to those reported by Lonka and Lindblom-Ylänne (1996). We have previously shown that constructivist conceptions of learning and knowledge (Lonka, Joram & Bryson 1996) are related to ideas of writing resembling transforming (Lonka, Maury & Heikkilä 1997). Therefore, changing an approach to writing may call for changing the whole framework about what learning and writing are. Moreover, it may call for changing the writer's whole lifestyle (Boice 1990).

Academic teachers represent their own community of practice, and have their own domain-specific views about what constitutes a good piece of writing. Lea and Street even suggest that 'what makes a piece of student writing 'appropriate' has more to do with issues of epistemology than with the surface features of form to which staff often recourse when describing their students' writing. That is to say, underlying, often disciplinary, assumptions about the nature of knowledge affected the meaning given to the terms 'structure' and 'argument'.' (Lea & Street 1998:

162). Therefore, it is extremely important to make these tacit assumptions open to discussion.

In the beginning of our course, some medical doctors found the rhetorical goals of the course extraordinary, almost bizarre. This was because they originally appeared very fact-oriented, and were hesitant to transform their text by taking into account the point of view of the reader. This approach resembled misconceptions 4 and 5 (Sternberg 1988, see Table 1), very deeply rooted in their thinking: 'our purpose is to present the facts, not to convince the reader'. This position obviously reflects the culture of the Faculty of Medicine in general (Lindblom-Ylänne & Lonka 1999). However, the writing logs revealed that the conceptions of the participants changed during the course:

> 'This course has been truly interesting. During this course, I have understood writing in a new way, and I have seen the rhetorical power of the writer to a much greater extent than I did originally. Fortunately I have never found writing per se to be very difficult, but this course taught me many valuable hints for later use, for instance, how to have an impact on the reader, or how to make a difference in one's own writing.'

Learning to write texts for non-specialist audiences may be very difficult in the context of academic writing. One aim of the course was to report one's own research in an understandable way. For instance, one participant finished her doctoral dissertation on a very exciting topic, which newspapers would headline 'the killer bacteria'. The title of her abstract was, however, in Latin, and the press would not have understood it. After The Deer Problem of Moraga exercise (Björk 1997) the author realised that she might want to write her abstract differently:

> 'The exercise Deer Problem of Moraga totally opened my eyes about how and on what kind of writing strategy might affect the reader. It became perfectly clear! After that I wrote the assignment of Dangers of Cholesterol text, and consciously applied the same strategy... I was very happy about the feedback my small group gave to me.'

Later this doctoral candidate wrote a draft for a press release, and revised it according to the advice she was given at the course. She replaced all Latin terms with understandable expressions and wrote a short popular text about her results. The outcome was that she managed to get her research well known. At the time when her orals took place, her picture was in the newspapers, and she was interviewed in the national television. This rarely happens for those who publish a study in bacteriology.

The immediate course feedback was quite positive (Table 3). Almost everybody (10/11) found the interaction between peer writers to be the most rewarding aspect of the course. Reflecting on one's own writing was mentioned to be important by more than half of the participants (6/11). Very few negative aspects were mentioned. Interestingly, such issues as heterogeneous group, the loose structure of the course, and its time frame were sometimes mentioned as positive, sometimes as negative aspects of the course. Surprisingly, these extremely busy professionals wanted a denser schedule, more structure, more exercises, more discipline, and even more workshop sessions. Positive atmosphere, encouragement and inspiration were not marginal outcomes of the course but essential in its objectives. Self-confidence is crucial in writing.

Table 3. Students' feedback about the course.

Students' feedback

What helped your learning? (n = 11)
- Interaction with peer writers (10)
- Self-reflection on writing (6)
- Exercises (3), inspiring teacher (3)
- Heterogeneous group (2)
- Atmosphere, practical advice, starting/understanding the writing process, new ideas, loose organisation, course materials, concrete examples (each comment mentioned by one participant)

What hindered your learning? (n = 11)
- I was not able to organise my own schedule (2)
- My peer group was too heterogeneous, we had problems with time schedule, more sessions needed, repetition needed (the loose structure of the course), my own writing process was in a desperate phase (each comment mentioned by one participant)

How would You develop the course? (n = 11)
- The time frame should be more dense (n = 3)
- More structure! (n = 3)
- More exercises! (n = 3)
- More sessions! More information! More courses per student! (Each mentioned by one participant)

After four months, almost all the participants still emphasised the usefulness of peer feedback in their e-mail responses. One participant mentioned, for instance: 'It is an excellent idea! If I ever start a research group of my own, I will apply it.' The main use of the groups was typically to relieve anxiety: 'It was very comforting to notice that also other people have to start with very primitive drafts! For once I could observe the anxiety-driven process that is not observable in the final text.' Despite the positive attitudes, none of the original groups continued meeting after the course was over.

Three participants had finished their doctoral dissertations before the final e-mail inquiry. They were those whose ideas of writing were positive from the beginning, and who also gave the best feedback of the course. Their current feelings towards their own writing were very positive. But they felt the course came too late: 'I wish this course had taken place earlier. I will recommend it to all colleagues who are writing their thesis. Not too early, though. Those who attend should have some experience in writing.'

The comments presented above may be just right, because those participants who were just starting their dissertation were the least likely to benefit from the course in terms of productivity. They felt they needed a more rigorous course, because they became the most confused. They did not want to face the ill-defined and creative nature of the writing process, but rather, expressed needs for a more product-oriented approach.

Five participants finished the part of their theses that they had chosen to be the product of the course. They were pleased, but somewhat less euphoric than those who had graduated. Typical comments were, 'Gradually I have started to approach writing as a job that rewards effort and persistence. The course helped me to work through my ideas about writing and also to analyse my ways of doing things.'

The four participants who did not finish the intended part of their dissertation before the e-mail inquiry were mainly part-time students who also worked as clinicians: 'Because of the lack of time, I am not writing at the moment. But I find writing easier, the threshold to start is much lower.' These students planned to write more in the future, and were optimistic about doing this.

Blending doctoral candidates at different points of their work may not be a bad idea after all. Vygotsky's (1978) idea of the zone of proximal development indicates that those in the beginning of their thesis writing may develop their own writing by sharing the writing process with more advanced students. Further, fusing psychology, medicine, and dentistry may serve the same purpose. Mixed feelings about heterogeneous groups may reflect the participants' different stages of development and the constructive frictions that may follow, when different points of view challenge each other (Lindblom-Ylänne & Lonka 1999). Dysthe (2000 and in this volume) points out that new meaning, new insight, and understanding are dependent on the tension between different voices, viewpoints, and perspectives.

Finally, the conceptual change that took place in the participants' minds may be conceptualised into five main paradoxes of writing that emerged in the workshop discussions:

1. *Chaos and structure* are not as far from each other as we might think. Well-structured texts may be produced by a chaotic process; that is the creative process of knowledge transforming.

2. *Process and product* are intertwined. But if we are too keen on the product and outcomes, the process of writing may suffer.

3. *Confusion and confidence* are both needed. The participants found the course confusing, but the process of writing may itself be confusing. Confidence was needed to survive confusion and to keep up determination and positive mood to survive the process. Social support was essential to keep up confidence.

4. *Participation vs. acquisition*: Most participants expected concrete advice and rules about how to produce a perfect piece of work. They also expected the teacher to comment on everybody's work. However, the participation in small group sessions and the dialogue with peers emerged to become more important than the teacher transmitting a list of facts about writing.

5. *Group work shapes the individual mind*. This paradox has its roots in Vygotsky's (1978) thinking: it is difficult to become an independent writer without internalising the view of the others. It is very important to get new insights about the reader's point of view as well as the shared literal conventions. These

the reader's point of view as well as the shared literal conventions. These things may be easiest to learn in a group.

There is an obvious need to develop new ways to support doctoral candidates. Not enough has been done to help them so far. This pilot course was encouraging and rewarding for the teacher. It evoked many new insights for all parties involved in the process. The workload for the teacher was not too heavy. If such a small investment of time and effort on the part of the Faculty may help, procedures like this might be worth serious consideration. Not to mention programs that are more systematic, presented in other chapters of this book.

In Karolinska Institute, we have already started to include brief large-class writing workshops for doctoral students. The next step is to systematically train university teachers in feedback strategies and process writing. As Kruse (this volume) points out, writing instruction should not be left for linguists only, because it is tied to the knowledge construction process. Doctoral students often have the extra demand for writing in English as a second language. Teaching academic writing for them is clearly a multidisciplinary mission, calling for domain-specific, linguistic, educational, and psychological understanding.

APPENDIX

The Deer of Moraga exercise

Jim Chow 'The Deer Problem of Moraga'
(Cooper & Axelrod, The St. Martin's Guide to Writing)

(1) It was a cold winter night when a friend and I were driving home from a midnight movie. The headlights arced out a narrow path in front of the car. All of a sudden, a deer bolted onto the road. Swerving to avoid hitting the animal, we scraped a car parked on the side of the road. Total damages amounted to more than three hundred dollars. The troublesome deer of Moraga had struck again.

(2) All of us in Moraga are familiar with this problem. Many have not escaped as cheaply as we did from encounters with the deer. Winter nights can be especially treacherous when the weather worsens and the deer come to town in search of food. They leave their natural habitat in the canyons when the vegetation becomes scarce and come to dine on the proudly tended gardens and parks in town. Local gardeners rank deer as their most destructive pest, worse even than gophers and caterpillars. In addition to being a nuisance, deer are a health risk, since they carry diseases communicable to humans.

(3) In fact, the deer problem is potentially lethal to us and to them. Nocturnal creatures, the deer invade our town at night. Travelling along the sides of our winding roads, they add to the danger of driving at night. Occasionally, for example, a deer will be frightened by the headlights of a car, and, in a moment of panic, run onto the road. It is all too often that the deer gets hit, the car is damaged, or both.

(4) The question is, what can we do about the deer? The most cost-effective method of solving the problem is to allow hunters to shoot them. In fact, I have heard this suggestion offered several times, though I can't tell if those proposing it are serious. We must reject this proposal. For one thing, the possibility of a stray shot hitting a bystander is too great. Second, animal lovers would surely protest the inhumanity and cruelty of such a policy. Furthermore, this proposal would not even solve the problem, since it wouldn't prevent the surviving deer from coming to Moraga in search of food. We would have to shoot a good many deer in the area to solve this problem completely.

(5) Another possible solution that has been suggested is to capture the deer and relocate them to a national park or some other protected area. Although this is a more humane proposal, it is no more workable. Finding, capturing and relocating enough deer to solve the problem would be extraordinarily expensive. It has been estimated that this effort would cost our town over two hundred and fifty thousand dollars. The damage caused by the deer does not even approach that much money, so spending so much could not be justified. But even if we found the money, there is another reason why this proposed solution is not feasible. You see, we here in Moraga have a double standard: we want to keep the deer out of town, but we like having them in the canyon because it adds to the secluded, natural environment that helps to make Moraga special.

(6) I would like to propose a solution that is both economical and practical: during the winter when their natural food supply is low, we should feed the deer, regularly, in the woods. Before the cold season starts, we should stock about a hundred food stations in the woods, located in areas known to have high concentration of deer. These spots can be found by trial and error: if we discover a station is not being used extensively, then we can find another location that is more popular. Once winter hits the area, volunteers can regularly monitor the food supply in these food stations. Deer feed is mainly composed of vegetation and finely mashed oats or wheat and so is inexpensive. Local residents could contribute grass trimmings and the like. Wheat or oats should cost approximately two thousand five hundred dollars a year, a hundredth of what it would cost to relocate the deer. This plan would allow us to keep the deer while eliminating the trouble they now cause.

(7) Critics of this proposal might argue that the food stations would allow the deer to prosper too much, perhaps even creating a population explosion. This seems unlikely since the canyon is also populated with such natural predators as coyotes. My proposal keeps the deer out of town without requiring any physical handling of them. It is humane and economically feasible. It solves the problem by removing its cause: the deer's need for food.

Structure of 'The Deer Problem of Moraga'

Problem: destruction & traffic danger caused by the deer
Alternative solution 1: Shoot the deer
Counterarguments:
- Risk of personal injuries
- Resistance from animal lovers
- Surviving deer
Alternative solution 2: Relocate the deer
Counterarguments:
- Too expensive
- We want to keep the deer
Own Proposal/solution: Feed the deer at predetermined food stations
Possible counterargument:
- Population explosion
Refutation:
- Ecological solution: coyotes
Supporting arguments: The proposal
- is cheap
- removes the cause (hunger)
- is humane

Please analyse the structure of the text by using the basic features of problem solving text presented by Björk and Räisänen (1996). See table 4.

Table 4. Basic features of problem solving. Adapted from Björk & Räisänen 1996).

Basic features of problem solving

A clearly stated definition of the problem. Including:
- Description of the problem
- Causes of the problem
- Consequences should the problem remain unsolved

A clearly stated proposal to solve the problem. With
- Arguments in favour of your solution(s)
- Some hints as to how to implement your solution

Awareness of alternative proposals. Including:
- Alternative proposals for solving the problem
- Acknowledgement, partial acceptance or refutation of each alternative proposal

An evaluation of the benefits of your proposal. With:
- Positive effects of your proposal

Possible counterarguments to your proposal. Showing:
- Potential advantages of such alternatives
- Arguments against the alternatives

A careful analysis of your audience. With:
- Awareness of the needs, convictions and prejudices of your audience

A reasonable, sensible tone. With:
- No irony or sarcasm
- A fair and respectful attitude to counterarguments

PART TWO:
TEACHING ACADEMIC WRITING IN CONTEXT

CENTRES FOR WRITING & READING – BRIDGING THE GAP BETWEEN UNIVERSITY AND SCHOOL EDUCATION

GERD BRÄUER

Emory University, USA & Freiburg University of Education, Germany

Abstract. In this chapter, I will outline institutional structures that can enhance the emergence of success-ful academic writers. I suggest the development of writing (and reading) centres at both ends of the edu-cational pyramid: in grade school and at the university. For each writing (and reading) centre type, I pro-vide a thorough description of possible content, working methods, functions, and goals. I develop a set of recommendations for how to initiate interplay between these places of producing and reproducing texts that would prepare not only successful writers but also better learners.

Keywords: College writing centre, History of the writing centre movement, Institutional development, Institutional change, Secondary school writing/reading centre, School development, Writing across the curriculum, and Writing to learn.

> This mixing with worlds outside the curriculum
> is itself key to the learning of the transferable skills
> which education at all levels will in future
> place increasing emphasis on.
>
> *Mark Robinson,*
> Centre for Lifelong Learning
> (University of Durham, England)

1 INTRODUCTION

In this chapter, I will describe institutional structures that can enhance the emer-gence of academic writers. My motivation for this specific focus stems from recent insights by theorists on educational development (Bryk *et al*. 1998) and their knowl-

Bräuer, G. (2003). *Centres for Writing & Reading – Bridging the Gap between University and School Education. G. Rijlaarsdam (Series Ed.) & L. Björk, G. Bräuer, L. Rienecker & P. Stray Jörgensen (Volume Eds.), Studies in Writing, Volume 12, Teaching Academic Writing in European Higher Education, pp. 135-150.*

edge that during drastic curricular changes (such as the inclusion of academic writing instruction in European higher education) one needs to pay attention to the following aspects:
1. Increasing participation in the change: involving people in reaching a certain educational goal,
2. systemic restructuring: establishing structures which make the involvement and collaboration of those people possible,
3. innovative instruction: fostering new ways and subjects of teaching (Bryk *et al.* 1998: 206).

Even though I will concentrate on the aspect of systemic restructuring, it goes without saying that in practice this element of institutional development needs to be tied together with measures of increasing participation and innovative instruction. These two aspects have been covered by a number of authors in this book.

Courses on academic writing can certainly be taught without fundamental institutional changes, but they will mostly have limited and short-term impact on the educational agenda of an institution (Fullan 2000). Since I understand the teaching of academic writing to be part of a writing pedagogy, which carries a great potential or educational reform, I call for a thorough observation and discussion of the structural changes that seem necessary in order to make academic writing instruction sustainable in European higher education. This approach must include the other end of the educational pyramid: high schools. Future academic writers not only go through high school before they enter the academy, they also often return to secondary schools as teachers to prepare the next generation of academic writers. It would be an irresponsible waste of opportunities for education at large if the changes in writing instruction at colleges and universities would spare their most potential partners.

There is another reason for focusing this chapter on the establishment of specific institutional structures where academic writers can grow across disciplines. This reason is linked to cognitive science and its recent finding that imagination creates what Mark Turner (1996) calls a 'conceptual blending' of what and how an individual receives and understands information. A direct result of this complex cognitive operation, writing should be seen as a multi-faceted activity, not as a bundle of skills. 'Writing proceeds from thinking,' as Thomas & Turner (1994: 5) say, and writers must therefore 'work through intellectual issues, not merely acquire mechanical techniques.' (ibid.). These intellectual activities, nurtured by institutional structures such as the ones introduced in the following, generate skills that will remain within and further develop together with conceptual knowledge.

2   UNIVERSITY WRITING CENTRES: WRITING AS 'A MODE OF LEARNING'

Following the major findings of recent writing research, I will outline the main features of a writing centre within higher education.

Research on writing suggests that *learning to write* should not be thought of as a mere process that can be uniformly predetermined through a curriculum (Moffett 1968, Britton et al. 1975, Young & Fulwiler 1986). *How* the individual writer produces texts grows and changes not only throughout his/her educational career (Herrington & Curtis 2000) but actually throughout an entire lifetime (Elbow 2000). *Wo ?* University writing centres, seen as places for accompanying and accommodating the emergence of the individual writer and for individualising institutional writing instruction are, therefore, essential for a personally meaningful education.

Another important result of recent writing research lies in a growing understanding of the multi-faceted function of writing as a skill not only for copying, documenting or presenting knowledge, but also for *developing* it. *Writing to learn* has been examined in and applied to educational processes as a powerful means of unfolding thoughts and ideas in order to gain insights (Bishop 1999). Even though this procedure is being done by some naturally, using writing as part of their personal preference in the way they learn, current pedagogy suggests that *writing to learn* should be taught to *all* as an intriguing set of techniques, methods and strategies for determining one's most effective ways of acquiring knowledge (Sternglass 1997, Bishop 1999, Bräuer 2000). Writing centres are places advocating *writing to learn* techniques in peer tutoring as well as a means of bridging the gap between the private encounter of thought, knowledge and public work within academic discourses. Successful academic writers are the direct result of these two efforts.

Research on knowledge and learning has shown that play has problem-solving qualities (Piaget 1962, Polanyi 1983, Csikszentmihalyi 1990, Gardner 1993), something which, in writing pedagogy, is known for its performance enhancing aspects (see Peter Elbow's 'free writing technique' 1998). Experimenting with thoughts and ideas through different modes of expression (in this context Elbow uses the terms 'growing' and 'cooking' for writing) helps to experience – make visible – the emergence of the *voice* of a writer: his/her individual creative potential in regard to something to be learned. Writing centres as extra-curricular places provide a safe environment for exploration, experimentation and shared experience. They can also open up the academic setting of the university toward communication with the artistic realm.

Increasing knowledge of the writing process has led to the determination of its character as discourse specific (writing is defined by disciplines, and disciplines are shaped by writing) on one hand, and as overlapping discourses on the other (Bishop & Ostrom 1997, Bleich 1998). Therefore, generalized writing instruction has failed to be useful beyond introductory purposes. Entire generations of US college students and teachers fell victim of the 'myth of transience' spread in the era of the first general composition courses (Russell 1991: 3-34), and it was not before Jerome Bruner's (1960) concept of the spiral-shaped curriculum that the notion of learning to write as a singular, punctual event was seriously questioned. More than a decade later, out of the so-called 'literacy crisis' in 1975 (Berlin 1987: 180-84) grew the understanding that the development of advanced writing ability needs to be part of discrete academic disciplines, yet cross-disciplinary in its approach, if students are to master the specific discourses in and within academic fields. This requires the development of writing-intensive courses within the disciplines and the training of the faculty teaching those courses. Writing centres meet these expectations through a close relationship with *writing across the curriculum* programs.

Most of the recent curriculum development in European grade schools and certain institutions of higher education have started to take into consideration the research findings outlined above. Content and methodology of writing instruction and the teaching of writing have been changing over the past ten years as much as their roles and institutional recognition have begun to shift. Writing is no longer just a matter of formal language training but has become a means of academic endeavour and creative work. Therefore, the demand for pedagogical and methodological know-how concerning writing has never been greater. Writing centres are called upon to meet those demands through consultation, curriculum development, training, and networking.

3   HISTORICAL BACKGROUND

The demands for modern university writing centres as places for academic work (fostering individually meaningful learning; educating in writing-to-learn strategies; providing a place for shared experience; encouraging writing across the curriculum; and providing pedagogical training in teaching writing) are the result of a historical development, which – until just recently – took place to the greater extent in the US. I want to briefly introduce this institutional history in order to clarify afterwards the specific functions of the much younger European writing centres.

Even though the term *writing laboratory* was already known in early North American college English composition, it was not conceived as a place but rather as a method of instruction in the first decades of the 20th century. The method's exclusive focus on error elimination and pattern drill for the so-called under-prepared student writers remained long after the laboratory had also taken on a physical existence.

The lab's image as a 'fix-it-shop' did not start to change until the 1970's; at a time, when in composition studies the paradigm shift from product to process writing was finally brought underway. Stephen North's article 'The Idea of a Writing Center' (1984) calls for a move of the writing centre's focus from the text to the *writer*, demanding a change of character in the work done there from instructing to *advising*. Even though a number of publications, among them a history of the oldest American writing lab at the University of Iowa (Kelly 1980), had already appeared some years before, it was North's provocative article that started a profound and vehement discussion over the course of nearly two decades about the purpose and place of the writing centre in the academy. The first larger collaborative effort on the topic, 'Writing Centers. Theory and Administration' (Olson 1984), appeared to become the theoretical framework and reference in this dispute.

North's premise of producing 'better writers, not better writing' was in tune with an overall rather romantic view of the writer and of writing as an individual phenomenon in composition studies of the 1980s. Nevertheless, at the same time, in the context of then recent knowledge theory (Kuhn 1970, Vygotsky 1978), thoughts emerged on the impact of collaboration on learning in general and, more specifically, on writing centre practice. This was also a result of radical criticism over the previous decade on conventional teaching methods (lecturing) and on authoritarian structure (teacher-student relationship) in education. In this context, Kenneth A. Bruffee's article 'Peer Tutoring and the 'Conversation of Mankind'' (1984) first introduced the social component of learning as crucial for a modern concept of education.

As a consequence of these developments, a shift from the individual writer to the writer within discourse communities has been evident since the late 1980s, not only in composition studies but even more so in writing centres, *i.e.,* collaboration has become central to the currently dominating writing centre model. This model, for which Joan Mullin & Ray Wallace (1994) provide the larger theoretical and practical context, consists of two main strands: (a) Peer tutorials for one-on-one advising where the social context of the individual writer comes into play (Harris 1986, Rafoth 2000) and (b) Writing across the curriculum programs where the specifics of writing in and beyond the disciplines are being addressed (Barnett & Blumner 1999). Christina Murphy (1991) and, much later from a different perspective, Nancy Welch (1999) analyse the educational theory and politics underlying this change of focus in writing centre practice at the end of the 20th century. A publication by Linda Myers-Breslin (1999) shows different practical applications of the model and introduces rigorous scholarly investigations in the form of empirical data, program descriptions, and the analysis of major problems in order to better understand the writing centre's contribution to the knowledge structures of the academy.

A collection of articles uniting the pioneers of the writing centre movement, 'Landmark Essays on Writing Centers' (Murphy & Law 1995), provides a highly valuable documentation of the main shifts in writing centre pedagogy outlined above: from text, to writer, to social context, revealing writing centre history as a slow transformation from a marginalized institution into one that now challenges traditional instruction and learning and helps to redefine the role of the university toward an institution of interdisciplinary education.

Despite clearly defined areas of expertise and some signs of change, the existence of writing centres in Europe is still sparse. Their physical configuration and institutional recognition is often poor, and their long-term future is largely unpredictable. In a mainstream educational culture of clear-cut division between those who know how to write well and those who don't, or in other words, in an atmosphere of heavy content-driven and product-oriented teaching, the 18th century 'writer as a genius' of the literary Enlightenment seems to still linger today. Writing is thought of as a skill one must learn early in grade school and then master – in the form of academic writing – at the university level. Too few seem to care that novice university students are expected not only to be proficient writers in academic genres, but also to master the content of the newly joined discipline.

4   UNIVERSITY WRITING CENTRES:
PREPARING INSTITUTIONAL CHANGE

What are the specific needs and envisioned functions for writing centres in such a biased environment? Traditionally, the mission of university writing centres is geared toward the enhancement of higher education. Therefore, the exclusive focus on academic writing, as practiced by most centres in Europe and elsewhere, comes as no surprise. Nevertheless, with a growing understanding of writing as a complex individual and social phenomenon that neither appears all of a sudden when one enters university as a new student, nor disappears when one graduates, time seems ripe for writing centres to embrace the need for more than the instruction and facilitation of putting together academic papers. As much as a modern university in general cannot afford to be an ivory tower any longer, writing centres must connect with the different discourses and domains higher education evolves from and has an effect on. Taking the main shifts in writing centre history – from text, to writer, to social context – as corner stones for a more holistic approach, I would like to propose a university writing centre which reaches out to the larger community of a region by promoting concrete forms of lifelong learning and thereby contributes to the redefinition of the role of higher education beyond its traditional goal of building banks of knowledge (Bräuer, 2002). Such forms include (examples for each will follow throughout the remainder of the chapter):

- *Encouraging people* to read and write.
- *Networking among professions* for the purpose of sharing unique views on reading and writing.
- *Spreading knowledge* about reading and writing through the training of various educators.
- *Supporting the disadvantaged* through all of the above.

One of the most important domains higher education evolves from and has an effect on is teaching and learning in primary and secondary schools. Students in both places preparing for higher education shape the future of universities as much as today's student teachers at the university influence the quality of school education to come.

This calls for making better known at grade schools what is required of writers and for writing in higher education. Those insights can be provided through university writing centres, in workshops specifically designed for high school students, such as those at the University of Bielefeld (see Frank *et al*: this volume). Another way of spreading the word about academic writing consists of tutorials and workshops organized directly at the high school. In this scenario, university students become active as tutors and workshop facilitators in secondary schools. Here they not only apply what they have learned themselves about academic writing, but they also bring back to the university a better understanding of where prospective academic writers come from and what they might need for a successful transition from secondary to higher education.

5   SUGGESTING A WRITING (AND READING) CENTRE MODEL THAT SERVES BOTH ENDS OF THE EDUCATIONAL PYRAMID

In the following, I want to introduce an institutional model I have developed for bridging the gap between writing at secondary schools and universities. Therefore, my thoughts on what I call the Grade School 'Writing/Reading Centre' (WRC) are not only intended to propose ideas for primary and secondary education, but also set examples for what should be and could be done in order to broaden the outreach function of university writing centres. Even in this early stage of the WRC initiative, which I started in the fall of 2000 with support from the Germany-based Körber Foundation, it becomes evident that, based on more holistic grounds than their counterparts in higher education, reading/writing centres at schools seem to evolve quickly and, in the long term, might also initiate a stronger development of university writing centres and foster a more complex scope of those institutions.

My vision seems more realistic in the light of what primary and secondary school writing pedagogy has contributed over the past twenty years to theoretical and practical writing pedagogy in higher education, such as the use of reflective practice (learning log, portfolio) and the introduction of small group work and the workshop format. This also includes direct contributions to the teaching methodology in higher education, such as personal and explorative writing as preparatory stages for academic papers. How, if not in collaboration with university writing centres, should future schoolteachers learn to master what they are obligated to teach their students?

6   THINKING ABOUT A SPECIAL PLACE FOR READING AND WRITING

In the fall of 1998, I asked students who have visited my writing tutorial at the *Oberstufenkolleg* in Bielefeld, Germany, under which circumstances they prefer to read and write.

> Maja: Most of my poems come to my mind when I hang around in the library in the afternoons.

> Natasha: I write letters to my friends during the breaks.

> Zbigniew: Twice a week we sit together working on our term papers in the computer lab.

> Sven: I do homework somewhere right here after class. Then everything is still fresh in my head. And besides, someone is always there to answer questions.

The impression holds true: Most of the reading and writing takes place outside of the classroom, but still mostly in school. It is here where the preferred social contacts for learning happen; the school atmosphere takes care of the rest. Nevertheless, there isn't a special place for reading and writing. Even the library or computer lab, if they exist, aren't ideal, because conversation about reading or writing is considered disruptive there. Beyond that, classrooms, hallways, stairwells, or gyms don't necessarily enhance a *pleasant* reading and writing experience.

The fact that reading and writing require ever-changing social contacts in order to become an integral part of a student's learning experience is now well-known, as well as the fact that both key competencies show subject-specific features (Oomen-Welke 1998). The gradually accepted insight that the complexity of one's reading and writing history cannot be solely addressed through instruction in language and literature courses is neither an accusation nor an admittance of fault, but rather a realization of the importance of cross-disciplinary teaching. In the following, I want to introduce how such changes in the way of thinking about literacy and schooling can be practically implemented through a writing and reading centre.

My vision of a WRC, stimulated by what I have seen in North American grade schools, could look like the following:

> On the door a sign posting the hours of operation: Monday through Friday 8:00 to 8:00, Saturday 9:00 to 1:00. Also, the names and e-mail addresses of the centre's director and her tutors. Directly next to the entrance, a bulletin board with the monthly schedule and courses offered: In the first week student poets meet with a writer in residence. Teachers gather to exchange views on effective written assignments. Scheduled for the second week is the neighbourhood's self-help group and a public reading. On the agenda for the third week is a workshop for social workers and another for amateur playwrights. In addition, an evening of Spanish prose. The fourth week offers a day for professional translators, as well as a family weekend for sharing art and writing activities.

> The centre's facility is subdivided as follows: A circle of chairs in the middle, computer workstations along one side of the wall, book shelves on the other. A small library with class anthologies stretches to the back of the room, where sofa and armchairs are arranged. The presence of a teapot and coffeemaker, a shelf with dishes, and plants help create an inviting atmosphere. Toward the front of the room, next to the entrance, there are several office cubicles for tutorials.

> The full schedule indicates that the centre is constantly in use: Projects in the mornings and afternoons, individual tutorials during lunchtime and in the latter part of the afternoons, workshops and cultural events in the evenings. In between, especially during breaks between classes, students and teachers congregate to chat, discuss drafts, drink coffee or tea, and flip through literary magazines…[translated G.B.] (Bräuer 1998: 141).

7   WHAT HAPPENS FROM A THEORETICAL VIEWPOINT?

In a WRC, *learning by doing* (Dewey 1938) takes place, whereby problem-orientated action promotes meaning for the individual. Impulses, emotions, and desires gradually flow into problem-solving processes (ibid. 69). For example, 12 year-old Jane from Iowa City comes to the writing tutorial four times for help with her drafts of a project report. When she turns in her final paper, she makes the following remarks in her tutorial evaluation:

> This [writing project] was not any fun at all this time. I never did know what I was supposed to do. I would have been totally lost without my tutor. Next time I will just write the report together with my friend.

From her tutor she also finds out about an upcoming workshop on how to write project reports. She immediately assures her tutor that she will participate as she signs up for the workshop.

Both decisions (to work together with her friend and to take part in the workshop) have little to do with the conventional goals of the class requiring the written report, but far more with conceptual learning extending beyond the expectations of this class.

This writing centre, along with its tutor, the workshop offer, and the place for future collaboration of the two friends, sets the framework for combined theoretical and hands-on learning, including reflection upon experience and outcome (Kolb 1984: 42).

8   DEFINING THE WRITING/READING CENTRE (WRC)

The WRC is the model of an extra-curricular institution, whose underlying concept I developed based on the structure of the *learning workshop* from early 20th century European Reform Pedagogy, the writing and reading workshop as part of literacy instruction, and the American college and high school writing centre (Farrell 1989).

Even if certain character traits of the WRC correspond with those of a *workshop*, I choose to avoid this methodologically oriented expression, and instead prefer the term *centre* as indicative of its physical presence. I decided to link writing with *reading* as the two domains of the centre in order to counteract the conventionally reading-dominated language and literature courses in a holistic way.

The necessity of the WRC, however, is based on the growing realization of the fact that writing and reading competencies need at the same time complex socialization and extensive discipline-specificity, which, therefore, cannot solely be carried out by the traditional language and literature course. In addition, writing and reading are more and more accepted as paths toward a type of education, which reaches far beyond school to lay the ground for lifelong learning. What remains abstract here will become more concrete with the following paragraphs on goals, content, and suggestions for their practical realization.

9   WHICH GOALS CAN BE PURSUED?

An important aspect of the WRC lies in the linguistic socialization beyond class and school. The mingling and interacting of different groups of learners (age, native language and culture, social integration) allow education in general and reading and writing in specific to appear as something ordinary – as something which is no longer largely separated from the students' world experienced outside of the educational institution. Competence in writing and reading is therefore based on personal motivation, instead of being imposed by the teacher. Knowledge is being developed, tried and tested, and internalised in order to fulfil individual needs and desires and, last but not least, with the goal of receiving public recognition.

If successful as readers and writers, this can initiate curiosity and pleasure for further learning; if not successful, this could result in fear of failure, and goals can slip out of reach. In the latter case, students working collaboratively on a project will help each other because the outcome depends on each of the participants' perform-ance. Thus, self-reliance, individual responsibility *and* collaborative action are being encouraged, and all those characteristics are beneficial beyond school in general and for studying at the university in specific.

One of the most important goals of the WRC lies in the continual and diverse promotion of intercultural learning. To some extent, this already happens through the inclusion of second and foreign language tutorials in what is being offered at the centre. Intercultural education is intensified especially when languages and cultures existing in a school are experienced individually through projects and public events. This goal embodies another preparatory aspect for future academic work at the uni-versity. In a growing multilingual world of higher education, students need to be able to motivate and orientate themselves, develop language learning strategies, and tie a network of study support.

10   WHICH CONTENT CAN BE REALISED?

Much of the educational content realized by the WRC seems, at first glance, similar to what is being done in the traditional language and literature classroom. A closer look, though, reveals many aspects of cross-disciplinary character:

- Writing as a process (planning, drafting, revising, reflecting)
- Text types (description, narration, report, *etc.*)
- Sorts of text (literary, non-literary, academic)
- Writing strategies (associative, structured, *etc.*)
- Reading strategies (informative, selective, *etc.*)
- Strategies for the reading and writing of second and foreign language texts
- General learning methods and techniques (brainstorming, clustering, mind-mapping, *etc.*)
- Forms of cooperative work (peer, tutorials, workshop, project)
- Forms of reflective practice (diary, reading log, writing journal, portfolio)

The cross-disciplinary aspect of the content mentioned above lies in the specific character of the WRC, which is that writing and reading are undertaken not for the purpose of getting graded but for individually defined reasons, *e.g.*, the article for the school newspaper is being revised in hope of positive feedback from peer read-ers. This does not mean that the student would not also realize the chance of better performance and grading.

The fact that patterns of producing and reproducing texts in the WRC are called upon repeatedly, but within different contexts and requirements, not only ensures the development of problem-solving strategies, but also guarantees the accumulation of the latter as *dynamic* systems of knowledge which are adaptable and changeable and as such the base for any academic endeavour to come.

11   HOW CAN GOALS AND CONTENT BE PUT INTO PRACTICE?

The list of practical possibilities is long, which does not mean all have to be realized at once in order to benefit from the pedagogical potentials of the WRC. Each aspect listed below carries a general potential for cross-disciplinary learning and could therefore be used as a starting point for a newly established WRC. What should also be kept in mind (and even fostered) is the snowball effect most of the projects listed below develop. It is the interconnectedness with regard to content, methodology, and organization, which, to a great extent, creates the purposeful character of the WRC: What would a writers' workshop for the so-called 'Mini-Hausarbeit' (try-out thesis, as seen at the *Oberstufenkolleg* in Bielefeld, Germany) be without publication? What would that student publication be without a review in the school newspaper? Which academic writer 'in spe' would not be proud to know that her/his thesis can be checked out of the school library? Looking over the following list of practical possibilities for the WRC, it is rather easy to imagine many connections of this kind:

- Peer tutoring
- Training of tutors
- Counselling of learning disabilities in regard to reading and writing
- Maintaining a network of teachers who work as facilitators for high school student tutors
- Workshops about main features of reading/writing improvement in first/second and foreign languages
- Academic writing workshop ('Mini-Hausarbeit')
- Creative writing workshops
- Writers-in-residence
- Publication of student anthologies
- Introduction in the art of book making
- Student newspapers
- Public readings and presentations by students, teachers, and parent writers (literary, academic)
- Projects initiating intercultural learning
- Literary café (permanent)
- Research on writing/reading pedagogy
- Curriculum development (writing/reading across disciplines and languages)
- Coordination between reading/writing-intensive courses across the curriculum
- Teachers' training
- Cooperation with university writing centres
- Internships for university students
- Cooperation with other WRC's
- Annual book fairs, writing contests, and other events that connect the school with the larger community

12   CONCEPTUAL FOCUS POINTS

In order to negotiate successfully between the resources of a school and the maintaining of the basic WRC features, it is helpful to be aware of the corner stones of writing/reading as extra-curricular activities. They will not only support individual orientation, but also provide guidance for the collaboration of all those people needing to be involved in setting up and running WRC's, such as teachers, students, school administrators, parents, and members of the university writing centre. The following definitions are very brief for the purpose of providing clear and concrete explanations of what is being aimed at.

12.1 Help for Self-help

The WRC is not a service station where students go for last-minute help in order to fulfil due requirements. The WRC is rather a place where, within a permanent social network of peers, tutors, and facilitators, skills for independent learning are developed as a strong base for any academic or professional education.

12.2 Everyday Culture of Reading and Writing

Through the establishment of permanent places for the exchange of reading and writing, such as the literary café and writers' workshops, the traditional fixation on literacy courses as the only place for reading and writing instruction is fundamentally questioned: Reading and writing are perceived as skills whose importance reaches across the disciplines and far beyond school, into the daily life of the individual student and toward future training in higher education.

12.3 Aesthetic Experience

Writing groups, school newspapers, writer-in-residencies, student anthologies, and public readings, among other offerings, are many-layered opportunities to individually explore the aesthetic components of reading and writing. Those experiences help to balance an otherwise heavily knowledge-oriented writing and reading education at school and prepare students to aim for such a balance at the university and elsewhere.

12.4 Intercultural Learning

In a multicultural/lingual school, aesthetic experiences, such as the ones mentioned above, often enable the individual student to recognize cultural differences on a new level. If such recognition is reflected and dealt with purposefully through intercultural projects, an appreciation of existing cultural differences between students and/or among people living in the region of a school can be a valuable result, leading to a better understanding within the larger community.

12.5 Electronic Media Education

Students need to learn how to efficiently use electronic media such as film, computers, and the Internet, which serve as powerful resources for the expansion of their individual learning. Through online writing/reading instruction, collaborative writing over the Internet, and web-based research, the use of electronic media should become commonplace, forming an advantageous starting point for studying at the university.

12.6 Collaborative Action

Peer collaboration, the training of high school tutors, university student internships, and cooperation between teachers and university faculty render work at the WRC unique, because traditional hierarchies between those who learn and those who teach are helpfully disrupted, evolving toward a shared effort for a personally fulfilling education.

13   WHICH METHODOLOGY?

The WRC follows two different methodological strands within the context of tutorials, workshops, and peer projects:

- Cross-disciplinary: initiate learning to deal with general text-types, such as analysis, report, description, argumentation, *etc*.
- Discipline-specific: initiate learning to deal with specific genres, such as lab reports for science courses, literary analysis for literature courses, technical descriptions for practical work classes, *etc*.

For both strands, model reading/writing processes are introduced and practiced and, over time, individually altered. Through extensive reflective practice in diaries, writing journals, reading logs, and portfolios, students learn to recognize the individual character of their work with texts and their collaboration with other writers. They learn to identify current strategies as more or less effective, as well as the possible need for change. On a long-term basis, the result of such an ongoing theory-practice-learning methodology is a growing ability to adapt one's own knowledge and skills to varying situations and tasks.

14   WHAT DOES A WRC LOOK LIKE?

Most of the currently existing WRC's in Germany show that an independent location is almost essential for such a rather non-traditional educational enterprise. Newly established WRC's need this extra amount of visibility within the daily hustle of school life in order to sink into everyone's awareness as a place where reading and writing reach beyond the conventional boundaries of language and literature classes. A school library, if existing at all, could help draw enough attention to emphasize that reading and writing belong together. As new WRC initiatives in Germany have revealed, running a library and WRC in tandem can create advantages on an organizational level, such as shared staffing, funding, and the use of material and equipment. Nevertheless, even if located together, a library and WRC should reserve some of their space for individual purposes to prevent limiting each other in their potentials.

The following is a list of furniture and equipment, which is helpful, but by no means necessary in its entirety, in getting a WRC started. Over time, attention should be paid to maintaining a balance between manual and electronic equipment to ensure that text production, despite the wide-spread excitement over new media, can also be experienced *hands on* as a process of *making*. This striving for a more holistic approach to the WRC is stressed through the comments given in brackets, indicating the particular function of the individual equipment.

As the list of fixtures suggests, the WRC invites discovery through both the senses and the intellect and encourages lively exchange. Here, *experiencing* language and *experimenting* with language, *constructing*, *deconstructing*, and *reconstructing* are in the forefront, compared to other learning environments where presenting and processing knowledge is predominant. In agreement with Gerald Graff (1992), I envision *conflicts* taught in the WRC, along with the process of finding possible solutions. As a result, insights are closely linked to the learner's personal experience. He or she has engraved meaning into each 'text' – a phenomenon that has been determined by educators to be longer lasting than firm know-how handed down just to be swallowed.

14.1 Furniture

- Small and large tables for individual and group work.
- A couch, a few armchairs grouped around a coffee table (inviting, casual ambience).
- Small library with resources on writing and reading pedagogy (continuing education for tutors/teachers).
- Collection of student anthologies (sharing what has been accomplished).
- Boards with outlines and reports from work in progress (demonstrating writing as a process).
- Literary café with newly released books of different genres, journals, and newspapers, possibly in different languages (reading for pleasure).

14.2 Manual Equipment

- Art supply (fostering the connection between visual and linguistic metaphors)
- A few portable flip charts (inviting spontaneous writing and drawing)
- Collection of artifacts, possibly from different cultures (inviting tactile experience)
- Manual printing sets of different kinds, typewriters, and material for manual book binding (supporting kinaesthetic/acoustic experience)

- Material to encourage handwriting as art (encouraging aesthetic/artistic experience)

14.3 Electronic Equipment

- Computers with Internet access, software for collaborative writing and editing, language learning programs, reading tools (connecting with the larger community of learners)
- Printer and scanner (visibility of 'texts')
- Overhead and slide projector (presenting work)
- TV and video camera (documenting work processes and events)

15   WHAT IS THE PART OF UNIVERSITY WRITING CENTRES IN ALL THIS?

I want to elaborate some of the thoughts I indicated at the beginning of this chapter with regard to the outreach function which university writing centres should embrace more strongly in the near future.

Traditionally, the university has been the primary place of teacher education. In Germany, for example, many student teachers experience their first practical classroom encounter only late during the course of their training. With the help of the university writing centre, this preparation of future educators could become practice-oriented much earlier. Internships and projects at school WRC's could be organized and facilitated through the university writing centre and in collaboration with faculty from various disciplines. In fact, those internships and projects, if designed as integrated parts of the school curriculum, could convince schoolteachers and administrators over time of the necessity of a WRC as an organizational counterpart of the university writing centre. In other words, any effort at bridging the gap between school and university does not have to wait for a WRC to be formally in place but, rather, fosters its emergence over time.

The latter indicates the advantage of university writing centres getting involved in reading and writing at schools with *more* than just the purpose of preparing future academic writers in mind. With research as one of its main foci, the university should indeed feel obligated to share various findings in applied forms with school education. By doing so, something that is known in the US as *Teachers-as-researchers* could be further developed in Europe. This would not only foster the existence of reflective practitioners, but also initiate cross-disciplinary thinking, as such providing the basis for better reading and writing instruction in both school and the university.

As a rather practical consequence of all the aspects mentioned above, university writing centres should secure specific resources for their outreach function. At many US university writing centres, one faculty member focuses primarily on the outreach activities of the centre, spending much of his/her time coordinating what is called the *National Writing Project* (NWP) (Gray 1986), which consists of regional networks of school writing programs and centres, promoting especially the idea of *writ-*

ing across the curriculum. Workshops are held to develop network coordinators, who then organize cooperation between the disciplines at their school. NWP's annual *summer writing workshops* bring together teachers from different academic areas to help them explore ways of integrating writing (and reading) in cross-disciplinary fashion.

To sum up, I would consider the following aspects important for the grade school-oriented outreach function of university writing centres:

- Organization and coordination of internships for student teachers at local schools.
- Promotion of the long-term project of establishing grade school WRC's.
- Training of teachers to run a WRC and bringing them together in summer academies for the purpose of sharing their experience.
- Helping to train/supervise the first set of peer tutors for a school.
- Initiation and support of a network among local school WRC's (perhaps through a website).
- Coordination of the search for funding and sponsoring.

Recalling the writing research findings I listed toward the beginning of this chapter, I see many of these aspects already promoted individually in a variety of ways within the European education system. It is now time to *link* them with each other and give them a *home* – a permanent place where people across the disciplines can read and write together and think about literacy in its largest possible meaning, including the *art* of academic writing. Such a move promises to make better use of reading and writing as powerful tools for learning and instruction as well as for bridging the gap between school, university, and the many worlds outside the curriculum.

WRITING AT NORWEGIAN UNIVERSITIES IN AN INTERNATIONAL PERSPECTIVE.

FROM INDIRECT STRATEGIES OF STRENGTHENING WRITING TO THE 'QUALITY REFORM'

OLGA DYSTHE

University of Bergen, Norway

Abstract. This chapter outlines the historical and contextual background for why writing has not had a prominent place in Norwegian higher education and tells the story of what strategies the professional development unit at the University of Bergen has chosen in order to increase and improve the use of writing. The choice of the 'Integration model' for strengthening writing is underpinned in sociocultural theories of learning. Three strategies are focused, firstly the integration of writing-to-learn and learning to write in the compulsory course for new university teachers, secondly the initiation of discipline based action research projects and thirdly 'Start writing' workshops and writing groups for master students. In spite of the success of such measures, it has not affected the mainstream of university teaching and learning until the government in 2001 announced the 'Quality Reform for Higher Education' which will transform Norwegian higher education. After briefly sketching some of the new reform proposals, some consequences for the state of writing at Norwegian universities are discussed, particularly the effect of changing the evaluation system.

Keywords: Dialogism, Integration model, Master students, Portfolio assessment, Professional development, Quality reform, Sociocultural, Training the trainers, Writing groups, and Writing project.

1   BACKGROUND: THE BERGEN PROGRAMME FOR RESEARCH ON LEARNING AND INSTRUCTION

None of the four universities in Norway has established a writing centre or a specific writing programme, but strengthening writing has been one of the tasks of the professional development units, which exist at all the universities. At the University of Bergen, this centre is called Programme for Research on Learning and Instruction (PLF). We have chosen an indirect route to strengthen writing, and this article is

Dysthe, O. (2003). Writing at Norwegian Universities in an International Perspective: From Indirect Strategies of Strengthening Writing to 'The Quality Reform'. In: G. Rijlaarsdam (Series Ed.) & L. Björk, G. Bräuer, L. Rienecker & P. Stray Jörgensen (Volume Eds.), Studies in Writing, Volume 12, Teaching Academic Writing in European Higher Education, pp. 151-164. © 2003 Kluwer Academic Publishers. Printed in the Netherlands.

therefore about how to build up the competence of university teachers in various disciplines to teach writing in their own discipline, to use writing as a tool for learning and to supervise students' writing. I believe that even though my account focuses on contextual constraints and opportunities in one particular national setting, it may be useful as a 'thinking tool' for others in their settings.

The introduction and organization of writing centres or writing programs at universities or the lack of such can only be understood in the context of the university history, traditions and practices in each country. Without knowledge of this context, it is not possible to judge the viability of transfer of practices from one country to another. Likewise, it is also important to know from which position and perspective the author is viewing the topic, and I will therefore first place myself in my university context.

The unit where I worked from 1994, 'Programme for Research on Learning and Instruction' (hereafter PLF), is an equivalent to what internationally is called 'Centre for Teaching and Learning', 'Professional Development Centre' or 'Centre for University Pedagogy'. While such centres or units now exist at many universities world wide, what is unusual about Norway is that all new academic staff is required to take a basic course in 'university pedagogy'. Organizing and teaching this course is part of PLF's responsibility. We were four academic staff members who also work as consultants for the central administration of the university, departments and institutes.[33] We also worked directly with students and this is a feature, which distinguishes this unit from the majority of our international counterparts, where student support centres are separate units, and where the staff work either with students or with faculty. This double responsibility has important implications; because the direct and continuous contact with students gives us access to student centred perspectives, which are very useful in our work with faculty. It also gives us a double perspective on writing; an understanding of the needs of the students combined with a realistic sense of what changes are possible within the system and to what extent we need to work for systemic changes.

In PLF, I have been the only one with qualifications in the teaching of writing. With a long history of teaching Norwegian, including writing, and a somewhat shorter as a writing researcher, I have worked closely with colleagues at the other Norwegian universities in order to find viable strategic approaches to the much needed strengthening of writing in higher education in Norway. The story I tell from Bergen is just one example of what has been going on at the other universities in various forms.

2   SOME ASPECTS OF THE NORWEGIAN UNIVERSITY TRADITION

2.1 German and American Influences

The Norwegian university tradition is strongly influenced by the German Humboldt idea of a university, emphasizing institutional independence, academic freedom and

---

[33] *From the year 2000, I have been involved in building up a new Department of Education and only worked part time for PLF.*

research based teaching. 'Academic freedom' has been a key concept in all countries, but it may be interpreted differently depending on the system. It always, however, involves some measure of institutional autonomy, which guarantees freedom of teaching, learning and research. At our universities, academic freedom is interpreted by many faculty members to also include students' freedom to choose whether to attend lectures or write papers. An exception is medical schools with compulsory attendance and also certain required lab courses in the sciences. The following quotation from an interview study of faculty attitudes towards writing and supervision at the University of Bergen (Dysthe & Breistein 1999) illustrates the reluctance to make written papers a compulsory part of undergraduate education:

> I would prefer my students to do more writing, but if you ask whether I would organize writing intensive courses where students had to attend and had to write, my answer is an absolute no. Professional colleges invite their students to follow a structured plan for their education; they have courses with compulsory attendance and they may demand written papers. But the university should be different. If we mean anything at all with academic freedom, this must also be a reality for students; we cannot claim it for the teachers only. And as I see it, without academic freedom, the university idea is broke. (Professor 'Lund' 6.13.98).

Students, as well as a majority of university teachers agreed with professor 'Lund' in his defence of this interpretation of academic freedom, and the rationale behind it is that learning and research in principle is the same sort of intellectual activities. Academic freedom is seen as a necessary prerequisite for development of students' critical thinking as well as for professors' innovative research. Opposition towards compulsory attendance and required written papers has therefore often been couched in such terms, even though an underlying reason may simply be that more writing would involve more work for teachers.

The American universities were also influenced by the German model but have shown great flexibility, for instance by embracing applied research and including disciplines, which traditionally had no academic status. The more functionalistic and utilitarian American university tradition has competed with the German tradition in shaping the modern Norwegian university (Bleiklie 1997). We have for instance adopted the departmental system of organizing teaching and research instead of continuing the German 'professorial chair' system. A number of applied disciplines are now included in the universities, but it is worth noting that Norway has a two-tier higher education system, with a considerable number of local colleges. The two levels offer the traditional academic subjects, but also include a great variety of applied disciplines, like nursing, teacher education and engineering. The colleges are generally more open to pedagogical innovations, and the attitude of professor 'Lund' is representative of faculty who sees academic freedom as one of the few remaining characteristics of the university.[34]

---

[34] *This view is strongly stated in an article 'Turning Academics into Teachers?' where the authors argue for research-based teaching because only an active researcher can involve students in real and engaged learning processes (Rowland et al. 1998).*

While our intellectual links were strong with Germany before World War II, they have been equally strong with the USA after the war. Our first university, the University of Oslo, dates back to 1813, but our other three universities, located in Bergen, Trondheim and Tromsø, were all founded after 1948. Many graduate students have taken their PhD. at American universities and a great number of university professors spend their Sabbatical year in the same places. This means that many university teachers have experience from the American system at the top ranking universities, and come back impressed by the rigorous demands of the course credit system, including the writing of papers and the provision of teaching assistants, but questioning the continuous assessment system which entails the power of the professors to decide student grades. This also means that a lot of faculty have regretted that Norwegian students do not write enough, and would like to change this.[35] Whether they will now endorse the 'Quality Reform' which advocates compulsory papers and participation is still to be seen, and I will return to this at the end of this chapter.

2.2 The 'Exam Giving' vs. the 'Instruction Giving' University

The Norwegian university model has been called 'the exam giving university' in contrast to the Anglo-American 'instruction giving university' (Øverland 1989, 1994). Somewhat exaggerated it can be said that while American university students 'take courses', students at Norwegian universities 'take exams'. For Norwegian students the 'contract' with the university is the curriculum list of texts on which exam questions are based. What students do in the meantime in order to acquire the required knowledge, is in principle their own responsibility. It follows from such a system firstly that students' grades only depends on the final exam, and secondly a very strong emphasis on external assessors in order to secure a fair evaluation. This explains to a certain extent why students have not been expected to write as much and as regularly in our universities as in Great Britain and the USA. Even though handing in written papers is advocated as a good way of preparing for the exam, there is resistance both among teachers and students to make papers compulsory, on the grounds I have mentioned before. Besides, however good papers the student writes during term, it counts nothing toward her final grade. Obviously, this does not motivate students to write much, or teachers to put in a lot of effort into assigning or responding to such papers.

Because the final exam has been a comprehensive one at the end of each term and not a separate assessment in each course (with the exception of the natural sciences), there has been no tradition for integrating papers. Teachers who want to introduce 'writing intensive courses' therefore had to convince their students that this was worth their effort, even though their writing did not count towards their final grade. What has worked well in all disciplines where it existed, however, is the term paper, which may count 50% of the final grade.

---

[35] This is brought out through the interview study 'Writing and Supervision. Attitudes and experiences by faculty and students' (Dysthe 1997).

The implications of this for efforts to strengthen writing at Norwegian universities will be discussed later, but we will first look more closely at what has been the state of writing at Norwegian universities.

2.3 Undergraduate Students Lack Practice in Academic Writing

At most universities, writing has traditionally been considered one of the skills students were supposed to possess when they entered academic life and specific teaching was therefore not deemed necessary. The change from elite to mass university changed this in many countries.

In Norway, however, the expansion of the number of university students did not lead to a similar emphasis on the teaching of academic writing, which is surprising in light of the fact that the student population grew from approximately 8 000 in 1946 to 80 000 in 1996. One interpretation is that because writing has a very prominent place in the Norwegian high school, students entering the university are quite experienced in extended writing.[36] High school writing, however, provides a general but insufficient basis for the demands of writing at the university, especially for the Master's degree thesis. Many students have complained that they do not know the demands of academic writing, and this becomes critical when they start the work on their Master thesis. A survey I made in 1995 showed that a considerable number of students never wrote any papers at all except their final exam, which in most cases was a sit-down exam of 6-8 hours. The picture is, however, somewhat more diversified due to the introduction of 'home exams' and 'term paper' in the Humanities and Social Sciences.

In the math and science departments, there has been even less sustained required writing at undergraduate level. Lab reports and site observation reports constituted the bulk of writing. In some subjects like physics, lab reports often require very little writing, as the students fill in a standard form, while in chemistry some reports may be quite elaborate.

2.4 High Demands on Writing at Master Level

The Norwegian Master degree has been based on a dissertation with a time frame of 3 to 4 semesters. Writing thus gains vital importance at graduate level. Over the last few years, pressure on the universities for introducing productivity measures, efficiency and quality control, has put a focus on factors, which explain why many students exceed the normal time frame. A major incentive for strengthening writing at Norwegian universities is the fact that Master degree students need more experience in academic writing in order to finish on time. The Writing Project, which I initiated in 1994, therefore focused on Master students.

---

[36] *The final exam at the end of twelve years of schooling consists of to national, five-hours essay exams, which carry a lot of prestige.*

3 CHARACTERISTIC FEATURES OF THE STRATEGIC AND PRACTICAL
   WORK TO STRENGTHEN WRITING AT THE UNIVERSITY OF BERGEN

In this section, I first want to outline the rationale for choice of strategy and the
theoretical underpinnings for our work to strengthen writing. Then I will discuss
some central elements of our work. The University of Bergen was the first Norwegian university to employ an academic staff person with expertise in writing.

3.1 Choice of Strategy: 'Expert Model' or 'Integration Model'?

Due to my year as adjunct professor at San Diego State University in 1985/86 and a
second year at the Centre for the Study of Writing at the University of California,
Berkeley, I was very familiar with Writing Across the Curriculum in the US and the
debate about choice of models, and we had thorough discussions at our PLF unit
about which strategy to choose. It was not a trivial decision, as it also involved the
whole field of 'study skills' and the international controversy of an integrated or a
centre based approach. The obvious advantages of the expert or centre model, is the
development of professional staff in academic writing (and study skills) which
would ensure a high quality in the services to students and faculty. The integration
model means that the responsibility for teaching and follow-up of writing was integrated in the disciplines. The danger of this was that nothing would happen, since
new money was not available and reallocation of staff involved other problems. The
advantage, if successful, was that discipline specific writing expertise would be able
to deal more holistically with students writing problems in light of that particular
discipline.[37]

An interesting question is what factors influence a choice between such models
and the decision in our PLF unit may serve as an example. My analysis indicates
that the choice of the integration model was due to a combination of the dominating
pedagogical philosophy at PLF, our university context and practical issues. The expert or centre model is often based on a cognitive view of learning, which traditionally focuses on the individual. It is not unusual that 70 % of the time of staff at
Communication and/or Study Skills units work with 'problems' of individual students (Ballard 1984). Our unit was located in the Psychology department, with its
bias towards what Wertsch (1998) calls 'methodological individualism'. One of my
colleagues is a cognitive psychologist; one has his background as an astrophysicist
and one as an architect. My own background is in comparative literature and applied
linguistics, and my pedagogical practice is grounded in sociocultural theory. We
have in our unit developed a balance between cognitive and sociocultural perspectives and share a basic belief in the importance of contextualising both writing pedagogy and study skills. An integration model was therefore clearly most in line with
our basic ideas. Our university tradition with very little compulsory writing at undergraduate level meant that a writing centre would primarily serve graduate stu-

---

[37] *The discussion of choice of model for strengthening writing at our university was published
as a chapter in a report (the title in English: 'Graduate writing—a challenge for the university' 1997).*

dents. And the practical constraints were that a writing centre would have to serve the whole university with its great variety of academic writing, not just the humanities and the social sciences. All these factors pointed in the direction of an integration model. I will later return to an evaluation of the results of this choice.

3.2 Dialogism as Theory Basis: Important in Gaining Academic Support

'Dialogism' is an epistemological approach to the study of language and mind, which focuses on how dialogue shapes both language and thought. Three characteristics of dialogism are: 1) a view of mind and consciousness as socially constituted, 2) a view of meaning and knowledge as products of interaction and sociocultural conditions, instead of objective, decontextualised entities, and 3) an emphasis on the connection between language and thinking. Vygotsky and Bakhtin as well as the Norwegian psychologist and linguist Ragnar Rommetveit provide the key theoretical basis for the close connection between language and learning, as well as for a socio-interactive view of the writing process (Bakhtin 1981, 1986, Vygotsky 1986, Rommetveit 1974, 1996, Linell 1998). Martin Nystrand's social interactive model of writing has also been a major influence (Nystrand 1989, 1992).

My own study 'Writing and Talking to Learn. A theory based, interpretive study of three classrooms in Norway and the USA,' (1993, English original) and the books published in Norwegian 'Ord på nye spor. Innføring i prosessorientert skriving' (1987) [Introduction to Process Writing] and 'Det flerstemmige klasserommet' (1995) [The Multivoiced Classroom], have provided a theoretical as well as empirical grounding of writing in Norway, together with the writing research group at the Institute of Applied Linguistics at the Technical University of Trondheim (NTNU), which includes Torlaug Løkensgard Hoel[38], Lars Sigfred Evensen, Jon Smidt, Finn Bostad and others. It is worth noting that Norwegian writing research is thoroughly grounded in sociocultural theory and that the researchers are at the same time and without exception, leading practitioners. (See also *Written Communication* nrs *3* and *4*, for five reports on Norwegian writing research.)

This solid theoretical and research basis has been important for three reasons. Firstly, there is scepticism particularly among university professors towards pedagogy in general, but specifically towards pedagogical methods, techniques and strategies which are not theory and research based. There is a suspicion that pedagogical qualifications, general or specifically in the teaching of writing, are used by the administration as part of their accountability and efficiency program. In our times of technical rationality and management view of educational institutions, this is understandable. Dialogism gives a rationale, which goes to the core of how knowledge is created—in interaction and dialogue with the 'texts' of other members of the disciplinary community, both students and teachers.

Secondly, dialogism includes both written and oral texts (Bakhtin 1986), and the potential for learning in the interaction of writing and talking is readily accepted.

---

[38] Hoel (1994, 2000)

Thirdly, since Norwegian research on writing and supervision at university level was non-existent ten years ago, local, empirical studies based on a sociocultural understanding of educational processes, have been welcomed as a contribution to understanding and solving problems of a mass university where students are less prepared than before for academic demands. Even though limited in scope, it is our experience that our local studies carry more weight as a basis for in service training of teachers than for instance American and Australian research. A series of reports and papers have been published from the research project 'Writing and supervision in the disciplines' (Dysthe & Kjeldsen 1997, Dysthe & Breistein 1999, Dysthe & Lied 2001, Dysthe 2002).

3.3 The Integration Model and Sociocultural Theory

In this brief space I will just focus on two aspects, firstly the concept of discourse society and academic writing as an inculturation into the disciplines (Bartholomae 1985, Ballard 1984, Bazerman 1994), and secondly the concept of situated learning and its implication for the teaching of writing (Lave & Wenger 1991, Lave 1997, Kvale 1997). Because the focus of our writing project has been on graduate students, it was obvious that writing a thesis was just as much about becoming a member of the particular disciplinary culture as about writing skills. Learning what questions were important and which were not, how to frame questions and answers and arguments within the particular discipline, involves identity formation, which is closely linked to the ability to write well. Writing, as learning, is situated in a community of common skills, knowledge and cultural practice, and from this theoretical perspective, students have to be taught and trained within the community of practice, not by external writing experts.

This theoretical stance has been confirmed by my own experience conducting a great number of writing workshops for graduate students across the disciplines. Focusing on writing processes and on commonalities of academic writing has been useful to a point, but it has convinced me that the responsibility for writing at that level can only rest with the teachers in the disciplines. The Writing Project therefore changed its focus to 'training the trainers', which in this context primarily meant making the teachers conscious of their own disciplinary practices, helping them verbalise it for their students and finding institutional solutions.

3.4 The Writing Project at the University of Bergen

The Writing Project was located within PLF, and this ensured integration into the professional development activities as well as a central place in our student assistance endeavours. Our strategies over the last 8 years can be placed under two headings:
1. Utilising the room of change within the present system.
2. Working for systemic changes.

Part of our agenda at the University of Bergen has been to place 'writing to learn' and 'learning to write' high on the university agenda at all levels, through committee work, well-advertised workshops, and publishing reports of empirical studies.[39] One direct result of this was that the Strategic Plan for the University of Bergen (1999) identified 'writing-to-learn' as a major strategy to improve learning. Such documents do not in themselves create change, but they serve important functions by legitimising and validating writing initiatives and making funding for action research easier.

Challenging our 'exam-giving-system' has also been high on our agenda, because the assessment system has a strong limiting effect on student writing and the teachers' engagement in writing. Exams are regulated in a national Higher Education Act. We have advocated a more diversified exam system, which combines internal and external assessment without the rigidity of having an external assessor for each exam. Interestingly, our advocacy of portfolio assessment met with official support in the government appointed Mjøs Committee's recommendations for changes in higher education, and this was followed up in Parliament Proposition 27/2001, also named 'The Quality Reform of Higher Education'.[40] Leaving the question of systemic change for the end of this chapter, the characteristic features of the Writing Project at the University of Bergen can be summed up in the following points:

- Integration of 'writing to learn', 'learning to write' and supervision strategies in the required courses for all new faculty
- Discipline based action research projects in order to create models and document results
- Special emphasis on 'Start writing' workshops and 'Writing groups' for master students

Integration of Writing-to-learn in the Work of Teaching and Learning Units with Academic, Tenured Positions. There are no separate Writing Across the Curriculum programmes in Norwegian universities, but our approach is to make writing an integral part of the activities of the units, which are given a special responsibility for teaching and learning at our university, whatever their names are.[41] This is not as

---

[39] *Dysthe 2002. The reports from the University of Bergen are all published in Norwegian: Dysthe (1997), Dysthe & Kjeldsen (1997), Kjeldsen & Dysthe (1997), Dysthe & Lied (1999), Dysthe & Breistein (1999), Lyngra (1999), Dysthe & Lied (2001).*

[40] *The Mjøs Committee Report was released on May 12th 2000 and proposed the greatest changes in higher education in Norway for the last 50 years. A long debate about the future of higher education followed. A year later, the government followed up with the official Stortingsmelding 27 (Parliament Proposition), which mostly is referred to as the 'Quality Reform' because the major purpose of all the proposed measures was to improve the quality of higher education.*

[41] *That such units are controversial, at least when they are non-academic, is brought out in an article in 'Teaching in Higher Education', where Stephen Rowland among others argues against 'service units' and 'institutes of teaching' which in his opinion reduces teaching to*

self-evident as it may sound, because the academic staff of such units often has their PhDs in Education or Psychology, and they do not necessarily know much about language and learning or writing. At the University of Oslo, for instance, they rely on the expertise of a professor in Norwegian linguistics.

It is worth noticing that Norwegian universities have not established non-academic 'service units' or ad hoc organisations for pedagogical improvements, but the policy is to build this work into the academic structure of the university. Such units are academic and located within university faculties (at the University of Bergen it is located in the Psychology Faculty, at the University of Oslo in the Education Faculty). This has four important implications, which have been worth fighting for. Firstly, it means that the formal requirement for positions in such units is a PhD. Secondly the positions are in principle tenured. This secures continuity of academic staff, and thus the possibility of gaining influence in the university system. Thirdly, our job description designates 45 % for research and 45 % for teaching (including consultancy work and supervision) and 10 % for administration. As a result, our teaching is in principle research based, like all university teaching. This provides the basis for equal status with the colleagues in other departments with whom we work as consultants. Fourthly, as there is no 'service staff' tied to these units, cooperation with the teachers and students in the different disciplines is therefore the only option.

Integration of Writing Across the Curriculum (WAC) in the Required Courses for New Faculty. For the last ten years all new faculty at Norwegian universities are required to take a course in 'Teaching and learning in higher education'.[42] This is controversial, as are all compulsory courses. There are at the moment two models for how WAC is integrated in these courses.

The Bergen University model means giving all participants a WAC-workshop focused on writing to learn. Since all participants are required to write a publishable report on a development or evaluation project, get-started techniques as well as response strategies are tied to their own work with the report. They give feedback to one another, and in that connection feedback to students and supervision in general

---

skills and strategies unrelated to the dynamics of each subject: 'Locked into this dichotomy [of teaching and research; my comment] a confusing array of 'service' units have grown in universities in many countries with the aim of improving university teaching. Variously described as Staff Development Units, 'non-academic' units have come to see themselves as embattled in the task of raising the importance of teaching in institutions which have traditionally rewarded academics primarily on their productivity in research.' (Rowland et al. 1998). When the author laments this development, it is on the one hand by arguing that good teaching must be research based, and therefore there should be no conflict between teaching and research, and on the other hand by arguing that staff from the aforementioned units lack the disciplinary basis which is the foundation of all good teaching. It is implied that their so-called 'services' therefore are of little use.

[42] *Cp the Dearing Report in the UK, entitled 'Higher Education in the Learning Society' which proposes the successful completion of a period of Teacher Training as a condition for gaining accreditation as a university lecturer.*

are discussed. Combining their own needs as writers with their role as respondents to students has worked well.

The Oslo university model is to offer the participants of the course a choice of workshops on specific topics, of which WAC is one. The advantage of this is that those who attend are interested, and that they all try out writing-to-learn strategies and come back to discuss on the basis of their experiences. The advantage of the Bergen model is that everyone gets exposed to the ideas. There has been an increasing interest in such workshops after the 'Quality Reform' with its new emphasis on writing.

Discipline Based Action Research Projects to Create Models and Document Results
One example of such action research projects is in the Department of the History of Religion, where there traditionally was no undergraduate writing except final exams. A writing intensive student seminar in the first semester resulted in statistically significant higher marks than for students who did not. Then a compulsory paper with teacher feedback was added to the 3. semester course, and for the first time none of the students failed. Initially some students and teachers were strongly opposed to making the paper compulsory, but students were unanimous in their support after they had gone through the experience. This underlines an important finding in my interview study 'Discipline specific writing and supervision': When students and teachers experience using different forms of writing they often change their negative attitudes towards compulsory papers.

Special Emphasis on 'Start Writing' Workshops for Master Students. 'Start Writing' workshops are intensive, discipline-specific workshops for master students who are just beginning their work on the thesis. They were initiated because many students waste a lot of time in the initial phases, partly due to writer's block. The workshops give students practice in writing-to-think as well as response strategies and are followed up by organised writing groups. In order to ensure integration of these workshops into the curriculum of each department, our policy was to teach such workshops only if two teachers agreed to be present and to co teach the next workshop and then to take over responsibility for the third. Over a three-year period, this strategy proved successful and contact was been established with such diverse subjects as economy, microbiology, art history, computer science and geography. Each subject established its own model, varying from a three day teacher directed 'Start writing' workshop where economy students test out their topic ideas, to a three week intensive workshop in microbiology at the end of the students' experimental phase, organized as writing groups discussing each others' drafts. In History of Religion, the students were very active partners in an action research project in order to try out a series of writing related initiatives at all levels, from first year to graduate students.[43]

---

[43] *A report was published describing this project (Lyngra 1999).*

Writing Groups. While writing groups or response groups are practiced in a process approach to writing in Norwegian schools, systematic use of such groups at university level was first used in the Writing Project at the University of Bergen. The focus was on building writing groups among Master students. We also sought out leaders in order to develop their competence to coach new groups as well as to teach writing workshops. An important element in the response groups has been the systematic training in response strategies and group interaction. Many Master students experience isolation as a major problem during the year when they worked on their dissertation. Our study of writing groups showed that writing groups counteracted this and helped them overcome writers' block.[44] An important side effect is that many students, who have experience from writing groups, become eager supporters of more emphasis on writing and act as agents of change both among students and faculty.

4   A NEW ERA FOR ACADEMIC WRITING AFTER THE 'QUALITY RE-
      FORM' OF HIGHER EDUCATION

The 'Quality Reform', which formally was introduced through Parliament Proposition 27/2001, affects both the structure and length of undergraduate and graduate studies, our assessment system, teaching, supervision and student learning. Internationalisation and globalisation of higher education are key factors behind the reform. Examples of alignment to international systems (ECTS) are that students will now get their Bachelor's degree in 3 instead of 4 years, and that our grading system will change from a very detailed numerical scale to a letter scale (A-F). Modulisation of all courses will also make it easier to include modules from other universities at home and abroad.

   In order to secure high quality of teaching and learning, the reform makes the following demands on all higher education institutions: 1) closer connection between teaching and assessment 2) more use of student active teaching methods 3) more student writing 4) close follow-up of each student and regular feedback on papers 5) increased student responsibility for attendance and participation 6) increased use of information and communication technology 7) more emphasis on formative assessment and alternatives to traditional exams 8) alternative ways of using external assessors. All these measures are clearly in line with international trends in higher education. Even though many university teachers endorse them and have advocated for instance increased use of writing and better follow-up of each student combined with clear demands on student responsibilities, there is a great deal of scepticism towards the reform in the academic community. Firstly, because there is so far no assurance that the reform will be followed up with increased resources, secondly because the reform will limit the traditional freedom of teacher as well as students (cf. the earlier quotation from professor 'Lund'), and thirdly because resource allocations will now be linked to student performance.

---

[44] *The Writing Project published a report based on a combination of observation and interviews of writing groups (Kjeldsen & Dysthe 1997) as well as a booklet on writing groups (Dysthe & Lied 1999). A useful basis for understanding writing groups was provided by Løkensgard Hoel's doctoral dissertation (1994, 2000).*

Changes in assessment are closely related to the increased emphasis on academic writing and will probably be the strongest driving force in changing actual teaching and learning practice. Portfolio assessment is specifically advocated as an alternative to traditional end-of-term exams because it leads to students working more regularly throughout the whole semester, because portfolios tie teaching and assessment closer together and because writing is seen as a way to learn. Many disciplines are now discussing what kind of portfolio models to choose and what the implications will be, for instance how to meet increasing demands of feedback and how to manage the logistics of an increased paper load. We try to encourage them also to discuss the need to teach a greater variety of genres in the disciplines, what kind of criteria they will use for assessing student collections of texts and to consider introducing multimedia texts and digital portfolios. The demand for change in so many areas at the same time poses formidable challenges on faculty, but this is also a unique opportunity for improvement. The deadline for implementing the 'Quality Reform' is the second semester of 2003, and in the meantime, development projects have been launched and writing courses for new students are being tried out.

One of the development projects, which involve writing, is a new course in Academic writing at the Humanities Faculty for first semester students. The course is workshop based and draws on process oriented writing pedagogy. It is taught by regular faculty and graduate students and focuses partly on general, partly on specific features of writing. Traditional educational systems where students specialise early have had no space for general writing courses at university level (Russell & Foster 2002). Norway occupies a middle position between the United States, where students specialize late, and England and France where students start their specialisation in secondary school. Norwegian students choose their field as they enter university, and the first semester consists of a general philosophy course in addition to the introductory course in Natural Science, Humanities, Social Sciences, Law or Medicine. Due to the reform, there is now an interest also in other faculties than the Humanities to include writing as part of their introductory course for new students.

Another major development project at the University of Bergen, which foreshadows the changes called for in the reform, is the First year compulsory philosophy course. In the year 2000, students were for the first time offered a choice between a traditional, lecture-based course with a sit-down exam at the end, and a group based model with compulsory attendance. The students choosing the latter had to submit a portfolio for assessment, consisting of three papers written during the course. The groups were combined discussion and writing groups, and every student also got individual coaching by the teacher. The main goal of the course was still on learning philosophy, but combined with learning to write an academic paper. This pedagogical experiment turned out to be an astounding success in terms of student satisfaction as well as very reduced rates of failure. The teachers, the majority being hired in part time staff, experienced however high works load. The change in teacher role from distanced lecturer to a combination of counsellor, writing supervisor and disciplinary oracle, was not easy. In spite of the high cost of the new writing workshop model, it will probably replace the traditional lecture-exam model. Since universities and colleges are now competing for students, taking good care of new students is of great importance in itself. One unanswered question, however, is whether such a tightly organised course will work for all students. The fact that students had a choice, could well have contributed to its success. Changing from a system with extreme student freedom to an unprecedented system of control, may, however, be problematic.

As can be inferred from my brief account of the 'Quality Reform', higher education in Norway is in a period of transition, which will greatly affect the status and amount of undergraduate student writing. It would be nice to interpret this as a fruit of the advocacy work of a number of writing specialists like myself scattered at different institutions of higher education. But the reasons behind the reform are of course to be found in the wider political and socio-economic contexts of higher education at the turn of the century. An analysis of these tendencies is beyond the scope of this paper, but increased awareness of the demand for communication skills in the students we 'produce' is one factor, another is competition for student enrolment, both among disciplines, institutions and nations.

It is obvious, however, that our work in the field of academic writing which I have described in this article and similar efforts at the other Norwegian universities, provide a basis of expertise which can be drawn on in our present situation.[45] All the three strategies I have focused on as characteristic of our work, now prove their usefulness: The university teachers who have attended the workshops for new faculty have at least got some insight in writing pedagogy which now turns out to be valuable when each discipline discusses how to integrate more writing. The small-scale action research projects provide local and easily accessible experience and expertise. Some of the graduate students who have experience from 'Start writing' workshops and writing groups are now key persons in training first year students. For many advocates of writing who have felt like lone voices in the wilderness, it is nice to see that writing in higher education now is becoming everybody's business.

---

[45] *One example of the close cooperation of writing experts at different universities is the book 'Writing to learn. Writing in Higher Education' (2000) which was written by three professors, Frøydis Hertzberg, University of Oslo, Torlaug Løkensgard Hoel, NTNU (Trondheim) and Olga Dysthe, University of Bergen. This book is being used as a resource book both by students and teachers across disciplines.*

CONTACTS – CONFLICTS – COOPERATION

A REPORT FROM THE WRITING LAB OF THE UNIVERSITY OF BIELEFELD

ANDREA FRANK*, STEFANIE HAACKE**
& CHRISTINA TENTE**

*Teaching and Studies at the University of Bielefeld,
**Bielefeld Writing Lab, University of Bielefeld, Germany

Abstract. In this chapter, we present the Writing Lab of the University of Bielefeld and its work as an interdisciplinary advice centre attached to a central university institution for research and development in higher education. We report in particular about our efforts to make academic writing an explicit subject of teaching in the faculties. Our approach is that we cooperate with staff with the members who take an interest in the issue of writing instruction. We have found that interest in the Writing Lab has constantly grown, contrary to our initial fear that the establishment of writing instruction within the individual departments would eliminate the lab.

We shall describe our experiences of cooperating with the academic staff and recount how we coped with the difficulties that arose and what procedures we found useful in helping to increase awareness of the importance of teaching academic writing in universities.

Keywords: Academic staff, Cooperation, Faculties, Interdisciplinary, Note taking, and Students' writing projects: do's and don'ts, implementation, and strategy.

1 THE WRITING LAB OF THE UNIVERSITY OF BIELEFELD
   – FINANCIAL AND INSTITUTIONAL FRAMEWORK

The Bielefeld Writing Lab is an interdisciplinary advice centre for the learning and teaching of academic writing. It was founded in 1993 as a pilot project modelled on Writing Labs or Writing Centres in the USA, as outlined by Gerd Bräuer in 1996.[46] North-Rhine Westphalian Ministry of Science initially financed the lab out of spe-

---

[46] See Bräuer (1996) for the history and concept of Writing Labs in the USA.

Frank, A., Haacke, S. & Tente, C. (2003). Contacts – Conflicts – Cooperation: A Report from the Writing Lab of the University of Bielefeld. In: G. Rijlaarsdam (Series Ed.) & L. Björk, G. Bräuer, L. Rienecker & P. Stray Jörgensen (Volume Eds.), Studies in Writing, Volume 12, Teaching Academic Writing in European Higher Education, pp. 165-174. © 2003 Kluwer Academic Publishers. Printed in the Netherlands.

cial funds designated to promote innovative university projects. Since 1998, the University of Bielefeld has borne the costs for one position, including the necessary infrastructure. These costs are shared among all university departments. In taking on financial responsibility for the Writing Lab, the University of Bielefeld has not only recognized the students' need for advice but has also accepted the need for institutional change in the field of writing instruction.[47]

The Writing Lab is linked to the Interdisciplinary Centre for Research and Development in Higher Education of the University of Bielefeld. The Writing Lab has been 'adopted', so to speak, by this institution, which offers courses in higher education methodology all over North-Rhine Westphalia. In addition, this centre is also involved in university research with regard to pedagogical issues. The Writing Lab has been given two offices and a seminar room, as well as valuable infrastructural services, such as photocopying facilities. For the establishment of a writing centre, we consider the link with an already existing institution as highly desirable. Without this connection, the viability of the Writing Lab would be considerably reduced.

We regard the interdisciplinary approach of the 'adopting' institution as even more significant. From the very beginning, the Writing Lab set out to be an institution for the benefits of students and teaching staff of all university departments. Being attached to any one single academic field would therefore have undermined this aim, as students and instructors of all other disciplines would not have felt they were being addressed. We believe, moreover, that the interdisciplinary approach is a vital element on which the success of the advice itself depends. This applies above all to the students. A non-discipline specific advice centre offers them a framework in which they can discuss their writing problems openly without having to fear adverse comment in their department: the advisor is thus in a position to intervene constructively. In addition, an interdisciplinary orientation is also an important prerequisite for cooperation with teaching staff in ensuring that writing problems can be addressed regardless of specific subject content (see section 3 in this chapter).

In universities without an interdisciplinary institution for university teaching methods, the students' advice centre could offer to act as partner to cooperate in writing projects. The Bielefeld Writing Lab has explored this option in an inter-university project for cooperation with students' advisors of other universities.[48]

---

[47] *Peggy Jolly (1984) gives insight into the diverse models of funding for writing centres in the USA. The motivation to finance writing centres or other developmental programs in the USA seems to be quite different from the motivation to do the same in Germany. This difference seems to depend on general differences in the financing structure of institutions of higher education in the USA and in Germany, where universities are financed by the states and not partially through charging fees to the students: The longer a student studies at a university in the USA, the more money he will bring to the university. So the main argument for writing centres in the USA, cited by Peggy Jolly, is that: '... it will increase the holding power of the college...' (Jolly 1984:104). In Germany, the main argument is that writing centres help students to shorten the time they have to spend at the university.*

[48]*See 'Schreiblabor Bielefeld' (1999) and Tente (1999). Tente & Büker (1999) contains material about writing advice geared to the specific advisory situation of the general students' advice centres.*

2   THE WRITING LAB'S FIELDS OF ACTIVITY

From the beginning, the Writing Lab has pursued two aims: firstly to support directly students who have difficulty in producing their writing assignments, and secondly to increase the awareness at the university concerning the major problems of academic writing and the need for staff to address them specifically in their teaching.

The Writing Lab, therefore, addresses students, tutors[49] and academic staff with their activities. Whereas the response from students has been considerable from the beginning, there have been a few obstacles to overcome with regard to the collaboration with and among instructors. However, we have in the meantime been able to establish a very diverse cooperation network. We shall highlight this aspect of our work,[50] as we regard cooperation with academic staff as being a matter of great strategic importance for the process of institutionalising the Writing Lab. In order to elucidate the framework of the Writing Lab as a whole, we first present the institution's fields of activity.

2.1 Help for Students

As an advice centre for students, the Writing Lab has developed two basic forms of assistance: we have fixed times when we are available for consultation without previous appointment and we offer individual consultation as well as workshops. The entire advice programme is designed to enable students to resolve their writing problems as independently as possible.

We advise people who come to the Writing Lab's consultation with general writing problems and extensive questions about writing assignments to take part in a workshop, where basic skills for academic writing are taught. The workshops are practically oriented; they make clear that writing is, by its nature, a process, and they provide training in constructive writing techniques.

The workshops take the form of two-day intensive courses. The group members usually come from different departments; the number of participants is restricted to 14. It has proved beneficial to offer seminars for two different types of participants: a) for students who have not yet reached an advanced level of studies (but who have, however, already had some experience of writing) and b) for students in the final phase of their course of studies, where they prepare a thesis.

Individual advice is only given to students with more considerable writing difficulties where the lack of orientation is too overwhelming for them. The intervention with individual advice aims at determining more exactly the causes of the writing

---

[49]*In the German system, tutors are undergraduates, usually in the advanced phase of their studies, who work with junior students in small groups*

[50] *Detailed accounts of the Writing Lab's other fields of activity have already been published: for instance Furchner, Großmaß, & Ruhmann (1999) and Ruhmann (1997a) on the concept of writing advice. Frank et al. (1999) and Frank, Hollmann, & Ruhmann (1995) contains an account of the project.*

problems and at enabling the students to come to terms with their problems through special writing assignments.

A variety of other problems are often related to general writing difficulties – they can be related to study techniques; motivation, content, and they can be emotional in nature. If we get the impression that serious problems exist on other levels, which impair the student's working ability, we recommend recourse to the university's general and psychosocial advice centre.

2.2 Help for Tutors

We believe that tutors play a special role in teaching academic writing. It is often their task to help students produce their first term paper or respond to other writing assignments. As they are often closer in many respects to the students than members of the teaching staff can be, they provide a framework in the tutorials in which students can speak more openly about their insecurities and can ask what they may consider as embarrassing or very basic questions.

That is why we organise training seminars for tutors of the University of Bielefeld – this takes place within the framework of the tutor programme organised by the Interdisciplinary Centre for Research and Development in Higher Education. Here we discuss with the tutors how they can deal with specific questions about academic writing and how they can help the students to produce texts successfully.[51]

2.3 Help for Academic Staff

We offer advice to members of staff for the planning of writing-intensive teaching. We present appropriate material for writing tasks and discuss the integration of our methodological and pedagogical concepts into the seminar plan. Furthermore, we ourselves take on teaching units within the instructors' seminars and – often in the presence of the teachers – practise various phases of the writing process with the students. What we offer in these demonstrations depends on the level of the students: We might for instance practise note-taking, using secondary literature, finding and elaborating an issue for analysis, or we work on text revision. Afterwards, we discuss the questions arising from the exercises with the students and their teacher.

In addition, we distribute among instructors a brochure once or twice per semester in which we report on new developments in the field of writing methodology, on current publications concerning academic writing, on concepts for writing-intensive seminars, and on our current offers of assistance.[52] With these brochures we want to continue to highlight the significance of writing as a key qualification for learning and at the same time demonstrate ways of teaching the practice of it. Furthermore,

---

[51] *See Mangasser-Wahl (1997) regarding the concept of writing tutorials. See Knauf & Schmithals (2000), pp. 92-122 for more on the content aspect of tutorials in the training of writing skills.*
[52] *These brochures (P.S.: Post aus dem Schreiblabor [Post from the Writing Lab]) are available at the following Internet address: http:/www.uni-bielefeld.de/slab/index.htm.*

the brochures ensure that the presence of the Writing Lab maintains acknowledged by the university.

3   COOPERATION WITH ACADEMIC STAFF

As described above, we have been pursuing two aims with the Bielefeld Writing Lab concept. Firstly, students are to receive support in coping with writing problems. Secondly, the Writing Lab aims, in the long term, at structural change in the university instruction, making writing not only an integral part of the courses but also a subject of teaching. We hope to achieve this quite substantial change through cooperation with the academic staff – not by institutional decree, but as a direct result of individual teaching experience.

Our cooperative approach is designed to make the repertoire of writing methodology available to staff members who take an interest in the issue. This material has partly been developed in the Writing Lab itself deriving from the work of our student advice service; the material also comes from university writing projects in the USA.[53] The Writing Lab also depends on dialogue and exchange with academic staff of the various departments for the development of their own discipline-specific concepts.

What steps has the Writing Lab undertaken in order to set the dialogue with academic staff in motion? And what difficulties have to be overcome thereby? At first, we tried to establish contact with the staff through a wide distribution of written communications and invitations to workshops. However, there was little response in the beginning. This made us contact those teachers directly, who had, in one form or another, already offered seminars on academic writing. Out of this exchange, a study group on academic writing arose in which a number of instructors from various departments participated. Questions concerning academic writing were discussed in this group and training exercises were developed for the different phases of the writing process – some of this work was done in short workshops.

As the Writing Lab has become better known at the university, we find ourselves advising a growing number of individual teachers with regard to the training of writing skills. It seems to make sense to initially focus on those teachers who have shown an interest in writing issues and to support them in teaching the appropriate skills. Such cooperation can, under positive circumstances, have a long term impact on curricular structures, bringing other staff to include writing-oriented seminars in their repertoire or having them use their influence to ensure that writing practice is included in introductory classes.[54]

Needless to say, academic teachers who approach the Writing Lab tend to be those who regard the teaching of academic writing techniques as meaningful and necessary, and who see our practically oriented methods as likely to reinforce their own forms of teaching.

---

[53] *See for example the guidelines on the home page of the National Writing Centers Association in the USA: http://departments.colgate.edu/diw/NWCA.html.*
[54] *See Furchner, Ruhmann, & Tente (1999).*

It is more difficult to establish cooperation with the very large number of academic teachers who expect students to be able to write their papers without explicit guidance[55] and to whom our practically oriented style of teaching seems rather alien. Most university teachers are unfamiliar with teaching strategies that provide training in the structuring of the writing process. In Germany, higher education traditionally involves intensive preoccupation with content and methods of specific academic subjects, but very little explicit concern with the techniques of academic writing. A recent German publication[56] by university teachers reports, for the benefit of students; on the university teachers' own experience of academic writing. It describes the do-it-yourself-methods employed by them – in these cases mostly, of course, with virtuosity – and the fear, lack of enthusiasm and indeed antipathy with which many of those who are now professors had to contend while writing their theses. Whereas this publication gives insight into the difficulties of the writing process – encountered by 'professional' writers(!) – in general, however, little is said about writing pedagogy.

It often proves necessary in discussion with academic teachers to point out that students have problems with writing and how these problems arise. Many teachers believe that the skills required for academic writing are, or should be, taught in school.[57] We therefore try to explain why the qualifications attained in school are usually not enough to produce academic papers without further support. We pass on the impression we receive through our advisory work that students very often begin the work on their papers rather unsystematically. For instance, due to inadequate knowledge about the writing process, they fail to distinguish between the different phases of text production, trying to work concurrently on steps belonging to different stages of the writing process, and thereby overtaxing themselves.[58] We also explain that students often do not know what is expected of them: for instance the ability to limit an academic topic, to structure it, to establish a central theme, and to select appropriate secondary literature from the wealth of publications available.

In our conversation with the teachers we begin with their perception of the major writing problems by enquiring about their experience with providing advice to students. In this context, they often express dissatisfaction with the students' work, which can lead to a discussion of the underlying difficulties and students' insecurity. Thus the teachers often come to recognize themselves that explicit teaching of writing skills is meaningful and important.

In order to ensure that the help we offer corresponds as closely as possible to the needs of our partners, we always discuss directly with them what we do in the teaching unit we organise for their seminar. We make every effort to respond flexibly and creatively to the various teaching contexts and specific requirements of the teachers.

In order to be able to adapt to the concrete situation in the seminar, we find out what aims the teacher is seeking to achieve in terms of the subject, what semester

---

[55] See Kruse & Jakobs (1999).

[56] Narr & Stary (1999).

[57] Those staff members who argue thus often seem to be implying that students who have not been adequately prepared in school to write academic papers are not qualified to study.

[58] See Kruse & Jakobs (1999) and Ruhmann (1996).

the students are in, and what questions and writing problems we should address in our unit.

This forms the basis for our work in designing appropriate exercises and planning the class together with the teacher.

We believe it is vital for successful cooperation that we are very clear as to our own role. We try to draw the line very precisely between advice regarding the subject or content and advice pertaining to the writing process as such. This distinction is essential to prevent teachers getting the impression that we are trying to interfere with their role as instructors and to call into question what they demand from their students.[59] Many teachers are most surprised to hear, for instance, that a regular part of our advisory work consists of helping students prepare for discussions with their academic supervisors so that they can clarify the questions they have regarding the content of their papers. To cooperate constructively with academic staff it is essential to establish very clearly how we perceive each other's competence and the limits of that competence as a basis to complement one another and to learn from one another.

The following example illustrates how certain scepticism of academic staff towards our advice service can be overcome:

At a meeting of an interdisciplinary group, an academic teacher vociferously challenged the Writing Lab on the grounds that it claimed to impart competence to students which they had already acquired in school and that it took upon itself to advise students without having any professional competence in the academic discipline the students are coming from. The teacher argued that having a study technique advisory service for students outside each individual academic discipline was neither meaningful nor feasible.

After extensive discussion, he agreed to invite us to his preparatory seminar so that we could give a presentation on how to use secondary literature in writing academic papers. With the students of his course, we practiced different aspects of note taking, and how to incorporate secondary literature into their writing.[60] The ensuing seminar discussion, which took place in the presence of the teacher, demonstrated that students felt a considerable need for clarification as to the proper academic use of secondary literature. 'How can I be sure that I have properly understood what I have read?', 'How can one express something in one's own words which has been perfectly formulated in the book?', 'How can I clearly indicate in my paper what I think of the passage I have quoted?' and 'May I, must I express my own opinion in a term paper?' These were some of the questions raised by the students. It thus became evident that one field of academic work which the teacher had regarded as being quite unproblematic for students (that of note taking in the process of reading) was by no means altogether clear, and that students had merely lacked an opportunity to raise the issue. Furthermore, we were able to demonstrate to this teacher, who

---

[59] *Stephen North describes several aspects of this distinction in his famous essay 'The Idea of a Writing Center' from 1984 and points out: '... we never play student-advocates in teacher-student relationships...' (North 1995, orig. 1984: 79).*

[60] *Kruse & Ruhmann (1999).*

had originally been so critical of our advisory service, that it is indeed possible to discuss questions pertaining to the writing process without interfering in the academic subject of the assignment.

Productive experiences with new forms of teaching are an important prerequisite for institutional change – among the latter, we would welcome for instance the inclusion of essay training in introductory courses. Such experience forms the basis of training, which the Writing Lab is planning to design for junior members of the academic staff within the framework of the preparatory training programme for young university teachers.

4   STRATEGIC CONSIDERATIONS FOR THE ESTABLISHMENT OF WRITING CENTRES

The fact that the original Writing Lab pilot project was implemented after six years (even if with only a relatively small staff) and has now attained the status of an established institution is due to particularly favourable local circumstances and also to the various strategic initiatives undertaken by the Writing Lab. We want to present some considerations briefly in the context of current trends in the politics of higher education in Germany.

North-Rhine Westphalia's plan of action[61] was among the favourable circumstances, which made it possible in the first place for us to try out an American idea for the improvement of university teaching.

At least some of the states of Germany were prepared in the 1990s to promote experimental university reform projects, which seemed likely to bring about a speedy increase in the number of students completing their studies. We have the impression that this interest has meanwhile abated. This is due in the main to the financial straits of the states, which are generally subject to budgetary restrictions. However, it may also be due to the fact that the promotion of individual projects has not led directly to visible structural change in the universities. It is therefore not surprising that at present almost all organisations involved in academic policy-making hope to achieve the decisive university structural reform through the introduction of consecutive courses of studies like the BA and the MA rather than Diploma courses.

It could make sense to set up future writing projects in this context. Awareness of the key role of writing competence may be heightened if a distinction is made between professional and academic degrees, and if it is thereby clarified what students in each case need to learn in very specific ways that will include the use of writing in rather specific ways. The University of Bielefeld is a modern campus university where all departments are located in one building. Here everything literally happens under one roof. Any seminar room or office can be reached from any university location within five minutes, and, therefore, the psychological inhibitions against entering into 'foreign territory' are much lower and the communication network among the departments and programs is much closer than in universities where buildings are scattered all over the city.

---

[61] *In the German federal system, the 'Länder' (states) are responsible for university finance.*

This architectural fact is of quite some importance for the impact of the Writing Lab: both students and teachers are accustomed to communication across departmental borders, and interdisciplinary projects are commonplace. Nevertheless, even under these favourable circumstances continuous propagation of the project Writing Lab remains essential.

From the beginning, the Writing Lab has therefore sought contact and cooperation with academic staff – if only to investigate their view on the major writing problems among students. Over time, various forms of cooperation (see sections 2 and 3 of this chapter) developed out of those contacts. In addition to such cooperation with individual teachers, it is also necessary to establish contact with university administrators, who would influence decisions about the establishment of a writing centre: for example, we invited representatives of the President's Office to meet for an exchange of information and views on the role of writing in higher education. In this regard, it proved to be useful that from the beginning of its activities, the Writing Lab always documented its work, which provides evidence of the importance of such an entity.

The Writing Lab also initiates or supports other projects in the faculties. It was, for instance, able to prevail upon the Senate Commission for Teaching, Student Affairs and Further Training to use the annually available 'Special Fund to Support Outstanding Activities for the Improvement of Teaching' for projects promoting students' writing competence. It was thus possible to assist other projects involved in developing writing skills. Among these is an essay-writing training course organised by the Philosophy Department and a project on domain-specific writing. A number of additional initiatives have taken shape, such as an interfaculty writing advisory centre for foreign students and a project called 'Writing and Speaking Workshop' in the Faculty for Linguistics and Literary Studies. These initiatives make use in various ways of the Writing Lab's competence and of the expertise developed here initially for the field of academic writing. A network of cooperating initiatives has been established for the purpose of imparting writing skills.

5   PRACTICAL EXPERIENCE IS MORE IMPORTANT THAN ABSTRACT PRINCIPLES

No idea is so good that it can be put into practice under any circumstances. That is why no pilot project can be directly transferred into a different context. Every idea must be adapted to the specific conditions of its environment and further developed within the framework of the given options. That is why a writing centre will be different in every university.

We would like to pass on what we have above all learnt from our own experience: a) how important publicity is, so that people hear about the activities being undertaken; b) how necessary it is to win allies and partners through appropriate public relations work. Everybody involved in the issue – teachers, advisors, student representatives, the President's Office – should be informed about the insights that have been obtained about present service and future plans. It is also important to involve these people directly in the work of the writing centre and to make use of their specific competence. In regard to the different conditions under which academic teachers operate it is furthermore essential to demonstrate that training writing competence as a component of the regular teaching is neither superfluous nor an unreasonable demand, but that it actually enhances the students' ability to cope with the content of any academic subject.

As the Writing Lab has become increasingly known at Bielefeld University, we find ourselves advising a growing number of individual teachers with regard to the training of writing skills. Such cooperation can have a long-term impact involving instructors including writing-oriented seminars in their repertoire and demanding that writing practice become part of any introductory class.[62] Needless to say, academic teachers who approach the Writing Lab tend to be those who regard the teaching of academic writing techniques as meaningful and necessary, and who regard our practically oriented methods as likely to reinforce their own ways of teaching.

In contrast, it is more difficult to establish cooperation with a very large number of academic teachers who expect students to be able to write their papers without explicit guidance.[63] We are afraid that only 'institutional decree', making the teaching of writing a required part of the curriculum, will help us to offer our service also to those instructors.

From the beginning the Writing Lab has sought to counteract the tendency innate in some university reform projects to establish a monopoly in a given problem area. This kind of specialization must be avoided in order to prevent institutional isolation. The Writing Lab at the University of Bielefeld began its work under the paradoxical premise that it will have furnished proof of its success once it has rendered itself superfluous. Now we know that this pint can never be reached as long as we improve our own problem awareness as well as that of instructors, students, and administrators.

---

[62] See Furchner, Ruhmann, & Tente (1999).
[63] See Kruse & Jakobs (1999). Gary A. Olson (1984:155) points out, how damaging the attitude of such professors for the motivation of staff members of a writing centre can be.

AN ANALYSIS OF THE DISCOURSE OF
STUDY SUPPORT AT THE LONDON INSTITUTE

SUSAN ORR & MARGO BLYTHMAN

The London Institute in London, UK

Abstract. In this chapter, we describe two approaches that exist in the UK framing discussions of student writing development in higher education. The first one is known as the 'academic literacies' approach and the second one can be referred to, as the 'standards are falling' approach. Our own research locates within the former paradigm. We then describe the context within which we work at the London Institute and we problematise the discourse that subject lecturers use to describe study support. The final section identifies the implications of our research.

Keywords: Academic literacies, Conceptions, Discourse, Literacy, Pedagogy, and Study support.

1   AN ACADEMIC LITERACIES APPROACH: AN OVERVIEW

Our research is located within an academic literacies approach. Researchers within this perspective construct literacy in radically different ways relative to previous researchers. It would be a simplification to represent the main proponents of this approach as speaking with one voice but several themes do emerge that are well represented by Lillis, who sees literacy not as a single autonomous entity. She argues that literacy is not functional or fixed; instead, it is contested and socially constructed (Lillis 1997). Thus, literacy is invented and reinvented by people who use it (Bartholomae 1985). This leads one to look at issues beyond that of grammar and spelling, in fact, these are rarely the focus of study within this paradigm. Academic literacy theorists focus on issues of voice, identity, and power relations, and they point to the centrality of epistemology:

> 'Epistemological levels of knowing what to say and how to say it in a specific disciplinary context' (Lea & Street 1998).

Orr, S. & Blythman, M. (2003). An Analysis of the Discourse of Study Support at the London Institute. In: G. Rijlaarsdam (Series Ed.) & L. Björk, G. Bräuer, L. Rienecker & P. Stray Jörgensen (Volume Eds.), Studies in Writing, Volume 12, Teaching Academic Writing in European Higher Education, pp. 175-184. © *2003 Kluwer Academic Publishers. Printed in the Netherlands.*

The moral outrage expressed in other research on literacy in higher education (see below) is acknowledged and dismissed (Creme & Lea 1999).

Academic literacies literature does not use the skills-based deficit vocabulary of *poor* literacy or problem writing (found in Winch & Wells 1995). Instead, it addresses the mismatch between what the student brings to the learning situation and what the lecturer expects. There is no attempt to quantify students' literacy; instead, this approach aims to probe into students' experience of writing as a social practice (Lea & Stierer 2000). This relativist approach draws on post-modern ideas thus standing in contrast to the other groups interested in literacy in higher education.

The use of the plural 'literacies' is significant to show that literacy is not a fixed commodity, 'it has many aspects and many expressions.' (Street 1993). John Clancy argues that:

> 'Literacy has many forms and literate behaviour, by the same individual, may vary markedly according to context, content and intention' (Clancy 1985).

2   THE 'STANDARDS ARE FALLING' APPROACH: AN OVERVIEW

In contrast to the approach outlined above there are those within education who adhere to the 'standards are falling' approach. For example, Lamb publishes about the alleged decline of literacy standards in higher education (Lamb 1992). Lamb's studies attempt to measure students' literacy skills today and benchmark them against the literacy skills of an apparently mythical golden era. Proponents of this model tend to focus on the surface features of writing such as grammar, punctuation and spelling, and there is an implicit assumption that surface mistakes should not be made by any one who has left school, particularly if they expect to study in higher education. Within this paradigm, writing is portrayed as a skill that is essentially a technique. Researchers argue that there are categorically correct and incorrect ways of writing (Lamb 1992). This contrasts to the relativist approach of the academic literacies proponents.

Winch and Wells seek to evidence 'poor current standards of literacy among higher education students.' (Winch & Wells 1995). Their abstract offers insight into this model of literacy:

> 'This paper records both dissatisfaction and evidence of current poor standards of literacy notably in the areas of the written word among higher education students.' (Winch & Wells 1995).

Their pejorative notion of 'poor' is very hard to quantify and is, after all, a relative concept. Indeed the use of the word 'poor' in addition to the use of the word 'current' implicitly compares the literacy levels of today to that of another era. They conclude:

> ' ... there is a prima facie cause for concern that standards of student literacy are not what one might expect at the level of higher education.' (Winch & Wells 1995).

What is expected? Is there a set level? How is this defined? These questions remain unanswered. As such this paper typifies the morally outraged, 'standards are falling' approach to literacy in higher education.

The following lecturer quotations from the work of Clark and Lorenzini resonate with moral overtones of a pejorative nature:

> 'Some students don't seem to appreciate that clarity and accuracy actually matter – I get comments like 'All my teachers have said things like that,' indicating a certain complacency with defective writing!

> It seems to me that the problems we are increasingly finding are much more deeply rooted than (…) stylistic infelicities (…) the problem is that students have so little understanding of sentence structure, which my generation were taught at primary school.' (Lecturers cited in Clark & Lorenzini 1999).

As Evans and Crivello argue:

> 'Higher education is caught up in a battle to prevent the so called 'skills deficit' of new students bringing down overall 'standards''. (Evans and Crivello 1995).

The academic literacies model and the standards are falling model are mutually oppositional. It is, however, important to note that there are other paradigms within which researchers analyse writing development in higher education. For example, Lea and Stierer identify three approaches, namely the study skills model, the writing in the disciplines model and the academic literacies model (Lea and Stierer 2000). Evidently, the two outlined above represent polarities between which there lies a range of perspectives.

3   STUDY SUPPORT AT THE LONDON INSTITUTE

As practitioners working within an academic literacies model, we wrestle with the tensions inherent in viewing literacy in the way described above, whilst supporting students within a system that places emphasis on grammar, spelling and the conventions of the academy. We aim to develop students' self awareness, to encourage students to understand/challenge the role of the academy; while at the same time equipping them with the skills they need to survive and achieve by the rules of the dominant educational ideology (Lillis 1997, Lea 1994). We work with students in one to one support and small group support with an emphasis on the whole writing process at deep (compositional) and surface levels.

Within this paradigm we ensure that study support:[64]

> ' … takes account of the variations in literacy practices amongst students and gives value to their different backgrounds and the different literacies they employ in their home contexts.' (Street 1993).

In our chapter on micro-politics in this book, we describe study support within the London Institute and we stress how important it is for the study team to work closely with course teams in the college. This is for several reasons:
* Working with course teams ensures that study support is situated within the students' curricula

---

[64] *By study support, we refer to one to one and small group support that is offered to students in addition to their learning programme. The aim of study support is to enhance student achievement and raise levels of retention.*

- We offer support to course teams in a number of ways, for example we help them write assignments that facilitate learning
- On a day-to-day basis we liaise with course teams about individual students and their learning needs.
- We rely on course teams to suggest to students that a visit to us might improve their grades. We are too small a team to pass this message on to every student throughout their studies.

The factors listed above underline the importance of a partnership model of study support. Our practice is predicated on this principle.

4   RATIONALE FOR OUR PERSPECTIVES

A micro political analysis of study support at the London Institute has shown us that successful partnerships have been developed with some lecturers while in other cases we have been less successful. A related point is that, as stated above, we rely on lecturers to pass on messages to students about study support. We therefore reflected on the fact that, whilst we had advertised the study support service to colleagues and students, we had never asked them what their understanding of study support was. Thus, we sent out what we considered to be clear messages to course teams but we were not listening to how those messages had been mediated to lecturers or students. In this section, we discuss these issues with a particular focus on subject lecturers' conceptions of study support and study support pedagogy. The aim of this section is to better understand the messages that might be passed onto students about our service. We speculated that subject lecturers' conceptions of study support might impact on their approach to working in partnership with the study support team. In this section, we seek to problematise subject lecturers' discourse[65] of study support. As Bakhtin argues:

> ' ... language is not a neutral medium that passes freely and easily in to the private property of the speaker's intentions; it is populated, overpopulated, with the intentions of others.' (Bakhtin 1986).

The discourse of the study team will not be analysed here but it can be characterised as the discourse of student potential (Skidmore 1998) that promotes an inclusive non-categorical view of the student as described by Harris and Thorp (1999) and Simpson (1996).

5   DISCUSSION

In the section below, we will address the following areas: (1) Conceptions of expertise, (2) Conceptions of pedagogy, (3) Conceptions of the students, and (4) Conceptions of decline.

---

[65] *Discourse as expressed by Gee (1990): 'discourses speak to each other through individuals and the individual gives body to it every time he or she acts or speaks and thus carries it and ultimately changes it through time.'*

5.1 Conceptions of Expertise

In our contacts and work with subject lecturers over a period of over ten years, we note that study support can be characterized in three ways that reveal the subject lecturers' conceptions of expertise.

The Content/Skills Conception

We have encountered the content/skills conception where lecturers describe the study support team as the study support experts. Within this orientation, the subject lecturers are the content experts and the study support team are the skills experts. A hidden message contained in the view is that we are the non-experts about the subject. Lecturers in this category clearly separate the work of the study support team and the work of the course team as the following quotations, extracted from an interview with a subject lecturer, underline:

> 'It is not our responsibility to pick up weaker skills-numeracy, literacy, communication … I deal with what I know'

> 'the focus is on the content'

They describe the study support team as experts within their own domain:

> 'They [the students] should do whatever the study skill tutor felt was appropriate … the study support people are experts at it.' (Orr & Blythman 2000).

This lecturer views himself as a non-expert in the area of study support. He strives to delegate this area to others to the extent that he feels he has no expertise what so ever, not even allowing himself to speculate on the nature of the problem or why pupils might leave school still experiencing difficulties with writing. His conception of himself as a non-expert concerning anything beyond his subject area is widespread in our institution, and we suspect that it relates to the vocational curriculum. The London Institute is comprised of two colleges (amongst five) that are specifically designed to prepare students for employment in fashion or print related industries. As a result of this vocational bias, the London Institute sometimes recruits lecturers directly from industry rather than from other universities. This may explain why this lecturer does not appear to be acculturated into educational discourse. He feels ill equipped to articulate the nature of student difficulty and proposes that there are clearly delineated distinctions between the work of study support teams and the work of his course team:

> 'At the end of the day, what we [subject lecturers] are looking for is subject matter … I'm looking to see if they know the subject matter. The focus is not on skills as such. I deal with what I know.'

The implication is, that *content* is autonomous and can be seen in isolation from other factors. How *content* is researched, understood, mediated, applied and constructed is not articulated. The lecturer suggests that he is able to look at a text for *content* in isolation from form. The mutual exclusivity of these categories (content/skills) is further underlined by his comment that study support does not need to have any vocational relevance. When asked about the materials we should use in study support to support his students effectively he replies:

> 'I wouldn't have a clue about materials; it doesn't matter if they are vocational.'

Thus, content can be delivered without recourse to the process of studying and study skills can be taught without recourse to a subject area. This implies that the two are independent and can exist alone, skills with no subject and subject with no skills.

These words suggest that a partnership approach with his course would be doomed to failure. There are no words used that describe partnership or an overlapping of responsibilities. Thus, his conception of study support appears to dictate our practice.

The Partnership Approach

Other lecturers use the language of partnership. We interviewed one course leader who has worked closely with the study support team and the extracts from her interview employ the discourse of partnership (Orr and Blythman 2000). Her views suggest that she thinks that there is an overlap between the expertise of the study support team and course team. In addition there is a reference to the additional expertise that belongs to the study team:

> 'I am hoping that when a student comes to me with a piece of writing that is full of all sorts of mistakes you are able to explain to them what mistakes they have made and why ... perhaps you have strategies to help them recover that.'

This lecturer signals that the boundaries between her course and study support are less clearly defined than they were for the lecturer quoted above:

> 'Sometimes we think we use words they understand, but we don't ... you offer support for language; written skills, research skills, study processes.'

This is expanded later in the interview when she says that the study support team does the following:

> 'Correcting misunderstandings about the nature and direction they [the students] are going.'

This suggests that the study team facilitates study and that the study team and the course team have a common interest.

The Leftovers Approach

Thirdly, we have encountered what we have labelled as the leftovers approach. An example of this approach emerged in earlier research (Orr and Blythman 2000). One lecturer interviewed was articulate about the work of the study team and used words that reflected the language of the study support team. However she was clear that she is the 'content' person. The study team is responsible for what is left over:

> 'Content is my job.'

They [the study team] are dealing with the things I haven't got time to deal with in my lessons

'Essay writing skills? I haven't got the time.'

This identifies the study team as the non-experts who are doing things that are squeezed out due to lack of time. A lower status is conferred onto the study team who has no control over their curricula. In this case, what we do in the study support service is dictated by what the lecturer does not do in class.

5.2 Conceptions of Pedagogy

Subject lecturers' conceptions about study support pedagogy vary. One of the lecturers interviewed spoke extensively about study support pedagogy so we will focus on her perspective. Unlike the other lecturers interviewed, she had actually asked students what they do when they come to study support. She described the work of the study team as follows:

> 'According to one student, ... you read over her assignment, rather than saying, 'I am going to teach you this,' you ask them what they have done so far and then you work together on it. You read over what has been produced so far and point out mistakes, suggest ways of going about it such as how to structure an essay, a two way street. From what I can gather, you don't write it for them, which is what they would like.'

The language accurately reflects study support pedagogy at the London Institute. What is significant about this quotation is that it is the student who has passed on the message, not the study support team. This has implications for our publicity and dissemination strategy.

5.3 Conceptions of the Student

In our years of working in the field of writing pedagogy, we note that many subject lecturers describe student-writing difficulties in terms of weaknesses. Thus, it is not a question of students having weak skills instead; they are described as the weaker students. (This may seem a trivial semantic distinction, but fierce battles have been fought to recognise that people have disabilities or people live with AIDS instead of being the victims, the disabled, the AIDS sufferers). Lecturers' discourse can imply that there is a fixed group of weak students who are different in some essential but unspecified way. This suggests a fixed ability conception of student learning. Fixed ability models of learning preclude the possibility that a weak student could become a high achieving student. It seems that they will be weak for the duration of the course (... their life ...?). This is contrasted with the anti-essentialist, non-categorical view of the study support team that stresses that students may need support for a wide variety of reasons but that they are not different in any categorical sense from those students who do not seek support (Harris & Thorp 1999).

Here we will focus on the views of two lecturers in order to illustrate two particular conceptions of writing difficulty. The first lecturer has a uni-dimensional view of student difficulty, which can be contrasted with the second lecturer's multi-dimensional model.

In the extract below, the lecturer does not attempt to describe the complexity of students' writing development and students' construction of knowledge.

'It's the weaker students ... they need help.'

Another lecturer offered a different perspective when she identified three types of students who might attend study support:

- It is a lack of basic skills (...) maybe it was introduced to them in a way that they couldn't take on board
- then there is another level of student difficulty, definitely learning difficulty, dyslexia, that kind of thing
- then there is a third group of students who doesn't have learning difficulties, it is not about grammar, it is a lack of confidence. (Orr & Blythman 2000).

This description of student difficulty has variety and depth. This is a more textured, developed perception of student need. Within this perspective students could move in and out of support and the distinctions between those who need support and those who do not are not categorical. This contrasts sharply with the first lecturers' language because her language echoes the discourse of student potential.

5.4 Conceptions of Decline

Our interviews and interactions with colleagues have revealed that many lecturers use the language of literacy decline using language that Turner would identify as *linguistic bigotry* (Turner 1999). The quotations below exemplify this stance:

'The Application of Number lecturer does say that generally today students are weak.'

'They have to know the difference between there, their and they're. And some of them don't ... you are kind of amazed that they get through school without it.'

'The terrible mistakes [made by students]'

'Some people just don't know, I am quite horrified actually; the standard of secondary education has dropped within my career span of seven years. I always ask them to word process and then they rely on the spell check an awful lot, my evidence of this is ask any student to write a lot and they always write allot [sic!].'

'You can sneak around not being able to read and write.'

These quotations are significant for three reasons. Firstly, these comments are not set in the context of the massification of higher education with attendant changes in student profile. The expansion of higher education relates directly to the profile of student on the course (see Blythman *et al.*, this volume on micro-politics for fuller explanation). Secondly, it is significant that surface errors are deemed to evidence general educational decline. As Turner argues 'Lapses in grammar, punctuation and spelling therefore indicate a much wider societal moral and educational decline.' (Turner 1999). Thirdly, the emotive use of the word 'horrified' again supports Turner's view that there is 'a pervasive tendency to comment on language use both in social and moral terms.' (Turner 1999). Moral outrage is expressed through the interview transcripts in subtle ways that confirm the views of Cameron and Turner (Turner 1999, Cameron 1995).

6   CONCLUSION

We are not claiming that we can generalise from these interviews and observations, but our findings do have implications for practice. We argue that lecturers have different conceptions about study support that may affect the messages they pass on to students about the service. For this reason we need to explore ways that we can use our *students* to publicise our service. As users of study support, they are particularly well placed to pass on messages about study support pedagogy. In this chapter, we have identified divergent pedagogic discourses that suggest that the study team is *contained* by the conceptions held by the lecturers. The conceptions that emerge serve to reduce the potential for the study support unit to be constituted within an academic literacies paradigm. Literacies are identified as functional in nature with particular emphasis on surface features (*grammar, spelling, English skills*). In the words of Turner:

> '... an emaciated conceptualisation of what is involved diminishes the status of writing development practitioners.' (Turner 1999).

The foregrounding of surface features may reduce the opportunities for us to work with students on deep, compositional features of their texts. Hinkle suggests that if subject lecturers locate student difficulty within surface features of the text, our opportunities to engage fully with student texts are diminished (Hinkle 1998). By exploiting opportunities for student mediated publicity we are disseminating a model of study support that matches the actual service provided (rather than lecturers' models of that service).

There was a very interesting 'slip', which occurred in the middle of one of our interviews with colleagues. The extract is as follows:

> 'I think they [the study team] are also helping out with the for... international students ... well they called them that in the last university, it was ok ...it was all right there.'

In this extract, the lecturer had started to call the international students *foreign students* or *foreigners*, then mid-word she corrected herself. This evokes a politically correct atmosphere where there are certain authorized codes of reference. She felt that she had to explain this 'slip', and she moved on to another subject promptly after this occurrence. Skidmore refers to the authoritarian discourse that this extract evidences (Skidmore 1998).

The 'slip' referred to in her narrative underlines a problem for study support. If no agreed discourse exists then there is clearly a danger that lecturers will want to get the language 'right' and yet not know how to do this. Thus, there is a danger that they may echo the words of the study team without understanding what the language connotes. It may be more effective if opposing discourses are allowed to emerge and be debated rather than burying variant discourses in the interests of political correctness.

Skidmore cautions against aiming to arrive at a 'single objective narrative' that locates within an authoritarian discourse and instead argues for an internally persuasive discourse that fosters debate and development and avoids the inhibiting context of 'political correctness'. In the London Institute this means that we do not want to impose a rigidly set discourse from above, *i.e.,* a single objective narrative, but we *do* want to work with colleagues in constructive ways so that we maximise opportunities for us to work together in a partnership model. We do this in a number of ways. Staff development and small scale research projects offer opportunities for us to discuss and share ideas with colleagues, and, by positioning ourselves on course committees and other academic, we multiply the opportunities for us to discuss pedagogy. Dialogue is the critical factor. It could be argued that the discourse of academic literacies that sits within the study team and the lecturers' discourse of decline is mutually constitutive, 'formed in the process of answering, challenging or responding to one another. Each discourse presupposes the existence of the other.' (Skidmore 1998).

In this chapter, we have identified that the success of study support may, in part, be dependant on subject lecturers' understanding of the service. By exploring and locating lecturer models of study support, we are able to engage and liaise with colleagues more effectively. This will surely be of benefit to all students who use study support.

CREATING A BASIS FOR A FACULTY-ORIENTED WRITING PROGRAMME

Approaches, Opportunities and Pitfalls in the Academic Writing Project in Groningen

FEMKE KRAMER, JACQUELINE VAN KRUININGEN & HENRIKE PADMOS

Academic Writing Project, University of Groningen, the Netherlands

Abstract. This article discusses the main features of a writing project at the Faculty of Arts of the University of Groningen in the Netherlands. We describe and discuss the way the project gradually developed, the problems we encountered and the ways in which we adapted our initial goals to the changing circumstances. In conclusion, we provide some recommendations for the development of a teacher-oriented writing programme within the setting of a European academic institution. The basic idea behind these recommendations is that educational renewals need a time-consuming, bottom-up approach, because they aim to change attitudes and raise consciousness among faculty members and administrators.

Keywords: Attitude change, Commitment, Dialogue, Electronic manual, Faculty-oriented approach, Hidden curriculum, Language and culture-specific conventions, Procedural approach, Problem-solution approach, and Standardised attainment level.

1   INTRODUCTION

In the academic writing project we carried out at the Faculty of Arts of the University of Groningen in the Netherlands (1997-1999), we developed a teacher oriented writing programme, to provide faculty and administrators with didactic and organisational support. In many respects, it was a trailblazing project, not because writing skills are often a neglected component in Dutch university programmes but rather because our view on the teaching of writing was unfamiliar to most faculty members, and because our institution-wide, faculty-oriented approach was unprecedented

185

Kramer, F., van Kruiningen, J.F. & Padmos, H. (2003). Creating a Basis for a Faculty-oriented Writing Programme – Approaches, Opportunities and Pitfalls in the Academic Writing Project in Groningen. In: G. Rijlaarsdam (Series Ed.) & L. Björk, G. Bräuer, L. Rienecker & P. Stray Jörgensen (Volume Eds.), Studies in Writing, Volume 12, Teaching Academic Writing in European Higher Education, pp. 185-194. © 2003 Kluwer Academic Publishers. Printed in the Netherlands.

in the Netherlands. In this chapter, we describe and discuss the project approach and the problems we encountered. The aim is to transform our experiences into recommendations for anyone who intends to initiate an institution-wide, teacher-oriented writing programme within the setting of a European academic institution.

2   BACKGROUND

2.1 The Occasion

The Academic Writing Project at the Groningen Faculty of Arts was part of a series of education reform projects, so-called 'Quality and Study Skills Project' [*Kwaliteits- en Studeerbaarheidsprojecten*], financed by the Dutch government between 1996 and 1999. All of these projects focused on the improvement of the quality of academic education. The main reason for paying special attention to writing skills was the observation that students' texts were often considered to be of worrying quality. Students' performance in composition was too much a matter of talent and/or of private initiatives by enthusiastic teachers. Moreover, many students seemed to experience writing assignments as difficult and time-consuming, and for too many, they were the cause of study delay. For those students who followed courses in different departments, the lack of conformity and the variety in standards, requirements, and genre designations were particularly confusing. Reports from the job market, finally, strongly suggested that alumni from our faculty were rarely able to fulfil their employers' expectations regarding writing skills. Obviously, it was assumed that these deficiencies could be reduced by a fundamental improvement in the writing components in the study programmes.

Up till then, explicit training in composition was either insufficient or absent in our programmes. Some programmes in our faculty had already developed more or less extensive writing components, but these were restricted to departments such as Dutch Language and Literature, English Language and Literature, and Communication Studies, and existed largely separately from each other, even within one department, thus causing the confusion mentioned above. This situation seemed to be typical of Dutch universities: with the paradoxical exception of several Technical Institutions, Dutch universities hardly ever provide structural education in composition. Most of them do provide writing courses in special study support centres, but these are of a strictly *remedial* nature and are usually frequented by students with severe writing problems. Writing centres and programmes such as those in the United States, now emerging in Europe, too, are still an unknown phenomenon in the Netherlands.

2.2 Context: the Dutch Education System

This insufficiency or even lack of writing components in university programmes becomes understandable when seen from the perspective of the Dutch system of education. Dutch pupils finish their secondary education with a standardised final exam at a certain level. A diploma at the highest of these levels, which is explicitly designated 'pre-university education' [*voorbereidend wetenschappelijk onderwijs*], guarantees admittance to university. Unlike the American situation, for example, where standardised admittance tests are used as a selection tool, Dutch universities do not work with admittance policies or entrance exams. Comparable to the situation in Norway and Germany (see Dysthe, this volume and Frank *et al.*, this volume), it is generally – though erroneously – assumed that during this 'pre-university education', general and practical skills such as writing have been acquired to a sufficient level and that explicit training in these skills is either not needed by university students or is undesirable – as a matter of principle, some university teachers are of the opinion that students ought to be able to acquire such skills themselves: 'if they are not capable of learning how to write proper texts on their own, they do not belong at a university.'

Another reason for the lack of writing courses in academic education is that, in the Netherlands, university programmes immediately focus on one specific field of study and less on general education or on the explicit training of 'general' or 'academic' skills. The absence of general or practical schooling further relates to the circumstance that the Dutch education system distinguishes between university study programmes and more practically oriented higher professional or vocational education; the latter type of education does comprise many practical skill components.

In the past, when there was no limit to the duration of academic studies, the lack of writing components in academic programmes hardly caused difficulties: students were able to learn the skills of academic writing over a long period of time, by trial and error. This style of learning – gradually, by doing and by copying the example of professional writers – fits the continental tradition of learning and of writing (see Rienecker and Stray Jörgensen about 'The (Im)Possibilities in Teaching University Writing...' in this volume). In the present situation, however, the duration of academic studies is now limited in most fields of study to four years: a period, which is much too short for the process of trial and error learning. Nevertheless, many senior faculty members tend to rely on this effective but implicit and time-consuming method and refuse to recognise the need for special attention to student writing in writing components or programmes.

3   MEASURES

3.1 The initial commission

The original commission the faculty board, on the advice of a planning committee, formulated for the project was, in short, to develop general standards for writing skills and a blueprint for a faculty-wide writing programme for the entire Faculty of Arts (consisting of 22 programmes; 3800 students). The intention was to provide departments with temporary support on a project basis in order to enable them to streamline and intensify the sparse writing components within the 22 separate study programmes. The limitations on time (two-and-a-half years) and money did not allow for the establishment of more structural support.

The faculty board wanted the individual writing programmes in the departments to be based on faculty-wide standardised attainment levels and to include a first-year writing course. Uniform competence levels seemed important for the quality of the outflow of students, and for a better flow of students between the study programmes; it would also prevent student writing problems due to the different views and expectations of teachers within the separate departments. More uniformity would create a clarity and consensus of aims and goals, which was previously lacking.

The project was supposed to enable the departments to maintain their own writing programmes. The faculty board and the planning committee insisted on preserving a situation in which the departments were responsible for their own writing programmes. They had always been autonomous at this level.

Concretely, the project aimed at the development of a manual for the teachers and the administrators, and at – temporary – assistance in improving their own (barely existent) writing programmes and methods of teaching writing. The manual was meant to provide a course description (first-year course), a range of writing assignments and guidelines for the coaching of student writing within the whole four-year curriculum. On a more abstract and less tangible level, however, the project aimed at gradually changing the teaching culture and the attitudes towards teaching in a complex, pluriform faculty.

For the realisation of this project, a project manager was appointed and a project team was established, consisting of nine faculty members from different departments. The choice of a team consisting of people from many different Arts disciplines was thought to guarantee a broad base for the project. Besides, roots in or at the very least strong ties with the departmental base of the faculty would provide easy access to the stray expertise already tacitly existing within the teaching community. The drawback of this option was that, considering the amount of available means, the team members were only appointed to the project on a part-time basis, and it was impossible to involve significant 'heavyweight' staff members.

3.2 Problems

Some but not all of the initial considerations and options proved to be valuable and feasible. The project team only gradually learned about the do's and don'ts, pitfalls and possibilities of an enterprise like this. After all, there were no examples of a faculty-wide, teacher-oriented project like this to hand, and the restrictions on money and time forced the team to make a rather quick, pragmatic start, not leaving much room for extensive literature studies or 'looking abroad'. With hindsight, we see can flaws and weaknesses in the basic principles of the original project plan which were not clearly distinguished beforehand.

One general and fundamental flaw which gradually emerged lay in the straight-forwardness of the way that was supposed to lead from the problem to its solution: there is a (writing/teaching) problem → in order to solve this problem we put a team of (writing) teachers from different departments (such as the department of Communication Studies or the English Language and Literature department) to work for a set period → they formulate standards and develop a standard course description and other related material → the problem will be solved. At first, it was not clear that such a time-limited and problem-solution-oriented approach is not suitable for the realisation of organisational changes of this type, which instead require a gradual, procedural change in teaching methods and attitudes towards writing and education.

Although much can be said for the establishment of writing programmes which are integrated within the curricula, geared to the specific study programmes, and maintained by the departments (see also Dysthe, this volume and Frank *et al.*, this volume), the constellation of such a programme is a very complex commission for a (temporary) project team, particularly when the fact that a large part of the teaching community initially did not feel the need for improvement and/or considered themselves as sufficiently expert is taken into account. Perhaps inevitably, some members of the faculty considered the project team to be a threat, a phenomenon that is recognised by many writing reformers (for example Frank *et al.* in this volume). The above-mentioned lack of 'heavyweight' staff members in the team and the unwillingness of the faculty board to impose measures on the departments (which were supposed to remain autonomous) gave the enterprise a noncommittal character which did not contribute to the authority of the team nor its proposals for reform measures.

During the preparatory phase of the project, the project team was not completely aware of these complicating factors. We thought that it would be possible to present a single writing programme for all the departments, maintained by the departments themselves and consisting of a generally applicable writing course and standardised requirements concerning writing skills. This aspiration turned out to be too difficult to realise in a complex faculty like the Faculty of Arts, which consists of 22 different languages, arts and history courses, and encompasses a range of approaches to writing.

Moreover, as the project proceeded, the team realised that the commission was in fact a very complex one in itself, and that improving people's teaching methods and refining their tacit preconceptions about writing really called for a much more subtle approach.

One of the causes of this 'evolution' was a change in perspective towards the complex nature of writing and the underlying functions of texts, and the consequences of this for the teaching of writing. Although process-oriented approaches and the advantages of interim and peer feedback were already part of the focus from the start, we learned more about a genre approach to the teaching of writing (Swales 1990; Rubin 1996) and about writing as a means for learning (Bean 1998). Through teaching and reading about writing pedagogy, and inspired by contacts with colleagues abroad, the team members themselves broadened their concept of writing and teaching writing. Starting off with a somewhat traditional view of writing as a cognitive, product-oriented process, we gradually developed a concept of writing as an activity in which affective and motivational factors are perhaps even more important than cognitive aspects. Accordingly, our view of writing pedagogy changed from a more or less prescriptive approach into one that aims at strengthening already present, though perhaps latent, skills. Obviously, this change in perspective did not make our 'mission' to incorporate writing programmes in a traditional academic context any easier.

Another factor in this process was our realisation of the fact that many aspects of academic writing are overruled by language and culture specific conventions. While investigating the perceptions and views of writing and the teaching of writing (through interviews and a questionnaire: see Van Kruiningen 1998), we found a whole range of different writing cultures and writing methods in our institution, some of which are based on a Continental writing and teaching style, and others on the increasingly influential Anglo Saxon tradition. This co-existence of many different writing styles is confirmed by Duszak (1997), Berkenkotter and Huckin (1995), Kaplan (1966), Cmejrková (1996) and Rienecker and Stray Jorgenson (this volume) who discuss the problem of this diversity in relation to writing and the teaching of writing at European universities. We noticed that teachers often fail to properly explain their discipline-bound notions and criteria to their students or, for that matter, to themselves: a phenomenon which is also described by Zirinsky (1987), Berkenkotter and Huckin (1995), Ruhmann (1997), Lewin and Fine (1996) and Rubin (1996). Many teachers, moreover, appeared to be attached to rather traditional, technical and product rather than process oriented ways of teaching. We feared that formulating and enforcing general teaching goals and attainment levels would scare these teachers off rather than make them enthusiastic.

3.3 Modifications

Considering the obvious complexity of the situation, the project team eventually decided to choose a more thoughtful but also more time-consuming approach. We decided to develop a more variegated programme consisting of a flexible framework for organisational and didactic support. In order to achieve this goal, we followed two approaches:

- We introduced an online 'manual' for teachers in order to provide flexible and freely interpretable guidelines and suggestions for the organisation and teaching of writing, with sample course schemes, course material, checklists, sample assignments, et cetera. This manual was made available through the electronic network in order to make it easy for the faculty to adjust the material for their own writing programme. It has not yet been possible to evaluate the feasibility of this manual on a faculty-wide scale because it was only partly finished by the end of the project period. Although the first version of the manual showed teething troubles, initial reactions to the benefits of this didactical approach are positive.
- We organised workshops and meetings with the faculty. These workshops and meetings were intended to facilitate the exchange of experiences, to improve didactic skills within the faculty, and to fine-tune and streamline the writing programmes of the departments. The approach in these workshops were aimed at intellectual exchange and demonstrating possibilities, although faculty members often seemed to expect us to show models of 'how to'. Given the fact that those in the faculty who were already interested mainly visited these workshops, it is

clear that not all of the faculty – and certainly not all of the sceptics in the faculty – were reached within this short project period.

The course material and the approaches chosen in the workshops and meetings were based on a range of didactical principles, which were developed during the project period. Inspired by reading and contacts we had with colleagues, especially in Germany, Denmark and the United States, these principles became rules of thumb that seemed to fit a diversity of writing and teaching styles and cultures:

- Provide students with insight into the intentions, functions and conventions of academic communication. This prevents them from committing the motivational and orientation errors that often lie at the root of writing problems. In the book 'Schlüsselkompetenz Schreiben', Otto Kruse and Eva Maria Jakobs typify writing as a 'für die Wissenschaft [...] konstituierende Handlung' (Kruse & Jakobs 1999: 20), which means that 'university socialisation' involves, to a great extent, socialisation in writing and speech. In our view, this process of socialisation requires teachers making students aware of the formal and functional aspects of academic texts. It also requires a programme in which explicit instruction and support in writing is provided. Further, students' socialisation works best if writing assignments are functional, realistic 'student variants' of professional scholarly communication: the writing of research proposals, conference proposals, actual real publications in 'student congress volumes' et cetera, instead of simply having to write an essay for a teacher.

- Teach students a professional and independent writing attitude. Student writers should consider it as 'not done' to bother readers/teachers with unstructured, sloppy texts. They have to make it a habit to write several drafts and to ask for feedback from a critical peer, though still take full responsibility for the final product. Teachers need to create room for a writing process in which they function as a coach not as a text editor.

- Provide a writing programme in which students can practice writing and significantly increase the frequency and variety of their writing. This will enable them to develop a writing fluency that can be applied in a variety of contexts. As Hilgers and Marsella put it: 'Quantity does not guarantee better writing. But we can guarantee that improved writing will not result from minimal experience with writing.' (Hilgers & Marsella 1992: 39). Furthermore, variation in writing assignments leads to more reflection, flexibility and 'transfer', which means that students will be able to apply their writing expertise in other, non-academic contexts. Moreover, frequent and varied writing gives students the opportunity to learn from their writing, to deepen their knowledge and insights and learn to explore themes from different perspectives.

As stated before, an effective approach to the development and transfer of the writing programme to the faculty gradually took form during the project. The project at the Faculty of Arts ended in 1999, with as tangible results the implementation of a first-year course and some renovations in ten study programmes, and a working version of an electronic manual for teachers. In addition, a new project for two other faculties at the University of Groningen was set up (see below). Despite some initial problems, teachers and students predominantly evaluated the renewed components and the writing skills of students positively. Qualitative evaluation data are hard to provide, however. For one thing, a zero measurement was never performed and the educational renewals revealed differences in characteristics and in intensity within the different departments. Therefore, it is not possible to get a clear picture of an improvement in student writing skills, or of an improvement in the study programmes. Besides, the project period was too short to measure long-term effects such as better graduate writing skills.

However, in our view, an even more valuable effect is the fact that writing and the teaching of writing has become an issue in the teaching community. Gradually, people are starting to realise that the teaching of writing is useful and not a waste of valuable teaching time. Several initiatives in the faculty show that the project has had an effect in depth:

- Several departments have continued discussing the possibilities to improve the writing components in their programmes on a more or less regular basis.
- Individual teachers are continuing to assess and reinforce their teaching methods and to strengthen their roles as teachers and as coaches.
- The faculty board consider the teaching of writing an important theme and have expressed this in faculty-wide evaluations, reports *etc.*

Unfortunately, a follow-up of this project in the Arts faculty does not have financial support, despite a positive evaluation by the faculties' administrators as well as by the university board. The question remains whether there will be any long-term effects. A renewal process has started which will have to develop further in the next couple of years. For such a process to succeed, much more is needed from the faculty board than just policy statements, which lack any obligation. This implies that renewals and initiatives will no longer be nourished and supported. Within the Faculty of Arts, with a few exceptions, the effects will gradually diminish in most departments. By their very nature, writing components just do not have enough status in themselves to survive in a (European?) academic culture.

Strangely enough, the university board is supporting and financing two new (four-year) writing projects in other faculties (Law and Sciences), to be co-ordinated and executed by the project team from the Faculty of Arts. These new projects are based on the experiences gained from the project in the Faculty of Arts. Thus, we are able to focus on creating a structural basis for a writing programme in these faculties.

4   RECOMMENDATIONS

In this last section we provide a rough outline of the most important do's and don'ts in projects such as the one dealt with above, based on our experiences. Some of these speak for themselves in the context of the problems mentioned. The basic idea behind the range of recommendations is that these educational renewals entail a time-consuming, procedural, 'soft', bottom-up approach rather than a technical, 'hard' approach (Wijnen *et al.* 1998). The start-up-phase of a writing programme can be considered as a project in itself. The ultimate goal of every project implemented in an organisation of any kind is to get the project results deeply rooted within the organisation. This requires a strategic and procedural approach, and this applies even more to projects, which aim to change attitudes and raise consciousness among the whole community in an organisation.

4.1 Anticipate Prejudices

One hindering factor, which was indirectly but strongly perceptible, is the well-known hierarchy of activities in the academic community. Within the academic culture, research enjoys the highest status. Of all the 'inferior' educational work, skills teaching have the lowest status. Symptoms of this hierarchy include the remuneration and the kind of appointments of 'skill' teachers, the extent to which didactic schooling of teachers is appreciated, and the financing of teaching matters. In principle, any kind of renewal in the field of university education is a difficult enterprise, but the low status of skill components is an extra handicap.

4.2 Create Commitments, Get Key Figures Involved and Start a Dialogue

Strong commitment from the faculty board, key figures and active pioneers within the institution is vital (Kapteyn 1996: 258). The authorities need to guard and guide the embedding and implementation in the institution, and the programme needs to start with key figures and pioneers who are open to educational changes, who respect students and – most importantly – who enjoy their colleagues' esteem and trust (Haring-Smith 1992: 183). It takes a lot of communication, fine-tuning, and often changes of attitude before the programme becomes a faculty-driven common property. Only then will the teaching community develop a shared responsibility for the programme (Walvoord 1992; Haring-Smith 1992). A 'dialogue model' with open discussions, meetings and workshops suits such goals better then a 'training programme' or a 'conversion model' (Walvoord 1992).

4.3 Be Flexible and Open with Regard to the Time Schedule and the Intended Results

Changes like the ones dealt with in this article require repeated activities; the dialogue has to continue, and you need to keep on (re) considering methods with regard to specific educational settings or changes to them. Complex problems cannot be 'solved' using a closed and structured, technical, problem-solution approach. Changes need to be implemented gradually: too many changes in a short time have a disturbing effect and work out the wrong way.

Moreover, to gain support and to create a faculty-driven writing programme, the timetable has to be flexible, leaving room for existing cultural and disciplinary differences between departments or study programmes. Rigid educational reforms, rules and methods which are enforced by the management board usually lead to unmotivated and artificial writing components, and to writing assignments which are perceived by members of the faculty as well as by students as obligatory appendages and not as natural components.

5   FINAL CONSIDERATIONS: THE EUROPEAN CONTEXT

If we look at the actual situation in Groningen and at some other programmes in Europe, it seems that, although European administrators and funding authorities are becoming gradually convinced of the need for changes in the teaching of academic writing, they are not yet convinced of the necessity of a procedural and structural approach to such renewals. Some interesting and valuable projects, unfortunately only with temporary funding, are being carried out in Europe. As a result, the programme committees of individual initiators are putting a lot of effort and energy into lobbying and finding financial means, energy that could be better used for further implementation and refining of the writing programmes and centres. What is even worse, the gradually developed expertise will probably just vanish when funding stops.

Let us hope that we are all just in the middle of a (tiresome) initial phase of educational changes in European higher education: a phase that resembles the initial phase that American writing programmes went through some twenty to thirty years ago (and which some of them are still going through). At that time, American administrators and funding authorities also only gradually acknowledged the value of writing programmes and provided (structural!) financial means for the establishment of writing programmes and writing centres. The same kind of reluctance could be sensed back then, and it took quite some time before writing programmes and centres became accepted as natural components of university programmes. Let us hope this acknowledgement gives the European initiators the strength and motivation to carry on. The recent initiative to establish a European network (EATAW) and the publication of European books on writing programmes and teaching methods will hopefully contribute to that.

IMPLEMENTATION ISSUES FOR STUDY SUPPORT

MARGO BLYTHMAN*, JOAN MULLIN**, JANE MILTON*** & SUSAN ORR*

*The London Institute in London, UK,
**The Writing Center at the University of Toledo, Ohio, USA,
***Nova Scotia College of Art and Design in Halifax, Nova Scotia, Canada

Abstract. In this chapter, we outline the underpinning principles of study support in two of the five colleges of the London Institute, and identify the micro-politics of implementation, thereby focusing on the process of moving policy to practice. We illuminate this outline with other examples from North America to illustrate that this is an international rather than local issue. Our key argument is that study support must be understood by staff and students, effectively situated organizationally and firmly linked within the wider institution. For these topics we offer some analysis and reflection based on our experience.

Keywords: Art & design, Micro-politics, Policy implementation, Study support, and Writing centres.

1   INTRODUCTION

In this chapter, we outline the principles by which we operate study support/writing centres and the practice we use to ensure the effective implementation of these principles. We explain the contexts of our various institutions and focus in detail on the one to one and small group support of student writing (study support) at two of the colleges of the London Institute. We argue that the issues we face are not unique to our institution or the UK and we relate our experience to that of the University of Toledo in the US and Nova Scotia College of Art and Design (NSCAD) in Canada.

2   UNDERPINNING PRINCIPLES

Study support is a model, which aims to give students extra support, particularly, but not exclusively, with writing. We take it as a given that high quality study support development maximizes student achievement and promotes independent learning; it also enables students to perform to their full potential and helps them overcome any

Blythman, M., Mullin, J., Milton, J. & Orr, S. (2003). Implementation Issues for Study Support. In: G. Rijlaarsdam (Series Ed.) & L. Björk, G. Bräuer, L. Rienecker & P. Stray Jörgensen (Volume Eds.), Studies in Writing, Volume 12, Teaching Academic Writing in European Higher Education, pp. 195-208. © 2003 Kluwer Academic Publishers. Printed in the Netherlands.

barriers to learning. We work within a model that develops cultural capital in our students (Bourdieu 1997). Bourdieu sees cultural capital as a theoretical concept that explains unequal educational achievement among different social classes, and he believes that the profits of the education system are based on differential class access to cultural capital. Cultural capital has three forms: an embodied form in terms of long-lasting dispositions of mind and body; an objectified form in terms of cultural goods; and an institutionalised state in the form of educational qualifications. It is domestically transmitted, requires an investment of time and labour by the accumulating people themselves, and, unlike economic capital, cannot be instantaneously transmitted. On a much less theoretical level, cultural capital could be seen as understanding the implicit rules of the game, learned through being a product of a family that has already mastered these rules.

The implications of this concept for study support is that many of the students who come to us are facing problems because they do not understand the implicit rules of higher education since they may be the first generation of their family to gain entry. Part of our role is to make the implicit explicit: for example, helping students interpret the coded language that many course lecturers use in feedback comments. We aim for a service that is non-stigmatised or that is not perceived as a deficit model. In the context outlined above it would be easy for study support to become associated with helping only 'weaker' students. We have tried to avoid this image because we reject, in agreement with Simpson (1996) and North (1984), the model that implies a fixed group of weaker students who need study support. On the contrary, we believe there is an ever-changing group of students who may use the study support services available. Olson (1984) and Simpson (1996) both argue for a focus on the inadequacies of the receiving institution rather than personal lack on the part of the student. The key issue is not whether the students are suitable for tutoring, but rather how the institution can respond to meet the learning needs of all students. For example, while some students may want to come to us with an essay that has been referred, others may want to bring us essays in order that they might earn higher grades; in each example, students will be working to improve their writing abilities overall, not just for the one essay.

In some universities study support fits within a counselling paradigm that focuses on the personal circumstances of the student. Whilst this context cannot be ignored, for us it is important to use the students' curriculum as the starting point rather than the students' personal circumstances. An academic focus for study support, one that locates it in the curriculum (through a writing across the curriculum program, through professional development, through course plan consultations) serves to concretise the link between study support and the curriculum. In this way, study support can have a visible profile within the college as opposed to the privacy and confidentiality that surrounds the counselling situation. Moreover, by stressing the academic mission of study support, we link ourselves with staff and management, which are also directly connected to the public, academic enterprise of higher education.

3   IMPLEMENTING THE STUDY SUPPORT MODEL

Many practitioners, having developed an effective model, face difficulty with implementation. Our concern is critically to examine how and why particular policy models evolve in the way they do in practice. We have:

> 'An analytical concern with education as a political process and the concomitant empirical interest in those conflicts which occur between groups and individuals who seek to define 'what is to count as education' in their own terms.' (Ball 1991:166)

Policy implementation literature indicates the variety of ways in which policy is mediated by those charged with its implementation (Ball 1994; Cerych & Sabatier 1986). Policy cycle models, within this literature, aim to present a framework for micro-political analysis of policy. One such framework is Cerych and Sabatier's (1986) which includes the following dimensions: consistency of the objectives, degree of change considered, adequacy of the underpinning causal theory, adequacy of financial resources, degree of commitment of those charged with its implementation, and of higher officials and politicians. The model has the underlying principle that many factors can intervene at the implementation stage and that, as a result, policies are reformulated at various levels. Ball, who argues that policy can be seen as 'awkward, incomplete, incoherent and unstable' (Ball 1997: 265), defines policy as

> 'The economy of power, a set of technologies and practices which are realized and struggled over in local settings. Policy is both text and action, words and deeds, it is what is enacted as well as what is intended.' (Ball 1994: 10)

Ball advocates a trajectory approach, which 'attends to the ways in which policies evolve, change and decay through time and space' (Ball 1997: 266).

As a main focus of the chapter, we concentrate on how to make high quality study support happen within an institution. We base this concentration on an analysis of key success factors through the perspective outlined above. We have used a variety of methods to evaluate our strategies. These are located within qualitative paradigms based essentially on 'thick description' (Geertz 1973) and 'the reflective practitioner' (Schon 1987). We see ourselves as teacher practitioners involved in research as

> 'A form of self reflective enquiry undertaken by participants in social (including educational) situations in order to improve the rationality and justice of (a) their own social and educational practices, (b) their understanding of these practices, and (c) the situations in which the practices are carried out.' (Kemmis 1993: 177)

We make no knowledge claims of cause and effect for any particular strategy, or combination of strategies, but set out to offer illumination on a complex situation and to use this to reflect on practical ways forward.

Equally, we make no attempt at traditional models of triangulation (Cohen & Manion 1980). We position ourselves closer to theory triangulation, the use of multiple perspectives to interpret a single set of data (Denzin & Lincoln 1998). We do not attempt the use of multiple perspectives on a single set of data but instead on a single issue, study support. Our validity locates in the reflexivity of the researcher and the openness of the research to critical peer judgment (Phillips 1993), and we would argue that validity comes from the use made by others of the insights (Nias 1993).

Within this context we all use a number of strategies. We collect data on the extent to which students use study support. We encourage students to evaluate formally how much study support helped them, and we also gather the views of course lecturers and study support tutors on the effect of study support on individual students. The University of Toledo collects the perceptions of course lecturers on the difference that writing centres have made to student grades. In the UK we are also, of course, open to external scrutiny with the highly regulated government quality assurance systems for higher education. In 1999-2000, both London Institute colleges were inspected and the areas of work described here received the highest possible grade with no recommendations for improvement.

As a result, we are building up a 'thick description' of our strategies as a basis for reflection, and we offer this as a new perspective. This approach is based on an understanding of the micro-politics of the organization. Micro-politics, in this context, is taken to mean the interplay, within an organization, of the status and power of the various groups based on their material interests and values, to achieve their preferred outcomes (Ball 1991, Ball & Goodson 1985, Hargreaves 1994, Blase 1991, Gronn 1986).

We argue, based on this literature, that currently in UK, US and Canadian higher education there is an inter-relationship of micro-politics, structure and policy operating in three ways. Firstly, there are competing policies and contradictory discourses (*e.g.*, numbers versus quality and widening participation versus a concern with standards; higher education's role to develop a body of knowledge and critical thought vs. developing the employability skills required by the knowledge economy). Secondly, practice is the outcome of conflict/struggle between competing interests (*e.g.*, a service resulting from tensions between professional practice and resource constraints). Finally, there are changing relationships between key players, which involve conflict/struggle not just between change and resistance to change but in a more complex pattern, which takes into, account both structural constraints and opportunities for individual action. A specific example of how this kind of alliance might occur is where a course manager is facing criticism for poor retention of students on the course (leading to a cut in resources) and we offer course-specific study support. This would meet our need to gain access to as many students as possible who wish to take advantage of our service and to work in close liaison with staff in the disciplines. But it also meets the course manager's need both to try to solve the retention problem and to show the senior management that action is being taken.

Structural constraints, therefore, might include the control of resources, the operation of the line management hierarchy or rigid disciplinary boundaries, but action results from strategic alliances, which enable different players to meet their own needs.

From our experience, there are four key issues that require a micro-political understanding in order to ensure effective policy implementation of study support. These are location, staffing, resourcing, and the role of senior management. It is important to our argument that these issues cannot be seen in isolation from one another; our model depends on striving to achieve on all of these axes. We have written elsewhere (Blythman & Orr 2001) about the importance of 'joined-up thinking'. This term, fore grounded in the UK by New Labour, indicates the fruitlessness of developing single stands of policy in isolation. We argue, therefore, that structural and cultural factors do not operate in isolation within an institution and that successful actors in micro-political terms must understand and operate within the wider picture. It is necessary to read the wider institution as well as the immediate local situation.

Our reading of the wider institutional picture, not only at the London Institute but also at NSCAD and the University of Toledo, indicates that, for successful study support to happen, we need to position ourselves advantageously in relation to the geography, or physical location, of the support, the composition of the study support team, the resourcing of this work and the achievement of management support.

4   THE CASE STUDIES' CONTEXT

4.1 The University of Toledo

While writing centres in the U.S. have a long history, they particularly expanded in the 1960s when the Civil Rights movement, a higher sense of equality for women and immigrant populations, and the need for educating soldiers returning from the Vietnam war forced open higher education's doors to new populations. Recognising the need to introduce these students to writing and thinking expectations of the academy, educators began to establish small tutorial centres where one on one work seemed most effective (Carino 1995).

Initially, writing centres in the U.S. were perceived as 'remedial centres' or 'grammar shops' where, according to the medical model of education, students could be 'fixed' by giving them an injection of grammar and comma instruction. However, as writing centre practitioners soon discovered, the complexities of language instruction went beyond the surface and there slowly grew a theoretical base from which writing theory emerged (alongside the parallel writing theory that was emerging from classroom teaching in composition). By 1984, Stephen North's landmark essay 'The Idea of a Writing Center' announced what most practitioner's had begun to understand: in writing centres there had occurred a paradigm shift in which writing tutors were focusing on the development of writers rather than only on correcting the paper in front of them.

This theoretical announcement gave to writing centres the 'currency' needed to be recognised within the academy; though not instantly. For years, writing centres had been marginalized – politically, physically, and as a discipline – in the academy. This context was still in force by the time the Writing Center started at the University of Toledo in 1987. Stuck in a room on the margins of campus with no supplies, no tutor training course and no tutors, the originating director was nonetheless supposed to fix students' papers as if by magic. Educating faculty and administration – shifting their paradigm to think of writing as a process – became primary for the establishment of a centre to which students could go without being stigmatised as remedial and to which faculty would willingly send students without fear of having someone else write the paper (*e.g.*, see Olson 1984).

This was especially true since the Writing Center, as is common in the U.S. uses students as peer tutors in the Center. Highly and continually trained, undergraduate and graduate tutors work with their peers and with those in programs at levels higher than they are. While the Center is also staffed with professional tutors, part time instructors and free-lance writers from the community, all receive equal training and pay for their work.

In order to educate the university community about the potential for the kind of study support possible in a (peer tutor) writing centre (North 1979, Mullin & Wallace 1994), the director had to establish herself as an academic: one who does research, teaching and committee work – rather than someone who holds students' hands and corrects their papers. This was accomplished over time through multiple conversations with individual faculty, chairs and administrators, through committee work to position the Writing Center as an academic centre, by obtaining grants that included faculty members' study of writing in their disciplines and by gradually establishing a required Writing Across the Curriculum programme in which writing was viewed as a central curricular mission of the institution (Mullin 1999, Mullin et al. 1994).

Currently, the University of Toledo Writing Center serves about 30% of the student undergraduate and graduate population each year through one on one (face to face) tutorials, in on-line tutorials, by attaching a tutor to writing intensive classes and by working with groups of senior students in capstone courses (*e.g.*, engineering team design courses). In addition, faculty use the Writing Center for their working papers, books grants, annual professional reports, and the Writing Center gives on campus workshops for faculty interested in incorporating writing into their teaching methodology, in course design, giving feedback to students and in assignment design. Not held to the university boundaries, the Writing Center has also started similar work in twenty-six school districts in northern Ohio. Despite shrinking budgets and staff support for higher education over the last several years, the Writing Center has continued to thrive. While government is only now emphasizing assessment and accountability, the Writing Center has continually proven its academic value on campus by integrating itself into the curriculum so the institution sees the results of work done in the Center, hears regular reports on liaisons with faculty and on the Center's academic accomplishments, and reads the research generated in the Writing Center that proves its value. As a result, the Writing Center is now located in the middle of campus in a newly renovated space with state of the art computers, desks, couches and a coffee bar far from its theoretical, pedagogical and physical origins at the margin of the institution.

4.2 *Nova Scotia College of Art and Design (NSCAD)*

The Nova Scotia College of Art and Design (NSCAD) is an open admissions institution, which means that anyone with a high school certificate can attend. Party because of increasing pressures from government to graduate and retain more students, and pressure on accountability due to scarce resources, there are moves to improve the quality of the students by establishing a minimum grade point average for entering students. However, the current situation indicates the need to improve the writing and thinking ability of current students, and the answer has been the establishment of a small writing across the curriculum effort.

In addition to taking required writing courses their first year, students who attend NSCAD take writing across the curriculum (WAC) courses. These courses are intended to use writing as a teaching method; in other words, course content is taught through a number of writing strategies. Besides this, WAC courses require that thirty pages of writing be generated during the semester (about nine thousand words); that there be frequent peer and faculty feedback on the writing in progress; and that there are formal as well as informal assignments (graded and non-graded). Within these classes, sit a peer (student) tutor trained by a faculty member to act as a writing consultant and peer and faculty mentor. These WAC tutors work closely with faculty, creating developmental writing assignments appropriate to the lecturer's objectives and the level of the discipline. The tutor also attends class, works with peer groups within the class and with students individually.

These efforts within the College have started very small because while all staff believes in the value of writing, the emphasis is still on art and design. This is the perception of students also. By integrating the teaching of writing into the classroom – and therefore, into the learning of course material – faculty is less likely to object to the educational support a tutor is providing. In addition, improved student performance by the inclusion of tutors in a WAC classroom helps faculty meet accountability standards called for by the institution.

4.3 London Institute

The London Institute is the biggest art and design higher education institution in Europe. It comprises five colleges, two of which are the London College of Fashion (LCF) and the London College of Printing (LCP). Both colleges have had study support for five years. Our conception of study support draws on writing centre development theory in the US, and our examples draw from Nova Scotia College of Art and Design in Canada and the University of Toledo in addition to the London Institute.

Study support is offered in addition to the main tuition on any course, and a member of staff can refer students, or they can self-refer. Study support can be offered to individuals or groups. It can happen outside the main course teaching or as double staffing through a study support tutor working alongside the course lecturer. The support offered includes all aspects of writing development and study skills. Study support aims to help students with planning and structuring work, reading and understanding texts, developing vocabulary, proof-reading (for grammar, spelling, *etc.*) and revising manuscripts, and organizing work with regard to time restrictions. In both UK colleges the staffing is based on a very small core of full time permanent tutors and a larger number of part-time hourly paid tutors, all qualified and experienced teachers.

Study support at LCP currently has 2.5 full-time and 10 hourly-paid part-time staff members while LCF has 0.5 full-time staff members and three hourly-paid part-time workers. A recent survey showed that 12% of students at LCF had used study support and an estimated figure for LCP is 8%. Study support is used by students from all schools (faculties) and all levels.

In five years, study support has grown from a very small start (0.5 staffing in each college and a small number of students) to its current size outlined above. Essentially this growth is linked to the social and political context in the UK. At the moment, higher education in the UK faces a coming together, or collision, of a number of forces: the mass expansion of higher education, a political commitment to keep down public expenditure, and a foregrounding of the rights of students as customers as typified by the charter movement (Green 1994) which gives formal status to customer entitlement. In addition, we now have the stated national policy aim of widening participation in higher education (CVCP 1998). The proportion of young people entering the higher education system has increased from one in eighteen in the 1960s to one in three now in England, with even higher proportions in Scotland and Northern Ireland (NCIHE 1997: § 3.9). In addition there has been growth in the numbers of mature students and those with 'non standard' entry qualifications. We therefore have a much more diverse student body than previously with a greater range of writing ability. Academic staff now expresses concerns about the quality of higher education entrants (NCIHE 1997: § 3.21) with the implication that they are more difficult to teach. R. Simpson outlines how increased student diversity can lead to a deficit model 'that sees learning development needs of students as problems, synonymous with falling standards and requiring remedial provision,' (Simpson 1996: 17) and argues that this comes from the continuing UK debate about alleged falling standards as well as the changing student profile.

At the same time, the pressure for enhancement comes from students and other stakeholders. In the 1990s a culture developed which saw users of public services as customers with rights. Students expect to be consulted on the quality of the provision they receive and have redress for complaints and dissatisfaction. Since 1998 in the UK (although subsequently abolished in Scotland) there has been direct payment of fees by students, which makes the customer relationship more explicit.

There has also been a foregrounding of government concern with the quality of teaching and learning. In higher education this foregrounding is embodied by the quality assurance systems developed across the sector since 1992. The history of these systems is outlined elsewhere (Brown 1998), but two points are relevant here: a concern with student retention and achievement and a focus on the student experience. At the institutional level, the London Institute has encouraged the constituent colleges to develop policies and strategies to support student retention and achievement, and the Institute has been the context for the development of study support.

5   MICRO-POLITICS OF STUDY SUPPORT IMPLEMENTATION

Given the case studies in three different countries, developed in three different ways, we will now examine how each locally addressed five key areas in the implementation of their study support: (1) Geographical and structural location, (2) Staffing, (3) Co-operation and liaison, (4) Resourcing, and (5) Strategic factors.

5.1   Geographical and structural location

For geography the key issue is the symbolic message sent out by the physical location. Is the location central and visible or difficult to find? Is it associated with the academic side of the institution or with services for students 'with problems'? Is the space well equipped and furnished or does its physical appearance indicate marginalisation? It is important that the geography reflect the mission of the study support service. As outlined earlier, it is our view that this service should not be seen as remedial nor about the personal psychological needs of the student, so our preferred location is within the library, a space used by all students and associated with learning rather than 'problems'.

However, in the geographic location it is also important to be visible to academic and resource managers so the location of staff offices for the study support team, offices which will inevitably be busy with students, should be as high profile as possible. Equally important, the study support accommodation should be high quality but not so much better than the average accommodation that it causes difficulty with course lecturers. An ideal situation has developed at the University of Toledo where the study support space, located across the corridor from the library, and tutors are also used by academic and administrative staff for advice and help with writing tasks. Alternatively, study support can go to the students. At NSCAD, as well as at the University of Toledo, writing tutors are situated in the classroom; they attend the class, work with the course lecturer and act as writing guides for that class of students. In the London Institute, study support is located either within the library or in central administrative areas to ensure its position within the academic culture.

5.2   Staffing

In the U.S. and Canada, the movement towards peers teaching peers is well established. Therefore, for budgetary and well as theoretical reasons, (a win-win situation for management and the writing centres) it is considered a triumph of teaching that students can provide study support. The UK model, however, depends on both students and course lecturers seeing the study support teachers as highly skilled, flexible and collaborative in their attitude toward both staff and students. We therefore need to ensure that we have a staff that brings these three attributes to their work. It is vital that both students and course lecturers immediately come to value the service. It is necessary to resist attempts, only too common, to transfer underperforming staff to the study support team. The study support tutors need to be specialists, so that there is an expertise to be observed and valued, but they also need to be flexible in what they are prepared to offer. It is useful if these staff has other roles within the institution such as staff development or a significant teaching role within the mainstream curriculum but it is also vital that they are recognized as academic staff in their own right.

As in the U.S. and Canada, staff in the UK recognise that different students have different approaches to learning, and therefore we aim to have an eclectic mix of teaching styles in the team. We also all aim to incorporate staff cohesion through development and meetings that include collaborative reporting and decision making where appropriate.

5.3 Co-operation and liaison

Study support/writing centre tutors must be able to develop effective relationships with course lecturers, a relationship which is supportive, collaborative and based on mutual respect. In practice, study support tutors need to interact with four key groups. These are students, course lecturers, academic managers (those who control the academic content of courses), and resource managers (managers who control the allocation of financial and human resources).

Study support (and writing centre) tutors should have well-developed formal and informal liaison skills; they should expect to spend time in liaison. Models for each course or programme need to be negotiated with the course or programme leader rather than attempting to impose one single support model. At the same time, however, the study support tutors must have the confidence to challenge proposed models if necessary. In the U.S., student-tutors can be less threatening to staff than would a director. In Canada and the UK, however, the staff status of the tutors or director will be used to mediate difficulties. In all cases there are likely to be situations of potential conflict at times over the needs of individual students, and study support tutors may be involved in a certain amount of advocacy, but they must recognise that there are boundaries, which should not be crossed. An issue, which often arises, for example, is the study support tutor's relationship to work set and assessed by a course lecturer. There can be disagreements about the nature and grading of the work, but in our view, while it is acceptable for the study support tutor to seek clarification over the tasks, it is not acceptable to challenge the course lecturer's grading even if privately we have reservations. A collaborative and mutually respectful relationship between professionals must recognise some boundaries of expertise.

On the other hand, the study support tutors need to question course lecturers who have unrealistic expectations of what can be delivered in a limited timescale. It is not only students who say 'Have you got ten minutes? Can you sort out this dissertation?' (Orr & Blythman 2000). Staff say this as well when they ask study support tutors to 'just sort out' a student's dissertation.

The University of Toledo found it helpful to establish, on a formal basis for each department or section, a liaison member of the course team who works closely with the study support team and eases their way into the department or section. This easing is enhanced if there is some training followed by one to one mentoring of the departmental liaison staff. In a much more subtle way, study support staff and tutors in NSCAD WAC program mentor staff on a daily basis through professional interactions.

5.4 Resourcing

It is difficult to achieve anything within an organisation unless one has access to resources. Study support requires space and staff, both often very limited resources in higher education institutions. In relation to resource managers, it is important that the study support team is seen to be in enormous demand by students, use resources efficiently and sparingly and, where possible, access external funding for development purposes. It is also useful to be seen to be delivering support to students regarded as particularly valuable by the institution; these might be high achievers aiming for a first class degree (UK) or they may be postgraduates or 'honour students' (U.S. and Canada). The study support tutor, or at least the manager of the team, needs to understand the funding principles and relevant resource allocation systems, and be able to use the appropriate financial discourse to argue the case within the constraints faced by the resource manager. Experience at the University of Toledo indicates that this strategy can protect study support activities at a time of general cuts in resources (Kinkead & Harris 1993).

Because resource is important and often in short supply, study support needs to control its own resources, and any attempt to use an internal market model where courses buy the service is likely to be problematic, particularly in the early days when its reputation is being established. The University of Toledo has its own budget, which it controls, while the NSCAD system works within the English Department. In the London Institute, we have our own budget, which comes from several government and college sources. Control is necessary because resourcing must be used flexibly to allow for instant response to both students and course lecturers and for different models and patterns of delivery. It needs to allow for liaison time with course lecturers and other college services but not be seen as resourced more generously than teaching on the main courses.

In the UK, liaising needs to be recognized as the study support equivalent of preparation and marking. Because of this liaison need, it is problematic to have a team who are mainly part-time hourly-paid staff. The utility of 'being around' should not be underestimated. It is important, however, that the study support team are as accountable, and seen to be as accountable, as any other section of the institution. In all counties, staffs know they need to keep excellent audit trails and develop performance indicators, which measure outcome (*e.g.,* improved retention) as well as process (*e.g.* number of students being tutored).

5.5 Strategic factors

Finally, it is important to have the active and visible support of senior management. Information about access to study support should be in all relevant literature given to students, have an active presence on the website of the institution (*e.g.*, http://writingcenter.utoledo.edu), and be mentioned in high profile induction talks given by senior staff. It should also feature regularly in communications to the staff in general by senior management. In these cases, the appropriate discourse must be used, avoiding unintentional use of remedial discourse. (See Orr & Blythman this volume). At NSCAD, second semester writing classes are described in the calendar (prospectus) as mandatory. The requirement is waived, in practice, in some cases, but by describing the course as mandatory rather than remedial, the intention is to convey the message that the college puts a priority on writing skills for all students. In return for this kind of management support, the study support team need to play their part by producing high quality information for internal and external quality assurance systems, in particular by trying to establish a link between study support and retention and achievement. Follow-up surveys of students who have used study support are particularly valuable. The University of Toledo is in the process of carrying out an alumni survey, which indicates useful long-term benefits of study support carrying through to employment.

The table below presents our model of the ideal situation, which we are working to achieve, and the interplay of these various issues on the groups involved (see table 1 below).

We recommend the following as starting points in achieving this model:

- Build up study support's relationship with the library so that this becomes the referent/location
- Set up a widely representative group to develop a policy and implementation plan
- Get the policy and implementation plan on agenda of every possible meeting
- Prioritise departments coming up for external or internal quality assurance inspection
- Gather, collate, analyse and publicise every possible statistic in relation to study support and give these to the institution's quality assurance manager and to course/programme managers
- Devote at least 10% of time to liaison with course/programme managers
- Identify key arguments for study support appropriate to the institutional culture.

6   CONCLUSION

Study support can make a considerable contribution to the academic success of individual students within higher education. To enable it to offer maximum benefit, study support needs policy and practice which recognises and understands the location of power within the institution, how this power operates and how to position study support so that it can make its full contribution to student success. By investigating the policies and practices of one's institution, applying to this the principles of micro-politics, and by using current research on student learning to develop best practices, the study support (or writing centre) models presented here can be effectively adapted to other contexts.

Table 1. Model of the ideal study support.

Group	Geography	Study Support Staff	How is it resourced	Management Support
Students	Physical location which is not remedial Permanent presence	Value the support – seen as 'good' Eclectic mix of styles and models Flexible in offer 'cultural capital' Some degree of advocacy, but understand limits of this.	Flexibly to meet different needs Instant response	Study support mentioned by 'important' people during induction In all relevant literature given to students
Mainstream staff	Status and referents of its physical location (not in student services) High quality accommodation	Perception as experts (dyslexia, ESOL) Seen as 'good' Good formal and informal liaison skills to ensure 2 way information flow Have other roles as well as study support *e.g.,* teach/staff development Ensure we use non remedial discourse	Allows for liaison time NOT perceived as more generously resourced than mainstream teaching Study support staff need to be 'around' therefore dangers of wholly VT staff	Public demonstrations of management support – need to ensure correct discourse in this
Academic managers	Visibility – constant reminders of its existence	Negotiate and discuss models – study support do NOT impose the 'study support model' Understand and respect the needs of academic managers but have confidence to challenge if appropriate	Study support team control own resources – NOT dependent on academic managers Resources used flexibly to meet needs of academic managers	Expectations of its use in QA reporting systems Profile of retention and achievement and link to study support

Group	Geography	Study Support Staff	How is it resourced	Management Support
Resource managers	Visibility Importance of being seen to support 'valuable' students	Be seen to be swamped by students Be seen to use all resources efficiently Try to partly 'pay your way' by accessing other sources of finance Understand the relevant resource allocation procedures, be able to use their financial discourse and know /use the funding principles in which they operate	Study support must be accountable, keep excellent audit trails and be reasonable in demands Study support must develop performance indicators which measure outcome as well as process Must understand the constraints under which resource managers are working	Need a powerful advocate Understand resourcing principles and keep up to date on national policy – and quote it! Understand their constraints

REFERENCES

Andrews, R., & Mitchell, S. (Eds.) (2001). *Essays in argument*. York and London: Middlesex University Press.

Angelil-Carter, S. (2000). *Stolen language? Plagiarism in writing*. Harlow, England: Longman.

Applebee, A. N. (1986). Problems in process approaches: Toward a reconceptualization of process instruction. In A. R. Petrovsky & D. Bartholomae (Eds.), *The teaching of writing. Eighty-fifth yearbook of the National Society for the Study of Education. Part II* (pp. 95-113). Chicago, Illinois: The University of Chicago Press.

Axelrod, R. B., & Cooper, C. R. (1998, 5ᵗʰ edition) *The St. Martin's Guide to Writing*. Bedford/St. Martin's.

Bakhtin, M. M. (1981). *The dialogic imagination: Four essays by M. M. Bakhtin*. Transl. C. Emerson & M. Holquist (Ed.). Austin TX: University of Texas Press.

Bakhtin, M. M. (1986). The Problem of Speech Genres. In C. Emerson & M. Holquist (Eds.), *Bakhtin. Speech genres and other late essays* (pp. 60-102). Austin TX: University of Texas Press.

Ball, S. J. (1991). Power, conflict, micropolitics and all that! In G. Walford (Ed.), *Doing educational research* (pp. 166-192). London: Routledge.

Ball, S. J. (1994). *Education reform A critical and post structural approach*. Buckingham: Open University Press.

Ball, S. J. (1997). Policy sociology and critical social research: A personal review of recent education policy and policy research. *British Educational Research Journal, 23, 3*, 257-273.

Ball, S. J., & Goodson, I. F. (1985). *Teachers' lives and careers*. Lewes: Falmer Press.

Ballard, B. (1984). Improving student writing: An integrated approach to cultural adjustment. In R. Williams, J. M. Swales, & J. Kirkman (Eds.), *Common ground* (pp. 43-53). Oxford/New York: Pergamon Press.

Barnett, R. W., & Blumner, J. S. (Eds.) (1999). *Writing centers and writing across the curriculum programs: Building interdisciplinary partnership*. Westport, CT: Greenwood.

Bartholomae, D. (1985). Inventing the university. In M. Rose (Ed.), *When a writer can't write: Studies in writer's block and other composing-process problems* (pp. 134-165). New York: Guilford Press.

Baume, D., & Baume, C. (1996). *Learning to teach. Assessing students' work*. Oxford, England: Oxford Centre for Staff Development.

Baurmann, J., & Weingarten, R. (1995). *Schreiben – Prozesse, Prozeduren, Produkte* [Writing – processes, procedures, products] (pp. 85-106). Opladen: Westdt. Verlag.

Bazerman, C. (1981). What written knowledge does: Three examples of academic discourse. *Philosophy of the Social Sciences 11*, 361-387.

Bazerman, C. (1994). *Constructing experience*. Carbondale: Southern Illinois University Press.

Bean, J. C. (1996). *Engaging ideas. The professor's guide to integrating writing, critical thinking, and active learning in the classroom*. San Francisco: Jossey-Bass Publishers.

Bean, J. C. (1998). *Schrijvend leren en andere didactische werkvormen voor actief leren* [Engaging ideas. The professor's guide to integrating writing, critical thinking, and active learning in the classroom]. Orig. 1996. Leiden: SMD Educatieve Uitgevers.

Bereiter, C., & Scardamalia, M. (1987). *The psychology of written composition*. Hillsdale, N.J.: Lawrence Erlbaum.

Berkenkotter, C., & Huckin, T. N. (1995). *Genre knowledge in disciplinary communication*. Hillsdale/New Jersey: Lawrences Erlsbaum Associates.

Berlin, J. A. (1987). *Rhetoric and reality: Writing instruction in American colleges, 1900-1985*. Carbondale: Southern Illinois University Press.

Bernstein, B. (1990). The structuring of pedagogic discourse. *Class, Codes and Control, 4*. London: Routledge.

Bernstein, B. (1999). Pedagogy, identity and the construction of a theory of symbolic control: Basil Bernstein questioned by Joseph Solomon. *British Journal of Sociology of Education, 20*, 265-279.

Bishop, W. (1999). *Ethnographic writing research: Writing it down, writing it up, and reading it.* Portsmouth, NH: Boynton/Cook, Heinemann.

Bishop, W., & Ostrom, H. (Eds.) (1997). *Genre and writing: Issues, arguments, alternatives.* Portsmouth, NH: Boynton/Cook.

Björk, L., & Räisänen, C. (1996, 1997). *Academic writing. A university writing course.* Lund, Sweden: Studentlitteratur.

Björk, L. (1997, August). Text-type awareness and academic writing. *A workshop at 7th European Conference of EARLI* (European Association of Research on Learning and Instruction). Athens, Greece, August 26 to 30, 1997.

Blase, J. (1991). The micropolitical perspective. In J. Blase (Ed.), *The politics of life in schools: Power, conflict, and cooperation* (pp. 1-18). London: Sage.

Bleich, D. (1998). *Know and tell: A writing pedagogy of disclosure, genre, and membership.* Portsmouth, NH: Boynton/Cook.

Bleiklie, I. (Ed.) (1997). *Kunnskap og makt: Norsk høyere utdanning i endring* [Knowledge and power: Norwegian higher education undergoing change]. Oslo: Tano Aschehoug.

Bloom, B. (1974). *Taxonomy of educational objectives: The classification of educational goals.* New York, Mackay.

Blythman, M., & Orr, S. (2001). Joined up policy: A strategic approach to improving retention in the UK. *Journal of College Student Retention. Research, theory & practice, 3*, 3, 231-242.

Boice, R. (1990) *Professors as writers. A self-help guide to productive writing.* Stillwater, Oklahoma: New Forums Press.

Boice, R. (1993). Writing blocks and tacit knowledge. *Journal of Higher Education, 64*, 19-54.

Booth, W. C., Colomb, G. C., & Williams, J. M. (1995). *The craft of research.* Chicago: The University of Chicago.

Bourdieu, P. (1997). The forms of capital. In A. H. Halsey, H. Lauder, P. Brown, & A. S. Wells (Eds.), *Education: Culture, economy and society* (pp. 46-58). Oxford: Oxford University Press.

Börner, W. (1987). Schreiben im Fremdsprachenunterricht. Überlegungen zu einem Modell [Writing in L2 instruction: Reflections on a model]. In W. Lörscher & R. Schulze (Eds.), *Perspectives on language in performance* (pp. 1336-1349). Tübingen: Narr.

Börner, W. (1989a). Planen und Problemlösen im fremdsprachlichen Schreibprozeß: Einige empirische Befunde [Planning and problem-solving in the L2 writing process: Some empirical results]. In U. Klenk, K.H. Körner et al. (Eds.), *Variatio Linguarum. Beiträge zu Sprachvergleich und Sprachentwicklung* [Contributions to comparative analysis of languages and the evolution of languages] (pp. 43-62). Stuttgart:Steiner-Verlag Wiesbaden

Börner, W. (1989b). Didaktik schriftlicher Textproduktion in der Fremdsprache. [Didactics of written L2 text production]. In G. Antos & H. P. Krings (Eds.), *Textproduktion. Ein interdisziplinärer Forschungsüberblick* [Text production: An interdisciplinary research review] (pp. 348-376). Tübingen: Niemeyer.

Bräuer, G. (1996). *Warum schreiben? Schreiben in den USA: Aspekte, Verbindungen, Tendenzen* [Why write? Writing in the USA: Aspects, connections, tendencies]. Frankfurt am Main: Peter Lang.

Bräuer, G. (1998). *Schreibend lernen. Grundlagen einer theoretischen und praktischen Schreibpädagogik* [Learning to write. Basis for a theoretical and practical writing pedagogy]. Innsbruck: Studienverlag.

Bräuer, G. (Ed.) (2000). *Writing across languages.* Stamford, CT: Ablex Publishing.

Bräuer, G. (2002). Drawing connections across education: the Freiburg Writng Center Model. *Language and learning across the disciplines, 5*, 2, 61-80.

Britton, J., Burgess, T., Martin, N., McLeod, A., & Rosen, H. (1975). *The Development of writing abilities* (11-18). London: Macmillan.

Brown, R. (1998). *The post dearing agenda for quality and standards in higher education.* London: Institute of Education.

Bruffee, K. A. (1984). Peer tutoring and the 'conversation of mankind.' In G. A. Olson (Ed.), *Writing centers. Theory and administration* (pp. 3-15). Urbana, Illinois: NCTE.

Bruner, J. S. (1960). *The process of education.* Cambridge, MA: Harvard University Press.

Bruner, J. S. (1973) *Beyond the information given.* Cambridge, MA: Harvard University Press.

Bryk, A. S., Easton, J. Q., Kerbow, D., Rollow, S. G., & Sebring P. B. (1998). *Charting Chicago school reform: Democratic localism as a lever for change.* Boulder, CO: Westview Press.

Büker, S. (1998). *Wissenschaftliches Arbeiten und Schreiben in der Fremdsprache Deutsch. Eine empirische Studie zu den Problem-Lösungsstrategien ausländischer Studierender* [Academic working and writing in German as a foreign/second language: An empirical study of international students' problem-solving strategies]. Baltmannsweiler: Schneider Verlag Hohengehren.

Büker, S. (2001). Writing consultation for foreign students. In Bräuer, G. (Ed.), *Pedagogy of language learning in higher education. An introduction* (pp. 171-184). Stanford:, CT.: Ablex Publishing.

Cameron, D. (1995). *Verbal hygiene*. London: Routledge

Carino, P. (1995). Early writing centers: Towards a history. *The Writing Center Journal 15*, 2, 103-15.

Cerych, L., & Sabatier, P. (1986). *Great expectations and mixed performance: The implementation of higher education reforms in Europe*. Stoke on Trent: Trentham Books.

Chatman, S. (1990). *Coming to terms: The rhetoric of narrative in fiction and film*. Ithaca and London: Cornell University Press.

Clancy, J. (1985). The development of student writing skills: Improving student writing. *The Higher Education Research and Development Society of Australasia, 7,* 3.

Clark, R., & Lorenzini, M. (1999). Focus on writing: An institution wide approach to the development of student writing skills. In P. Thompson (Ed.), *Academic writing development in higher education: Perspectives, explorations & approaches* (pp. 95-109). Centre for Applied Language Studies, The University of Reading.

Clyne, M. (1984). Wissenschaftliche Texte Englisch- und Deutschsprachiger: Textstrukturelle Vergleiche [Academic texts written by native-speakers of German and English: A comparative analysis of the text structure]. In *Studium Linguistik* [Studies in Linguistics], *15*, 92-97.

Clyne, M. (1987). Discourse structures and discourse expectations. Implications for Anglo-German academic communication in English. In L. E. Smith (Ed.), *Discourse across cultures: Strategies in world Englishes* (pp. 73-84). Hertfordshire UK: Prentice Hall.

Clyne, M. (1991). The socio-cultural dimension: The dilemma of the German-speaking scholar. In H. Schröder (Ed.), *Subject-oriented texts. Language for special purposes and text theory* (pp. 49-67). Berlin: de Gruyter

Cmejrková, S. (1996). Academic writing in Czech and English. In E. Ventola & A. Mauranen (Eds.), *Academic writing. Intercultural and textual issues* (pp. 137-152). Amsterdam/Philadelphia: John Benjamins Publishing Company.

Cohen, L., & Manion, L. (1980). *Research methods in education*. London: Routledge.

Creme, P., & Lea, M. R. (1999). Student writing: Challenging the myths. In P. Thompson (Ed.), *Academic writing development in higher education: Perspectives, explorations & approaches* (pp. 1-13). Centre for Applied Language Studies, The University of Reading.

Csikszentmihalyi, M. (1990). *Flow: The psychology of optimal experience*. New York: Harper & Row.

CVCP (1998). *From elitism to inclusion: Good practice in widening access to higher education*. Main Report. London: CVCP.

Danish Ministry of Education (1995). *Departmental order on grading scale and other evaluation. No. 513*, Copenhagen, Denmark.

Denzin, N. K., & Lincoln, Y. S. (1998). *Strategies of qualitative enquiry*. Thousand Oaks: Sage.

Dewey, J. (1938). *Experience and education*. New York: Collier.

Duszak, A. (1997). (Re)orientation strategies in academic discourse. In E. M. Jakobs & D. Knorr (Eds.), *Schreiben in den Wissenschaften* [Writing in the sciences] (pp. 63-75). Frankfurt am Main: Peter Lang.

Dysthe, O. (1993). *Writing and talking to learn. A theory-based, interpretive study of three classrooms in Norway and the USA*. Tromsø: Unikom, University of Tromsø.

Dysthe, O. (1995). *Det flerstemmige klasserommet* [The multivoiced classroom]. Cappelen Akademisk Forlag. (Swedish edition: Studentlitteratur 1996. Danish edition: Klim 1997).

Dysthe, O. (1996). The multivoiced classroom. Interactions of writing and classroom discourse. *Written Communication, 13*, 3, 385-425.

Dysthe, O. (1997). *Å skrive hovudfagsoppgåve – ei situasjonsskildring* [Writing the master thesis. A situation report] Report no. 2. Programme for Research on Learning and Instruction (PLF), University of Bergen.

Dysthe, O. (2000, September). 'Giving them the tools they need to succeed'. A high school teacher's use of writing-and-talking-to-learn in a literature class. *Paper presented at EARLI SIG-Writing Conference*, Verona, Italy, September 4-7, 2000.

Dysthe, O. (2001). *Keynote speech: European Association for the Teaching of Academic Writing*. Conference in Groningen, 2001.

Dysthe, O. (2002). Professors as mediators of academic text cultures. An interview study with advsors and master's degree students in three disciplines in a Norwegian university. *Written Communication, 19,* 4, 485-536

Dysthe, O., & Breistein, S. (1999). *Fagskriving og rettleiing ved universitetet. Holdningar blant lærarar og studentar ved Institutt for administrasjon og organisasjon* [Writing and supervision at the university. Attitudes among teachers and students at the Institute for Administration and Organizational Science]. Report no 1, PLF, University of Bergen.

Dysthe, O., & Kjeldsen, J. (1997). *Fagskriving og rettleiing i faget religionsvitskap* [Discipline specific writing and supervision in Comparative Religion]. Report no 5, PLF, University of Bergen.

Dysthe, O., & Lied, L. I. (1999). Skrivegrupper [Writing groups]. *Læring ved universitetet, 2* [Learning at the University]. PLF, University of Bergen.

Dysthe, O., Hertzberg, F. & Hoel, T. L. (2000). *Skrive for å lære – Skriving i høyere utdanning* [Write to learn – writing in higher education]. Oslo: Abstrakt forlag. (Danish edition: Klim 2002; Swedish edition: Studentlitteratur 2002).

Dysthe, O., & Lied, L. I. (2001). *Fagskriving og rettleiing ved universitetet. Intervjustudie ved Institutt for fiskeri- og marinbiologi ved Universitetet i Bergen* [Writing and supervision at the university. Interview study at the Institute of Fishery and Marine Biology at the University of Bergen]. Report no. 2, PLF, University of Bergen.

EATAW: European Association for the Teaching of Academic Writing (http://www.hum.ku.dk/eataw).

Eco, U. (1990). *Wie man eine wissenschaftliche Abschlussarbeit schreibt* [How to write a thesis]. Heidelberg: C. F. Müller.

Ehlich, K. (1995). Die Lehre der deutschen Wissenschaftssprache. Sprachliche Strukturen, didaktische Desiderate [The theory of the German academic language. Linguistic structures, didactical consequences]. In H. L. Kretzenbacher & H. Weinrich (Eds.), *Linguistik der Wissenschaftssprache* [Linguistics of academic language] (pp. 325-355). Berlin, New York: de Gruyter (Arbeitsberichte der Akad. d. Wissenschaften zu Berlin, 10).

Ehlich, K. (1999). Alltägliche Wissenschaftssprache [General academic language]. In *Info DaF, 26,* 13-24.

Elbow, P. (1973/1998, 2nd edition). *Writing without teachers.* New York: Oxford University Press.

Elbow, P. (1981). *Writing with power.* New York: Oxford University Press.

Elbow, P. (1991). Reflections on academic discourse: How it relates to freshmen and colleagues. *College English, 53,* 135-155.

Elbow, P. (2000). *Everyone can write: Essays toward a hopeful theory of writing and teaching writing.* New York, Oxford: Oxford University Press.

Entwistle, N., & Ramsden, P. (1983). *Understanding student learning.* London: Croom Helm.

Eßer, R. (1997). *'Etwas ist mir geheim geblieben am deutschen Referat.' Kulturelle Geprägheit wissenschaftlicher Textproduktion und ihre Konsequenzen für den universitären Unterricht von Deutsch als Fremdsprache* ['Something about the German text form "Summary" remained a mystery to me.' Cultural coinage in academic text production and its implications for L2 German instruction in tertiary education]. Munich: Iudicum

Evans, J., & Crivello, L. (1995). Do we need to teach numeracy and literacy and other academic skills in higher education? *Journal of Access Studies, 10.*

Farell, R. (Ed.) (1989). The High School Writing Center. Urbana, Ill: NCTE.

Flower, L. S., & Hayes, J. R. (1980). The dynamics of composing: Making plans and juggling constraints. In L. W. Gregg & E. R. Steinberg (Eds.), *Cognitive processes in writing.* Hillsdale, N.J.: Lawrence Erlbaum.

Flower, L. S., & Hayes, J. R. (1981). Plans that guide the composing process. In C. H. Fredriksen & J. F. Dominic (Eds.), Writing: The nature, development, and teaching of written communication. *Writing: Process, Development and Communication, vol. 2.* Hillsdale, NJ: Erlbaum.

Flower, L. S., Stein, V., Ackerman, J., Kantz, M. J., McCormick, K., & Peck, W. C. (1990). *Reading-to-write: Exploring a cognitive and social process.* New York: Oxford University Press.

Fluck, H-R. (1998). *Fachsprachen und Fachkommunikation.* [Discipline-specific language and discourse]. Heidelberg: Groos.

Frank, A., Furchner, I., Ruhmann, G., & Tente, C. (1999). Das Bielefelder Schreiblabor [The Bielefeld Writing Lab]. In O. Kruse, E. M. Jakobs, & G. Ruhmann (Eds.), *Schlüsselkompetenz Schreiben. Konzepte, Methoden, Projekte für Schreibberatung und Schreibdidaktik an der Hochschule* [Writing as a key qualification. Concepts, methods, projects for the tutoring and teaching of writing at the university] (pp. 290-292). Neuwied, Kriftel: Luchterhand.

Frank, A., Hollmann, D., & Ruhmann, G. (1995). Wenn die Worte fehlen. Das Schreiblabor: Beratung für Studierende und Lehrende [When words are missing. The Writing Lab: Consultation for students and teachers]. In *Handbuch für Hochschullehre*, [The Higher Education Handbook] *E 2.5*, 1-26. Bonn: Raabe Verlag.

Friedman, S., & Steinberg, S. (1989). *Writing and thinking in the social sciences*. Engelwood Cliffs, N.J.: Prentice Hall.

Fulkerson, R. (1996). The Toulmin model of argument and the teaching of composition. In B. Emmel, P. Resch, & D. Tenney (Eds.), *Argument revisited; argument redefined* (pp. 45-72). Thousand Oaks: Sage Publications.

Fullan, M. (2000). Schulentwicklung im Jahr 2000 [School Development in the year of 2000]. *Journal für Schulentwicklung, 4*, 4, 9-16.

Fulwiler, T. (1997). *College writing. A personal approach to academic writing*. Protsmouth, NH: Boynton/Cook Publishers.

Furchner, I., Großmaß, R., & Ruhmann, G. (1999). Schreibberatung oder Studienberatung? Zwei Einrichtungen, zwei Zugangsweisen [Consultation in the Writing Lab or in the Students' counselling Centre? Two institutions, two approaches]. In O. Kruse, E. M. Jakobs, & G. Ruhmann (Eds.), *Schlüsselkompetenz Schreiben. Konzepte, Methoden, Projekte für Schreibberatung und Schreibdidaktik an der Hochschule* [Writing as a key qualification. Concepts, methods, projects for the tutoring and teaching of writing at the university] (pp. 37-60). Neuwied, Kriftel: Luchterhand.

Furchner, I., Ruhmann, G., & Tente, C. (1999). Von der Schreibberatung für Studierende zur Lehrberatung für Dozent/inn/en [From writing tutorials with students to teaching consultations with teachers]. In O. Kruse, E. M. Jakobs, & G. Ruhmann (Eds.), *Schlüsselkompetenz Schreiben. Konzepte, Methoden, Projekte für Schreibberatung und Schreibdidaktik an der Hochschule* [Writing as a key qualification. Concepts, methods, projects for the tutoring and teaching of writing at the university] (pp. 61-72). Neuwied, Kriftel: Luchterhand.

Gage, J. T. (1991). *The shape of reason: Argumentative writing in college*. Second Edition. New York: Macmillan.

Galtung, J. (1983). Struktur, Kultur und intellektueller Stil. Ein vergleichender Essay über sachsonische, teutonische, gallische und nipponische Wissenschaft [Structure, culture, and intellectual style. A comparative essay on Saxon, Teutonic, Gallic, and Japanese science]. In Leviathan *Zeitschrift für Sozialwissenschaft*, [Journal of Social Sciences] *3*, 303-338.

Gardner, H. (1993). *Multiple intelligences*. New York: BasicBooks.

Gee, J. P. (1990). *Social linguistics and literacy: Ideology in discourses*. London: Falmer Press.

Geertz, C. (1973) Thick description: Towards an interpretive theory of culture? In C. Geertz *The interpretation of cultures* (pp. 3-30). New York: Basic Books.

Geertz, C. (1973) *The interpretation of cultures*. New York: Basic Books.

Graefen, G. (1997). Wissenschaftssprache – ein Thema für den Deutsch-als-Fremdsprache-Unterricht? [Academic language – a topic for L2 German instruction?]. In A. Wolff & W. Schleyer (Eds.), *Fach- und Sprachunterricht: Gemeinsamkeiten und Unterschiede* [Subject-related instruction vs. language instruction: Similarities and differences] (pp. 33-41). Regensburg. (Materialien Deutsch als Fremdsprache 43) [Teaching material for German as a foreign language].

Graefen, G. (1998). Wie formuliert man wissenschaftlich? [How to phrase academically?] In H. Barkowski & A. Wolff (Eds.), *Alternative Vermittlungsmethoden und Lernformen auf dem Prüfstand, Wissenschaftssprache – Fachsprache, Landeskunde aktuell, interkulturelle Begegnungen – interkulturelles Lernen* [Testing alternative teaching and learning methods: Academic language, language for special purposes, intercultural encounters, and intercultural learning] (pp. 222-239). Regensburg. (Materialien Deutsch als Fremdsprache 52) [Teaching material for German as a foreign language].

Graff, G. (1992). *Beyond the cultural wars: How teaching the conflicts can revitalize American education*. New York: Norton.

Gray, J. (1986). University of California, Berkeley: The Bay Area Writing Project and the National Writing Project. In *Modern Language Association, School-college collaborative programs in English*, pp. 35-45. New York: MLA.

Green, D. (1994). What is quality in higher education? Concepts, policy and practice. In D. Green (Ed.), *What is quality in higher education?* (pp. 3-20). Buckingham: SRHE/Open University Press.

Grieswelle, D. (1978). *Studenten aus Entwicklungsländern: Eine Pilot-Studie* [Students from developing countries: A pilot study]. Beiträge des Instituts für Soziologie, Band 1 [Contributions of the Institute of Sociology, vol. 1]. München: Minerva-Publ.

Gronn, P. (1986). Politics, power and the management of schools. In E. Hoyle (Ed.), *The world yearbook of education 1986: The management of schools*. London: Kogan Page.

Gross, A. G. (1991). Does rhetoric of science matter? The case of the floppy-eared rabbit. *College English, 53*, 2, 933-943.

Hargreaves, A. (1994). *Changing teachers, changing times*. London: Cassell.

Haring-Smith, T. (1992). Changing students' attitudes: Writing fellows programmes. In S. H. McLeod & M. Soven (Eds.), *Writing across the curriculum. A guide to developing programmes* (pp. 175-188). Newbury Park/London/New Delhi: Sage Publications.

Harris, M. (1986). *One-to-one: The writing conference*. Urbana, IL: NCTE.

Harris R., & Thorp, D. (1999). Language, culture and learning: Some missing dimensions to EAP. In H. Bool & P. Lyford (Eds.), *Academic standards and expectations: The role of EAP*. Nottingham University Press.

Hayes, J. R., & Flower, L. (1980). Identifying the organization of writing processes. In L. W. Gregg & J. Steinberg (Eds.), *Cognitive Processes in Writing* (pp. 3-20). Hillsdale, N.J.: Lawrence Erlbaum.

Healy, M. K. (1981). Purpose in learning to write: An approach to writing in three curriculum areas. In C. H. Fredriksen & J. F. Dominic (Eds.), Writing: The nature, development, and teaching of written communication. *Writing: Process, Development and Communication, vol. 2*. Hillsdale, NJ: Erlbaum.

Healy, M. K. (1986, August). *Jyväskylä writing project summer seminar*. University of Jyväskylä. Chair: Pirjo Linnakylä. August 5-8, 1986, Jyväskylä, Finland.

Herrington, A. J., & Curtis, M. (2000). *Persons on process: Four stories of writing and personal development in college*. Urbana, Illinois: NCTE.

Higgins, R., Hartley, P., & Skelton, A. (2001). Getting the message across: The problem of communicating assessment feedback. *Teaching in Higher Education, 6*, 2, 269-274.

Higgins, R., Hartley, P., & Skelton, A. (2002). The conscientious consumer: Reconsidering the role of assessment feedback in student learning. *Studies in Higher Education, 27*, 1, 53-64.

Higher Education Statistics Agency (HESA) (2000). *Higher education statistics focus*. Cheltenham, England: Higher Education Statistics Agency (HESA).

Hilgers, Th. L., & Marsella, J. (1992). *Making your writing programme work. A guide to good practices*. Newbury Park/London/New Delhy: Sage Publications.

Hildyard, A. (1996). Writing, learning and instruction. In E. de Corte & F. E. Weinert (Eds.), *International encyclopedia of developmental and instructional psychology* (pp. 562-564). Oxford: Elsevier.

Hinkle, A. (1998). Transcriptional and compositional responses to student writing. In C. Rust & G. Gibbs (Eds.), *Improving student learning: Improving student learning through course design* (pp. 164-171). Oxford: Oxford Centre for Staff Development.

Hoel, T. L. (1994). *Elevsamtalar om skriving i vidaregåande skole. Responsgrupper i teori og praksis* [Pupil conversations on writing in high school. Response groups in theory and practice]. Doctoral thesis, University of Trondheim.

Hoel, T. L. (2000). *Skrive og samtale. Responsgrupper som læringsfellesskap* [Writing and talking. Responsgroups as learning communities]. Oslo: Gyldendal Akademisk.

Hounsell, D. (1984). Learning and essay-writing. In F. Marton, D. J. Hounsell, & N. J. Entwistle (Eds.), *The experience of learning* (pp. 103-123). Edinburgh, UK: Scottish Academic Press.

Hounsell, D. (1987). Essay writing and the quality of feedback. In J. T. E. Richardson, M. Eysenck, & D. Warren Piper (Eds.), *Student learning: Research in education and cognitive psychology* (pp. 109-119). Milton Keynes, England: The Society for Research in Higher Education & Open University Press.

Hufeisen, B. (2000). Fachtextpragmatik: Kanadisch – Deutsch. Studentische Texte an der Universität [Pragmatics of Term Papers: Canadian and German. Texts written by university students]. In H. J. Krumm (Ed.), *Erfahrungen beim Schreiben in der Fremdsprache Deutsch. Untersuchungen zum Schreibprozess und zur Schreibförderung im Unterricht mit Studierenden* [Experiences in L2 German writing. Studies of university students' writing process and writing instruction]. Innsbruck: Studien-Verlag.

Hyland, K. (1998). Persuasion and context: The pragmatics of academic metadiscourse. In *Journal of pragmatics, 30*, 437-455.

Ivanic, R., Clark, R. & Rimmershaw, R. (2000). What am I supposed to make of this? The messages conveyed to students by tutors' written comments. In M. R. Lea & B. Stierer (Eds.), *Student writing in higher education: New contexts* (pp. 47-65). Buckingham, England: The Society for Research in Higher Education & Open University Press.

Jakobs, E. M. (1994). Conceptsymbols. Zitation und Verweisung im wissenschaftlichen Diskurs [Concept symbols. Citation and references in academic discourse]. In D. W. Halwachs & I. Stütz (Eds.), *Sprache – Sprechen – Handeln* [Language – Speech – Action] (pp. 45-52). Vol. 2. Tübingen: Nimeyer.

Jakobs, E. M. (1995). Text und Quelle. Wissenschaftliche Textproduktion unter Nutzung externer Wissensspeicher [Text and source. Academic text production and the use of externally stored knowledge]. In E. M. Jakobs, D. Knorr, & S. Molitor-Lübbert (Eds.), *Wissenschaftliche Textproduktion. Mit und ohne Computer* [Academic text production. With and without computer] (pp. 91-112). Frankfurt am Main: Peter Lang.

Jakobs, E. M. (1997). Lesen und Textproduzieren. Source Reading als typisches Merkmal wissenschaftlicher Textproduktion [Reading and text production. Source reading as a typical aspect of academic textproduction]. In E. M. Jakobs & D. Knorr (Eds.), *Schreiben in den Wissenschaften* [Writing in the sciences] (pp. 75-90.) Frankfurt am Main.: Peter Lang (Textproduktion und Medium, 2).

Jolly, P. (1984). The bottom line: Financial responsibility. In G. A. Olson (Ed.), *Writing centers. Theory and administration* (pp. 101-114). Urbana, Illinois: NCTE.

Kaplan, R. B. (1966). Cultural thought patterns in intercultural education. In *Language Learning, 16*, 1-20.

Kaplan, R. B. (1987). Cultural thought patterns revisited. In U. Connor & R. B. Kaplan (Eds.), *Writing across Languages: Analyses of L2-Text* (pp. 9-22). Los Angeles, CA.: Addison-Wesley.

Kapteyn, B. (1996). *Probleemoplossing in organisaties: Theorie en praktijk* [Problem solutions in organisations: Theory and practice]. Houten: Bohn Stafleu Van Loghum.

Kelly, L. (1980). One-on-one, Iowa City style: Fifty years of individualized writing instruction. *The Writing Center Journal, 1*, 1, 4-19.

Kemmis, S. (1993). Action research. In M. Hammersley (Ed.), *Educational research: Current issues* (pp. 177-190). London: Chapman.

Kinkead, J. A., & Harris, J. G., (Eds.) (1993). *Writing centers in context: Twelve case studies.* Urbana: NCTE.

Kjeldsen, J., & Dysthe, O. (1997). *Skrivegrupper på hovudfagsnivå – analyse av responssamtalar* [Writing groups at graduate level – analyses of response conversations]. Report no 3. PLF, University of Bergen.

Knauf, H., & Schmithals, F. (2000). *Tutorenhandbuch. Einführung in die Tutorenarbeit* [Tutor manual. Introduction to tutoring]. Neuwied, Kriftel: Luchterhand.

Kolb, D. A. (1984). *Experiential learning: Experience as the source of learning and development.* Englewood Cliffs, NJ: Prentice-Hall.

Kretzenbacher, H. L. (1995). Wie durchsichtig ist die Sprache der Wissenschaften? [How transparent is academic language?]. In H. L. Kretzenbacher & H. Weinrich (Eds.), *Linguistik der Wissenschaftssprache* [Linguistics of academic language] (pp. 15-39). Berlin, New York: de Gruyter (Arbeitsberichte der Akad. d. Wissenschaften zu Berlin; 10).

Krings, H. P. (1992). Empirische Untersuchungen zu fremdsprachlichen Schreibprozessen – Ein Forschungsüberblick [Empirical findings in L2 writing processes: A research review]. In W. Börner & K. Vogel (Eds.), *Schreiben in der Fremdsprache. Prozeß und Text. Lehren und Lernen* [L2 Writing. Process and product. Teaching and learning] (pp. 47-77). Bochum: AKS-Verlag.

Kruse, O. (1997a). Wissenschaftliche Textproduktion und Schreibdidaktik [Academic text production and writing pedagogy]. In E. M. Jakobs & D. Knorr (Eds.), *Schreiben in den Wissenschaften* [Writing in the sciences] (pp. 141-158). Frankfurt am Main: Peter Lang (Textproduktion und Medium, 2).

Kruse, O. (1997b). *Keine Angst vor dem leeren Blatt. Ohne Schreibblockaden durchs Studium* [Don't be afraid of the empty sheet. Studying without writer's block]. Frankfurt/N.Y.: Campus Concret.

Kruse, O. (1999, 7th edition). *Keine Angst vor dem leeren Blatt. Ohne Schreibblockaden durchs Studium* [Don't be afraid of the empty sheet. Studying without writer's block]. Frankfurt am Main: Campus.

Kruse, O. (2001). *Kunst und Technik der Erzählens. Wie Sie das Leben zur Sprache bringen können* [Art and technique of narration. How to turn life into language]. Frankfurt am Main.

Kruse, O., & Jakobs, E. M. (1999). Schreiben lehren an der Hochschule: Ein Überblick [Teaching writing skills at the university: An overview]. In O. Kruse, E. M. Jakobs, & G. Ruhmann (Eds.), *Schlüsselkompetenz Schreiben. Konzepte, Methoden, Projekte für Schreibberatung und Schreibdidaktik an der Hochschule* [Writing as a key qualification. Concepts, methods, projects for the tutoring and teaching of writing at the university] (pp.19-34). Neuwied, Kriftel: Luchterhand.

Kruse, O., & Ruhmann, G. (1999). Aus Alt mach Neu. Vom Lesen zum Schreiben wissenschaftlicher Texte [From old to new. Reading and writing academic texts]. In O. Kruse, E. M. Jakobs, & G. Ruhmann (Eds.), *Schlüsselkompetenz Schreiben. Konzepte, Methoden, Projekte der Schreibdidaktik an der Hochschule* [Writing as a key qualification. Concepts, methods, projects for the tutoring and teaching of writing at the university]. (pp. 109-120). Neuwied: Luchterhand.

Kuhn, D. (1989). Children and adults are intuitive scientists. *Psychological Review, 96*, 674- 689.

Kuhn, T. (1970). *The structure of scientific revolutions.* (2nd edition). Chicago: University of Chicago Press.

Kvale, S. (1997). Research apprenticeship. *Nordisk Pedagogik* [Nordic Pedagogy], *17*, 3, 186-194.

Lahtinen, V., Lonka, K., & Lindblom-Ylänne, S. (1997). Spontaneous study strategies and the quality of knowledge construction. *British Journal of Educational Psychology, 67*, 13-24.

Lamb, B. C. (1992). *A national survey of UK undergraduates' standards of English.* London: The Queen's English Society.

Lave, J. (1997). Learning, apprenticeship, social practice. *Nordisk Pedagogik* [Nordic Pedagogy], *17*, 3, 140-151.

Lave, J., & Wenger, E. (1991). *Situated learning: Legitimate peripheral participation.* Cambridge, England: Cambridge University Press.

Lea, M. R. (1994). 'I thought I could write until I came here.' Student writing in Higher Education. In G. Gibbs (Ed.), *Improving student learning: Theory and practice.* Oxford, Oxford Centre for Staff Development.

Lea, M. R., & Stierer, B. (Eds.) (2000). *Student writing in higher education: New contexts.* Buckingham, England: The Society for Research in Higher Education & Open University Press.

Lea, M. R., & Street, B. V. (1998) Student writing in higher education: An academic literacies approach. *Studies in Higher Education, 23*, 157-172.

Lea, M. R. & Street, B. V. (2000). Student writing and staff feedback in higher education: An academic literacies approach. In M. R. Lea & B. Stierer (Eds.), *Student writing in higher education: New contexts* (pp. 32-46). Buckingham, England: The Society for Research in Higher Education & Open University Press.

Ledin, P. (1996). *The concept of genre – a survey of research, 12.* Dept. of Scandinavian Languages, Lund, Sweden.

Lewin, B. A., & Fine, J. (1996). The writing of research texts. Genre analysis and its applications. In G. Rijlaarsdam, H. v. d. Bergh, & M. Couzijn (Eds.), *Theories, models and methodology in writing research* (pp. 423-445). Amsterdam: Amsterdam University Press.

Lillis, T. (1997). New voices in academia? The regulative nature of academic writing conventions. *Language and Education, 11*, 3, 182-199.

Lillis, T. (2001). *Student Writing. Access, regulation, desire.* London: Routledge.

Lillis, T., & Turner, J. (2001). Student Writing in Higher Education: Contemporary confusion, traditional concerns. *Teaching in Higher Education, 6*, 1, 57-68.

Lindblom-Ylänne, S., & Lonka, K. (1999). Individual ways of interacting with the learning environment. Are they related to study success? *Learning and Instruction, 9*, 1-18.

Linell, P. (1998). *Approaching dialogue. Talk, interaction and contexts in dialogical perspectives.* Amsterdam/Philadelphia: John Benjamins Publishing Company.

Lonka, K. (1996). *The writing process questionnaire.* Department of Psychology, University of Helsinki.

Lonka, K., & Ahola, K. (1995). Activating instruction: How to foster study and thinking skills in higher education. *European Journal of Psychology of Education, 4*, 351-368.

Lonka, K., Joram, E., & Bryson, M. (1996). Conceptions of learning and knowledge – does training make a difference? *Contemporary Educational Psychology, 21*, 240-260.

Lonka, K., Lindblom-Ylänne, S., & Maury, S. (1994). The effect of study strategies on learning from text. *Learning and Instruction, 4*, 253-271.

Lonka, K., & Lindblom-Ylänne, S. (1996). Epistemologies, conceptions of learning, and study practices in medicine and psychology. *Higher Education, 31*, 5-24.

Lonka, K., Maury, S., & Heikkilä, A. (1997, August). How do students' thoughts of their writing process relate to their conceptions of learning and knowledge? *Paper presented at 7th European Conference of EARLI* (European Association of Research on Learning and Instruction). Athens, Greece, August 26 to 30, 1997.

Low, G. D. (1996). *University written assignments and complex feedback situations*. Manuscript. English Language Unit University of York.

Lyngra, T. (1999). *Styrking av skriving på faget religionsvitenskap* [Strenghtening writing in the Discipline History of Religion]. Report no 4, PLF, University of Bergen.

MacDonald. S. P. (1987). Problem definition in academic writing. In *College English, 49*, 315-31.

MacDonald, S. P. (1994). *Professional academic writing in the humanities and social sciences*. Southern Illinois University.

Mangasser-Wahl, M. (1997). Saarbrücker Schreibtutorien [Saarbruecken writing tutorials]. In E. M. Jakobs & D. Knorr (Eds.), *Schreiben in den Wissenschaften* [Writing in the sciences] (pp. 183-192). Frankfurt am Main. Peter Lang (Textproduktion und Medium. Vol. 1).

McGovern, T. V., & Hogshead, D. L. (1990). Learning about writing, thinking about teaching. *Teaching of Psychology, 17*, 5-10.

McQuarrie, E. F., & Mick, D. G. (1999). Visual rhetoric in advertising: Text interpretive, experimental, and reader-response analyses. *Journal of consumer research, 26*, 37-54.

Moffett, J. (1968). *Student-centered language arts, K-12*. Portsmouth, NH: Heinemann.

Molitor-Lübbert, S. (1995). Anstelle eines Nachwortes: Überlegungen zum Schreiben in den Wissenschaften [Instead of a post-script: Reflections on academic writing]. In E. M. Jakobs, D. Knorr, & S. Molitor-Lübbert (Eds.), *Wissenschaftliche Textproduktion: Mit und ohne Computer* [Academic text production. With and without computer] (pp. 275-288). Frankfurt am Main: Peter Lang.

Molitor-Lübbert, S. (2001). Schreiben und Denken [Writing and thinking]. In I. Böttcher, O. Kruse, D. Perrin, & A. Wrobel (Eds.), *Schreiben. Von intuitiven zu professionellen Schreib-strategien* [Writing. From intuitive to professional writing strategies]. Wiesbaden: Westdeutscher Verlag.

Möhn, D., & Pelka, R. (1984). *Fachsprachen. Eine Einführung* [Technical languages: An introduction]. Tübingen: Niemeyer.

Mullin, J. A. (1999). Beginning, maintaining, assessing a writing across the curriculum program. In L. J. Meyers (Ed.), *Writing program administration*. Urbana, Il.: NCTE.

Mullin, J. A., & Wallace, R. (Eds.) (1994). *Intersections: Theory-practice in the writing center*. Urbana: NCTE.

Mullin, J. A., Lively, B. T., Holiday-Goodman, M., & Nemire, R. (1994). Development of a Teaching Module on Written and Verbal Communication Skills. *American Journal of Pharmaceutical Education, 58*, 257-261.

Mullin, J. A., & Momenee, L. (1993). The writing centers at the university of Toledo: An experiment in collaboration. In J. A. Kinkead & J. G. Harris (Eds.), *Writing centers in context: Twelve case studies* (pp. 45-77). Urbana: NCTE.

Murphy, C. (1991). Writing centers in context: Responding to current educational theory. In R. Wallace & J. Simpson (Eds.), *The writing center: New directions* (pp. 276-288). New York: Garland.

Murphy, C., & Law, J. (Eds.) (1995). *Landmark essays on writing centers*. Davis, CA: Hermagoras.

Myers-Breslin, L. (Ed.) (1999). *Administrative problem-solving for writing programs and writing centers: Scenarios in effective program management*. Urbana, Illinois: NCTE.

Narr, W. D., & Stary, J. (Eds.) (1999). *Lust und Last des wissenschaftlichen Schreibens. Hochschullehrerinnen und Hochschullehrer geben Studierenden Tips* [Pleasure and pain in academic writing. Pieces of advice from academic instructors to students]. Frankfurt am Main: Suhrkamp.

National Committee of Inquiry into Higher Education, NCIHE (1997). *Higher Education in the Learning Society*. Norwich: HMSO.

Nelson, J. (1990). This was an easy assignment: Examining how students interpret academic writing tasks. *Research in the Teaching of English 24*, 362-396.

Neman, B. S. (1995). *Teaching students to write*. USA: Oxford University Press.

Nias, J. (1993). Primary teachers talking: A reflexive account of longitudinal research. In M. Hammersley (Ed.), *Educational research: Current issues*. London: Chapman.

North, S. M. (1979). *Writing centers: A sourcebook*. Diss. State University of New York at Albany, DAI 40-02A: 0816.

North, S. M. (1984). The idea of a writing center. *College English, 46,* 433-46.

North, S. M. (1995, orig. 1984). The idea of a writing center. In C. Murphy, & J. Law (Eds.) (1995), *Landmark Essays on Writing Centers* (pp. 71 - 85). California: Hermagoras Press.

Nystrand, M. (1989). A social-interactive model of writing. *Written Communication, 6,* 1.

Nystrand, M. (1992). Social interactionism versus social constructionism: Bakhtin, Rommetveit, and the semiotics of written text. In A. H. Wold (Ed.), *The dialogical alternative.* Oslo: Scandinavian University Press.

Olson, G. A. (Ed.) (1984). *Writing centers. Theory and administration.* Urbana, Illinois: NCTE.

Olson, D. (1994). *The World on Paper. The conceptual and cognitive implications of writing and reading.* Cambridge, MA: Cambridge University Press.

Oomen-Welke, I. (1998). *'...ich kann da nix!' Mehr Zutrauen im Deutschunterricht* ['...I can't do that.' More self-confidence in German classes]. Freiburg im Breisgau: Fillibach Verlag.

Orr, S. (2002). *Keynote speech: Writing Development in Higher Education.* Conference in Leicester, 2002.

Orr, S., & Blythman, M. (2000). Have you got ten minutes? Can you just sort my dissertation? *Proceedings of the 6th Annual Writing Development in Higher Education Annual Conference 1999.* Leicester: WDHE.

Øverland, O. (1989). Norske universiteter må gi bedre undervisning [Norwegian universities must improve their teaching]. *Forskerforum, 2.*

Øverland, O. (1994). Skriving ved det undervisningsgivende og det eksamensgivende universitetet [Writing at the instruction giving and the exam giving university]. In O. Dysthe (Ed.), *Skriving på universitetet* [Writing at the university]. Report no 1, 1994. Tromsø: UNIKOM, University of Tromsø.

Phillips, D. C. (1993). Subjectivity and objectivity: An objective inquiry. In M. Hammersley (Ed.), *Educational research: Current issues. London:* Chapman.

Piaget, J. (1962). *Play, dreams, and imitation in childhood.* New York: W. W. Norton.

Polanyi, M. (1983). *The tacit dimension.* Gloucester, Mass.: Peter Smith.

Pörksen, U. (1994). *Wissenschaftssprache und Sprachkritik* [Academic language and language critique]. Tübingen: Narr.

Projektgruppe Ausländerstudium [Project group: Studying in a second/foreign language]. (Bockhorni, R., Ferdowsi, M. A., Schädle, W., & Steinitz, R. unter der wissenschaftlichen Leitung von [academic supervision] Opitz, P. J.). 2nd revised edition. 1987. Ausländerstudium in der Bundesrepublik Deutschland [International and foreign students in Germany]. Baden-Baden: Nomos-Verl.-Ges.

Prosser, M., & Webb, C. (1994). Relating the process of undergraduate essay writing to the finished product. *Studies in Higher Education 19,* 125-138. (http://owl.english.purdue.edu/)

Rafoth, B. (Ed.) (2000). *A tutor's guide: Helping writers one to one.* Portsmouth, NH: Boynton/Cook, Heinemann.

Rico, G. L. (1984). *Garantiert schreiben lernen* [Writing the natural way]. Reinbek bei Hamburg: Rowolt.

Rienecker, L. (1999). Research questions and academic argumentation: Teaching students how to do it; using formats and model-examples. In O. Kruse, E. M. Jakobs, & G. Ruhmann. (Eds.), *Schlüsselkompetenz Schreiben. Konzepte, Methoden, Projekte der Schreibdidaktik an der Hochschule* [Writing as a key qualification. Concepts, methods, projects for the tutoring and teaching of writing at the university] (pp. 95-108). Kriftel/Berlin: Luchterhand.

Rienecker, L., & Stray Jörgensen, P. (1999). *Opgaveskrivning på videregående uddannelser – en læreRbog* [Academic writing in higher education: A teacher's handbook]. Frederiksberg: Samfundslitteratur.

Rienecker, L., & Stray Jörgensen, P. (With contributions of L. Hedelund, S. Hegelund, & C. Kock). (2000). *Den gode opgave – opgaveskrivning på videregående uddannelser* [The good paper: Writing term papers in higher education]. 2nd ed. Frederiksberg: Samfundslitteratur.

Rienecker, L., & Stray Jörgensen, P. (2002). *Att skriva en bra uppsats* [The good paper: Writing term papers in higher education]. Malmö: Liber.

Rommetveit, R. (1974). *On message structures.* London/NY: Wiley.

Rommetveit, R. (1996). Læring gjennom dialog. Ei sosiokulturell og sosiokognitiv tilnærming til kunnskap og læring [Learning through dialogue. A sociocultural and sociocognitive approach to knowledge and learning]. In O. Dysthe (Ed.), *Ulike perspektiv på læring og læringsforskning*. [Different perspectives on learning and research on learning]. Oslo: Cappelen Akademisk Forlag.

Rowland, S., Byron, C., Furedi, F., Padfield, N., & Smyth, T. (1998). Turning academics into teachers? *Teaching in Higher Education, 3*, 2, 133-141.

Rubin, B. (1996). The writing of research texts: Genre analysis and its applications. In G. Rijlaarsdam, H. van den Berg, & M. Couzin (Eds.), *Effective teaching and learning of writing. Current trends in research* (pp. 36-50). Amsterdam: Amsterdam University Press.

Ruhmann, G. (1995). Das Bielefelder Schreiblabor [The Writing Lab in Bielefeld]. In *Tagungsbericht der ARGE-Tagung vom 6. bis 9. September 1995 in Osnabrück* [The report of the ARGE conference from September 6 till September 9 in Osnabrück] 69-79.

Ruhmann, G. (1996). Schreibblockaden und wie man sie überwindet [Writer's blocks and how to overcome them]. In K. D. Bünting, A. Bitterlich, & U. Pospiech *Schreiben im Studium. Ein Trainingsprogramm* [Academic writing for students. A training program] (pp. 108-119). Berlin: Cornelsen Verlag.

Ruhmann, G. (1997a). Ein Paar Gedanken darüber, wie man wissenschaftliches Schreiben lernen kann. [Reflections on how to learn academic writing]. In E. M. Jakobs & D. Knorr (Eds.), *Schreiben in den Wissenschaften* [Writing in the sciences] (pp. 125-139). Frankfurt am Main: Peter Lang.

Ruhmann, G. (1997b). Schreibprobleme auf der Spur [Identifying writing difficulties]. In *Handbuch Hochschullehre* (Ergänzung September) [The Higher Education Handbook: Supplement September], *E 2.5,* 1-26. Bonn: Raabe Verlag.

Ruhmann, G. (1999). Schreiben lernen, aber wie? Instrumentenkoffer zur Leitung von Schreibwerkstätten [Learning to write, but how? Essential tools for writing instruction]. In *Handbuch Hochschullehre,* (Ergänzung März) [The Higher Education Handbook: Supplement March], *E. 12,* 1-28. Bonn: Raabe Verlag.

Ruhmann, G. (2000). Aus der Schreibnot eine Tugend machen. Das Bochumer Modell der Schreibförderung [To turn the necessity to write into a virtue: The Bochum model for writing instruction]. In *Handbuch Hochschullehre,* (Ergänzung November) [The Higher Education Handbook: Supplement November], *E 2.13,* 1-15. Bonn: Raabe Verlag.

Russell, D. R. (1990). Writing across the curriculum in historical perspective: Toward a social interpretation. *College English, 52,* 1, 52-73.

Russell, D. R. (1991). *Writing in the academic disciplines, 1870-1990: A curricular history.* Carbondale: Southern Illinois University Press.

Russell, D. R., & Foster, D. (Eds.) (2002). *Writing and learning in cross-national perspective: Transitions from secondary to higher education.* NCTE and Lawrence Erlbaum Associates.

Ryan, L. (1994). *Bedford guide for writing tutors.* St. Martins Press: N.Y.

Scardamalia, M., & Bereiter, C. (1991). Literate expertise. In K. A. Ericsson & J. Smith (Eds.), *Toward a general theory of expertise. Prospects and limits* (pp. 172-194). Cambridge, MA: Cambridge University Press.

Schon, M. (1987). *Educating the reflective practitioner.* San Francisco: Jossey-Bass.

Schoonen, R., & de Glopper, K. (1996). Writing performance and knowledge about writing. In G. Rijlaarsdam, H. van den Berg, & M. Couzin (Eds.), *Theories, models and methodology in writing research* (pp. 87-107). Amsterdam: Amsterdam University Press.

Schreiblabor Bielefeld (1999). *Prävention und Intervention bei Schreibproblemen – Entwicklung eines Weiterbildungsangebotes für Zentrale Studienberatungsstellen nordrhein-westfälischer Hochschulen. Abschlußbericht* [Preventing and intervening in writing problems – in-service training for student counsellors at universities in Northrine-Westphalia. Final report]. Unpublished manuscript, University of Bielefeld, Bielefeld.

Scott, P. (1995). *The meanings of mass higher education.* Buckingham, England: The Society for Research into Higher Education and Open University Press.

Simpson, R. (1996). Learning development in HE: Deficit or difference. In S. Wolfendale & J. Corbett (Eds.), *Opening doors: Learning support in higher education.* London, Cassell.

Skidmore, D. (1998). Discourses of learning difficulty and the conditions of school development. *Educational Review, 51,* 1.

Skillen, J-A. (1985). Psychosoziale Probleme ausländischer Studenten. Interventionsmöglichkeiten innerhalb einer zentralen Studienberatungsstelle [Psycho-social problems of international/foreign students: Suggestions for student counsellors interventions]. *Zeitschrift für Theorie und Praxis der Studien-*

und Studentenberatung [Journal of theoretical and practical matters of student counselling] *2*, 1, 27-36.

Slotte, V., & Lonka, K. (1998). Using notes during essay writing: Is it always helpful? *Educational Psychology, 18*, 445-459.

Slotte, V., & Lonka, K. (1999a). Review and process effects of spontaneus note-taking on text comprehension. *Contemporary Educational Psychology, 24*, 1-20.

Slotte, V., & Lonka, K. (1999b). Spontaneous concept maps aiding the understanding of scientific concepts. *International Journal of Science Education, 21*, 515-531.

Slotte, V., & Lonka, K. (2001). Note-taking and essay-writing. In G. Rijlaarsdam (Series Ed.) & P. Tynjälä, L. Mason, & K. Lonka (Volume Eds.), *Studies in writing. Volume 7. Writing as a learning tool: Integrating theory and practice* (pp. 131-143). Dordrecht, The Netherlands: Kluwer Academic Publishers.

Stadter, A. (2002). *Der Essay als Instrument und Ziel geisteswissenschaftlicher Schreibdidaktik. Überlegungen zur Erweiterung des traditionellen Textsortenkanons* [The essay as instrument and aim for writing pedagogy in the humanities. Considerations on expanding the traditional text-type canons]. Paper presented at the writing conference in München, Schreiben für die Hochschule, 21-23 March 2002.

Sternberg, R. J. (1988). *The psychologist's companion. A guide to scientific writing for students and researchers*. Cambridge, MA: Cambridge University Press.

Sternglass, M. S. (1997). *Time to know them: A longitudinal study of writing and learning at the college level*. Mahwah, NJ, London: Lawrence Erlbaum Publishers.

Street, B. V. (1984). *Literacy in theory and practice*. Cambridge: Cambridge University Press.

Street, B. V. (1993) The new literacy studies special edition. *Journal of Research in Reading, 16*, 2.

Student Handbook. (2002). Registry, University of London Institute of Education.

Swales, J. M. (1990). *Genre analysis: English in academic and research settings*. UK: Cambridge University Press.

Swales, J. M., & Feak, C. B. (1994). *Academic writing for graduate students. A course for non-native speakers of English*. The University of Michigan Press.

Swales, J. M., & Feak, C. B. (2000): *English in today's research world. A writing guide*. The University of Michigan Press.

Tente, C. (1999). Beratung bei Schreibproblemen [Tutoring writing problems]. In Büro für Studienberatung (Eds.), ARGE-Tagung Herbst 1998. *Die Identität der Studien- und Studierendenberatung nach ca. 25 Jahren – Inventur, Kritik, Standards, neue Ziele* [The identity of the student counselling after 25 Years – stocktaking, criticism, standards, new aims] (pp. 45-48). Gießen.

Tente, C., & Büker, S. (1999). *Reader zur Schreibberatung* [Writing tutorial guide]. Unpublished manuscript, University of Bielefeld, Bielefeld.

Thomas, F. N. & Turner, M. (1994). *Clear and simple as the truth: Writing classic prose*. Princeton, N.J.: Princeton University Press.

Torrance, M., Thomas, G. V., & Robinson, E. J. (1993). Training in thesis writing: An evaluation of three conceptual orientations. *British Journal of Educational Psychology, 63*, 170-184.

Torrance, M., & Galbraith, D. (1999). *Knowing what to write*. Amsterdam: Amsterdam University Press.

Toulmin, S. (1958). *The uses of argument*. Cambridge: Cambridge University Press.

Turner, J. (1999). Academic writing development in higher education: Changing the discourse. In P. Thompson (Ed.), *Academic writing development in higher education: Perspectives, explorations & approaches* (pp. 36-48). Centre for Applied Language Studies, The University of Reading.

Turner, M. (1996). *The literary mind: The origins of thought and language*. New York: Oxford University Press.

Tynjälä, P., Mason, L., & Lonka, K. (2001). Writing as a learning tool: An introduction. In G. Rijlaarsdam (Series Ed.) & P. Tynjälä, L. Mason, & K. Lonka (Volume Eds.), *Writing as a Learning Tool: Integrating theory and practice* (pp. 7-22). Dordrecht, The Netherlands: Kluwer Academic Publishers.

Van Dijk, T. A., & Kintsch, W. (1983). *Strategies for discourse comprehension*. New York: Academic Press.

Van Eemeren, F. H., Grootendorst, R., Jackson, S., & Jacobs, S. (1993). *Reconstructing argumentative discourse*. London/Tuscaloosa: The University of Alabama Press.

Van Kruiningen, J. F. (1998). *What is a paper? Divergent views of faculty on genres in academic writing and the (un)clarity in writing assignments in the teaching of writing.* Unpublished, University of Groningen.

Virtanen, T. (1992a). *Discourse functions of adverbial placement in English.* Åbo: Åbo University Press.

Virtanen, T. (1992b). Issues of text typology: Narrative – a 'basic' type of text? *Text 12* (1992), 293-310.

Visser, I., Kruiningen, J., Kramer, F., & Nip, R. (1999). Towards a writing programme for the Faculty of arts, University of Groningen: Exploring the possibilities of a faculty-wide writing programme within a pluriform academic world. In O. Kruse, E. M. Jakobs, & G. Ruhmann. (Eds.), *Schlüsselkompetenz Schreiben. Konzepte, Methoden, Projekte der Schreibdidaktik an der Hochschule* [Writing as a key qualification. Concepts, methods, projects for the tutoring and teaching of writing at the university] (pp. 191-207). Kriftel/Berlin: Luchterhand.

Vygotsky, L. S. (1978). *Mind in society. The development of higher psychological processes.* Cambridge, MA: Harvard University Press.

Vygotsky, L. S. (1986). *Thought and language.* Translation newly revised by A. Kozulin. Cambridge, Mass: The MIT Press.

Walvoord, B. E. (1992). Getting started. In S. H. McLeod & M. Soven (Eds.), *Writing across the curriculum. A guide to developing programmes* (pp. 12-31). Newbury Park/London/New Delhy: Sage Publications.

Weinrich, H. (1995). Wissenschaftssprache, Sprachkultur und die Einheit der Wissenschaft [Academic language, language culture and the unity of science]. In H. L. Kretzenbacher & H. Weinrich (Eds.), *Linguistik der Wissenschaftssprache* [Linguistics of academic language] (pp. 155-174). Berlin, New York: de Gruyter (Arbeitsberichte der Akad. d. Wissenschaften zu Berlin; 10).

Weissberg, B. (2000). On the interface of writing and speech: Acquiring English syntax through journal writing. In Bräuer, G. (Ed.), *Writing across languages* (pp. 71-88). Stanford, CT.: Ablex Publishing.

Welch, N. (1999). Playing with reality: Writing centers after the mirror stage. *College Composition and Communication, 5,* 1, 51-69.

Werlich, E. (1976). *A text grammar of English.* Heidelberg: Quelle & Meyer.

Wertsch, J. (1998). *Minds as action.* Cambridge, MA: Harvard University Press.

Wijnen, G., Renes, W., & Storm, P. (1998). *Projectmatig werken* [Working in projects]. Utrecht: Het Spectrum.

Winch, C., & Wells, P. (1995). The quality of student writing in higher education: A cause for concern? *British Journal of Educational Studies, 43,* 1, 75-87.

Wolff, D. (1992). Zur Förderung der zweitsprachlichen Schreibfähigkeit [Supporting L2 writing competence]. In W. Börner & K. Vogel (Eds.), *Schreiben in der Fremdsprache. Prozeß und Text. Lehren und Lernen* [L2 Writing. Process and product. Teaching and learning] (pp. 110-134). Bochum: AKS-Verlag.

Young, A., & Fulwiler, T. (Eds.) (1986). *Writing across the disciplines: Research into practice.* Portsmouth, NH: Boynton/Cook.

Zirinsky, H. B. (1987). An investigation of student awareness of teacher criteria for evaluating writing as an element in the composing process. *Dissertation Abstracts International 39,* 186-A.

AUTHOR INDEX

223

SUBJECT INDEX

systemic restructuring, 136

tacit knowledge, vii, 113, 114, 117, 120, 212
task definition, 4, 75, 76, 80
task interpretation, 75
teacher oriented writing programme, 185
teacher role, 164
teaching culture, 188
teaching genre, 62
teaching-in-the-disciplines, 14
term paper, 7, 19, 21, 45, 47, 48, 51, 52, 56, 59, 61, 65, 73, 101, 102, 107, 141, 154, 155, 168, 172, 220
terminology, 21, 39, 45, 48
text format, 109
text revision, 54, 168
text type, vi, 4, 10, 11, 22, 29, 30, 31, 32, 33, 35, 36, 37, 38, 39, 40, 68, 108, 113, 120, 122
textual consciousness, 35, 39, 40
thesis writing, 119, 124, 127, 222
training the trainer, 158
trial and error, 7, 9, 23, 46, 60, 130, 187
tutorial, 71, 72, 93, 141, 142, 199, 222
tutoring, 1, 3, 5, 7, 11, 13, 43, 51, 72, 101, 102, 107, 108, 110, 111, 137, 145, 196, 212, 215, 217, 218, 220, 223
   individual, 4, 10, 41, 43, 50, 51, 54, 55, 56

University writing centre, 137

WAC, 1, 160, 161, 201, 205
with academic staff, vii, 167, 169, 171, 173
writing across the curriculum, vi, 9, 13, 14, 138, 150, 196, 201, 211, 219

writing assignment, 22, 37, 38, 51, 167, 168, 186, 188, 191, 193, 201, 223
writing block, 116
writing centre, 1, 2, 3, 5, 7, 8, 9, 10, 13, 14, 27, 71, 73, 101, 105, 106, 107, 109, 111, 135, 136, 138, 139, 140, 141, 143, 145, 146, 149, 150, 151, 152, 156, 157, 166, 173, 174, 194, 195, 198, 199, 200, 201, 203, 204, 207, 213, 219, 220
writing development, vi, vii, 13, 175, 177, 181, 183, 201, 213, 222
writing difficulties, 3, 4, 13, 41, 42, 44, 52, 56, 168, 181, 221
writing group, 6, 14, 151, 161, 162, 163, 164
writing in the disciplines, vii, 9, 11, 12, 13, 14, 177
writing instruction, 5, 6, 7, 11, 12, 13, 14, 15, 21, 29, 30, 32, 33, 37, 40, 60, 73, 108, 117, 119, 128, 136, 137, 138, 146, 149, 165, 166, 216, 217, 221
writing lab, iv, 42, 138
writing methodology, 169
writing pedagogy, 3, 5, 9, 10, 11, 13, 14, 15, 136, 137, 141, 156, 163, 164, 170, 181, 189, 212, 217, 222
writing programme, 1, 2, 3, 5, 7, 8, 10, 11, 13, 14, 15, 37, 108, 149, 151, 152, 185, 186, 187, 188, 189, 190, 191, 192, 193, 194, 216, 219, 223
writing project, 2, 3, 6, 8, 9, 13, 14, 142, 158, 165, 167, 169, 172, 185, 192, 216
writing skill, vi, 4, 8, 19, 23, 24, 25, 42, 56, 57, 118, 158, 168, 169, 171, 173, 174, 181, 185, 186, 187, 189, 192, 206, 213, 218
writing to learn, 13, 137, 159, 160
writing workshops, 59, 128, 145, 150, 158, 162, 164

LIST OF CONTRIBUTORS

Lennart Björk, Emeritus Professor of English, Gothenburg University, Sweden. lennart.bjork@eng.gu.se

Margo Blythman, Teaching and Learning Coordinator, London College of Printing, London Institute, UK. m.blythman@lcp.linst.ac.uk

Gerd Bräuer, DAAD Visiting Professor, Freiburg University of Education, Germany. braeuer@ph-freiburg.de

Stella Büker, Lecturer, Department of German Studies, Tokyo University of Foreign Studies, Japan. stellabueker@web.de

Kelly Coate, Research Officer, Centre for Higher Education Studies, Institute of Education at the University of London, UK. k.coate@ioe.ac.uk

Olga Dysthe, Professor of Education, University of Bergen, Norway. olga.dysthe@psych.uib.no

Andrea Frank, Consultant for Teaching and Studies, University of Bielefeld, Germany. andrea.frank@uni-bielefeld.de

Stefanie Haacke, Writing Consultant, Bielefeld Writing Lab, University of Bielefeld, Germany. stefanie.haacke@uni-bielefeld.de

Signe Hegelund, External lecturer, Department of Education, Philosophy, and Rhetoric, University of Copenhagen, Denmark. styrup@post11.tele.dk

Christian Kock, Professor of Rhetoric, Department of Education, Philosophy, and Rhetoric, University of Copenhagen, Denmark. kock@hum.ku.dk

Femke Kramer, Project worker, MA, Communication Skills Programme for the Science Faculty, Faculty of Arts, University of Groningen, The Netherlands. f.l.kramer@let.rug.nl

Jacqueline van Kruiningen, Project Manager, The Science Faculty and the Faculty of Law, Language and Communication Faculty of Arts, Groningen, The Netherlands. J.F.van.Kruiningen@let.rug.nl

Otto Kruse, Professor of Psychology, University of Applied Sciences, Erfurt, Germany. kruse@sot.fh-erfurt.de

Kirsti Lonka, Director, Development and Research Unit, Learning Centre, Faculty of Medicine, University of Helsinki, Finland. kirsti.lonka@lime.ki.se

Jane Milton, Writing Resource Director, Nova Scotia College of Art and Design, Halifax, Nova Scotia, Canada. jmilton@nscad.ns.ca

Joan Mullin, Associate Professor of English and Director of Writing Across the Curriculum and the Writing Center, University of Toledo, Ohio, USA. Jmullin@UTNet.Utoledo.Edu

Susan Orr, Learning and Teaching Coordinator, London College of Fashion, The London Institute in London, UK. s.orr@lcf.linst.ac.uk

Henrike Padmos, Project worker, MA, Department of Communication and Innovation Studies, University of Wageningen, The Netherlands. H.C.W. Padmos@let.rug.nl

Lotte Rienecker, Director of Academic Writing Center, Faculty of Humanities, University of Copenhagen, Denmark. rieneck@hum.ku.dk

Mary Scott, Senior Lecturer in Education and Academic Director of the Centre for Academic and Professional Literacy Studies, The Institute of Education, University of London, UK. m.scott@ioe.ac.uk

Peter Stray Jörgensen, Writing Consultant, Academic Writing Center, Faculty of Humanities, University of Copenhagen, Denmark. stray@hum.ku.dk

Christina Tente, Educational Consultant, Deutsche Bahn AG, Berlin, Germany. christinatente@web.de

Studies in Writing

For Volumes 1 – 6 please contact Amsterdam University Press, at www.aup.nl

KLUWER ACADEMIC PUBLISHERS – DORDRECHT / BOSTON / LONDON